Social and Behavioral Science Research

A New Framework
for Conceptualizing, Implementing,
and Evaluating Research Studies

David R. Krathwohl

Social and Behavioral Science Research

A New Framework
for Conceptualizing, Implementing,
and Evaluating Research Studies

 Jossey-Bass Publishers

San Francisco • Washington • London • 1985

SOCIAL AND BEHAVIORAL SCIENCE RESEARCH
*A New Framework for Conceptualizing, Implementing,
and Evaluating Research Studies*
   by David R. Krathwohl

Copyright © 1985 by: Jossey-Bass Inc., Publishers
                    433 California Street
                    San Francisco, California 94104

                    &

                    Jossey-Bass Limited
                    28 Banner Street
                    London EC1Y 8QE

Library of Congress Cataloging in Publication Data

Krathwohl, David R.
   Social and behavioral science research.

   (Jossey-Bass social and behavioral science series)
   Bibliography: p. 303
   Includes index.
   1. Social sciences—Research—Methodology.
2. Psychology—Research—Methodology.   I. Title.
II. Series
H62.K6794   1985   300 '.72   84-43028
ISBN 0-87589-637-5

Manufactured in the United States of America

The paper in this book meets the guidelines for
permanence and durability of the Committee on
Production Guidelines for Book Longevity of the
Council on Library Resources.

JACKET DESIGN BY WILLI BAUM

FIRST EDITION

Code 8513

The Jossey-Bass
Social and Behavioral Science Series

Consulting Editor
Methodology of Social and
Behavioral Research

Donald W. Fiske
University of Chicago

To my wife,
Helen Jean Abney Krathwohl,
who has so wonderfully increased the level of life's fulfillment
through our shared experiences of family, friends, travel, and work.

Preface

Increasingly, social and behavioral scientists are not just doing research but are also examining the nature of the scientific process itself, and more and more journals are publishing articles bearing on the subject. One index of this growth is the number of references in a given year to Kuhn's *Structure of Scientific Revolutions,* a treatise that did much to spark discussions on "What is science?" First published in 1962, this work was cited 122 times in periodicals indexed in the 1970 volume of *Social Science Citation Index.* The citation rate more than doubled in the 1980 index, and there were nearly 300 citations in 1982. *Science 83,* recognizing this increased attention, described Kuhn's influence in an article titled "Brother, Can You Paradigm," a pun on Kuhn's reference to new paradigms (Pollie, 1983).

There are many possible reasons for this interest. One is the slow accumulation of social and behavioral research knowledge, which has left policy makers underwhelmed by equivocal advice on how to ameliorate social problems. This snail-paced progress has called into question whether our research methods are the best ones for the purpose, whether we adequately understand how to use them, and whether our framework for developing and judging them is adequate. Another reason for the interest is that qualitative research methods are attracting adherents in areas where quantitative methods have long been dominant. This sparks heated debate on such questions as: Which orientation is better? By what framework of criteria do we judge? Is there more than one standard? Discussions of such basic questions as these make us realize that we have taken much for granted. They drive us to reexamine the bases on which our methods rest, to consider the adequacy of our frameworks for determining what constitutes effective research, and to seek reformulation where inadequacies are found. These questions suggest that there may be alternative views of what the social and behavioral sciences ought to be, with implications for what is considered sound research.

If there are different views of the social and behavioral sciences, one might suppose they would grow out of dialogues about quantitative versus qualitative methods. But since there are positive possibilities inherent in both methods, it is unfortunate that discussions of relative merits have so often sought to extol the virtues of one at the expense of the other. Even when the methods are treated evenhandedly, there has been no unifying framework. Such a framework would do much to put the methods in a single perspective and provide a basis for more productive dialogue about where and how they are best used. That is what this book seeks to do.

The goal of *Social and Behavioral Science Research: A New Framework for Conceptualizing, Implementing, and Evaluating Research Studies* is to contribute substantially to our understanding of how social and behavioral research proceeds—and, therefore, how it can be improved. As the title suggests, the book first *conceptualizes* the process by which findings become knowledge, examining what aspects facilitate acceptance of findings and within what structure decisions are made in planning, doing, and reporting research. The implications of that view for a typology of different research orientations are explored. The implications for *implementing* and *evaluating* research are described as the framework is developed.

The book began as an exploration of such basic questions as "What is knowledge?" and "How do social and behavioral scientists contribute to it?" In seeking answers to these questions, however, an analogy emerged—that of the research report as presenting a chain of reasoning analogous to a metal chain. This thinking led to an analysis of those characteristics that make for strong links in a chain, whether of metal or of the chain of reasoning in the typical research report. Further analysis of the research chain resulted in the formulation of an integrated set of research criteria—the "framework" to which the book's subtitle refers.

This framework, as well as reconceptualizing such previously recognized criteria as internal and external validity, provides an overview that shows the optimizing decisions involved in research. The framework includes the questions addressed by past conceptualizations but goes beyond them to offer a more complete picture of the critical decisions made in formulating and implementing a study. The criteria in the framework are intended to fit naturally the way researchers think about their work—how they "carve nature at its joints."

The framework has important implications for conceptualizing, for doing, and for improving social and behavioral science research. Researchers make many decisions that may have unforeseen consequences for the chain of reasoning they are trying to construct. By making the entire set of decisions explicit, the framework shows the interdependence of decisions and allows conscious and controlled decision making for the overall benefit of the study. The framework helps one decide where and how to place special effort.

Researchers often do their work "by the numbers," slavishly following what they believe to be the correct steps and lacking the confidence (or maybe not recognizing the need) to adjust their approach to the demands of their problem and situation. A better understanding of the way research findings become accepted as knowledge may put the steps in sufficient perspective to give such researchers enough confidence in their grasp of the overall process that they become free to develop their projects more appropriately.

Additionally, the framework helps make apparent the location and nature of some of the many trade-offs in research as well as the importance of those trade-offs. It gives new emphasis and meaning to some underemphasized aspects of research, provides new tools for analyzing research, and helps develop a sharpened sense of what is important in reporting it.

This book is designed for all social and behavioral scientists, those in basic disciplines, such as psychology, sociology, anthropology, and political science, as well as researchers in applied behavioral science fields. It is intended both for seasoned professionals and for those still studying or just beginning their careers in the social and behavioral sciences.

Beginning professionals will find this book an especially useful adjunct to research methods books. It provides a perspective that is broader and deeper than do books that are more concerned with providing the details and niceties of method. While in draft form, the book's overview has been supplying the conceptual cement integrating three conventional methods texts dealing with qualitative, quantitative, and statistical methods in a two-semester research methods sequence I have been coordinating. This book also includes a discussion of the important concept of causation, another typical casualty of the press of details.

A note about terminology: Although I am addressing all social and behavioral scientists, I have chosen to use the term *behavioral science* by itself throughout the book. The abbreviated form is less cumbersome (the primary virtue of its use); it does not exclude the other social sciences.

Overview of Contents

The book begins with an Introduction that summarizes the major points in a series of twenty statements. These statements orient readers to where they are in the argument as it progresses and also indicates where the argument is going. At two places in the book I suggest a rereading of the introduction as a way of fitting material into the broader context.

Chapter One seeks answers to such questions as "What is knowledge?" "What is science?" "How is it different from other ways of knowing, and how does it contribute to knowledge?" It notes the social character of knowledge building. Although the researcher may make a judgment that the research is new knowledge, its acceptance as knowledge requires a consensus. Therefore the scientist is in the business of creating a consensus about the interpretation of evidence.

Chapter Two takes the process a step further. It contrasts the discovery phase of research—a not-to-be-circumscribed creative act—with the validation, or confirmation, phase. In the latter, the expectations of the scientific establishment very strongly influence how one presents the knowledge claim. Research as a layperson might do it is explored and found to have direct parallels to what a behavioral scientist would do. It is in this chapter that I develop and explore the conception of the research write-up as a chain of reasoning analogous to a metal chain.

Chapter Three begins the process, which extends through Chapter Six, of examining the research chain of reasoning to determine by what criteria the successive links in the chain are judged when a researcher presents a generalizable knowledge claim. Chapter Three explores two key criteria: the characteristics of a study that enable one to demonstrate (1) that variables are linked in a relationship and (2) that the relationship has generality. The power of a study to show the linkage of the variables is its internal validity (linking power). Abbreviated as "internal validity (LP)," it is a relative of, but broader than, the currently used concept of internal validity. Similarly, the power of a study to show the generality of the relationship is its external validity (generalizing power), abbreviated as "external validity (GP)," which is also similar but not identical to its current criterion namesake, external validity. Each of these broader concepts is shown to depend on a series of five judgments.

Chapter Four develops in some detail the nature of the five judgments that make up internal validity (LP). It shows that they are a set of sequential judgments and explores their practical implications. One of the five judgments consists of four subjudgments, and these are also detailed. Chapter Five provides the same treatment for the five sequential judgments that make up external validity (GP). Chapter Six embeds these two concepts in a larger framework of criteria and describes the constraints within which one must work. This larger framework makes clear that, because of the conflicts among the criteria and the typical shortage of resources to conduct research, one typically finds it impossible to completely satisfy all the criteria simultaneously. Therefore one maximizes or optimizes overall satisfaction across the set: problem formulation, weighting internal validity (LP) and external validity (GP), building audience credibility, information yield, and resource allocation.

Having so far proceeded as though everyone subscribed to the same criteria ignores the differences in method and outlook noted at the outset—differences between quantitative and qualitative methods, for instance. Chapter Seven rectifies this omission by presenting a typology of orientations to what the social and behavioral sciences ought to be and how they are best developed. This typology was stimulated by and is in part based on the work of Mitroff and Kilmann (1978). Each of the types is described in terms of its guiding principle, its view of the nature of behavioral science knowledge, its criteria of excellence, its preferred research method, persons who exemplify the type, the role of values, its strengths, and its weaknesses.

In Chapter Eight the typology is related to the criteria described in previous chapters to show which criteria each orientation emphasizes. Chapters Seven and Eight provide new tools for social and behavioral scientists who have long suspected such differences but may not have had a framework that sufficiently articulated them. These chapters help one understand researchers' criticisms of one another's studies. As perceived by different orientations, the strengths and weaknesses of various methods become more apparent.

Chapter Nine is devoted to causal explanation, a concept routinely used in research methods books but rarely examined in them. The chapter begins by showing why some have suggested that the concept be abandoned, describing some of its complexities. A wide variety of relationships can all be considered causal even though we usually consider simply that "a cause results in an effect." The discussion of the way some of these different types of relationships show up in data alerts researchers to new possibilities to look for in ferreting out the meaning of data.

Chapter Ten, using the checklist that forms the Appendix, applies the framework to a quantitative and then to a qualitative study. This analysis demonstrates how the criteria apply to both as well as having separate implications for each. It also indicates the applicability of the framework to both causal and noncausal studies. The checklist should be especially useful to individuals constructing research proposals, to those seeking to improve existing ones, and to researchers structuring and presenting research reports.

Chapter Eleven relates the formulation in this book to its predecessors (Campbell and Stanley, 1963, and Cook and Campbell, 1979) and to Cronbach's concept of reproducibility (Cronbach, 1982). Similarities and differences are delineated and the advantages of the proposed formulation are suggested.

A concluding statement summarizes what has been attempted.

Acknowledgments

Basic ideas for this book were developed while I was a Fellow at the Center for the Advanced Study of the Behavioral Sciences, Stanford, California, in 1980–81. The center provided superb atmosphere, services, stimulation, fellowship, and freedom. I wish to thank the many other Fellows who contributed so much to my education and to acknowledge the Spencer Foundation and Syracuse University for the financial support that together made the year possible. It provided a tremendous boost.

A book that has been in progress over several years, as this one has, is significantly improved by the comments of and interactions with the many persons who have seen it. I would love to acknowledge them all, but since there is not sufficient space, let me single out a few. I particularly appreciate the help of Lee J. Cronbach. He shared drafts of his then-forthcoming book (1982), his thinking, and his files and provided significant encouragement the year I was at the center. I appreciate the risk he took in loaning a large number of his personal files to me. Exceptionally helpful comments and/or encouragement were received from Benjamin S. Bloom, Donald T. Campbell, Meredith Gall, Bruce Rogers, and Michael Scriven. Emily Robertson called my attention to David Lewis's helpful work, and her expert advice eliminated a number of significant problems from the chapter on causal analysis; if errors remain, it is because I did not profit adequately from her suggestions. Jay Millman provided very detailed comments that were used to improve discussions throughout the manuscript. Donald W. Fiske, consulting editor to Jossey-Bass, made a number of very helpful suggestions and called my attention to Chamberlin, from which the fitting quotation of Chapter Seven was taken. Suggestions on earlier drafts made by students in my classes have been extraordinarily helpful. Rephah Berg has markedly improved the clarity of the manuscript with her careful editing. I am very appreciative of the work of Virginia A. Hiscox, a senior in the Syracuse University illustration program, who did the drawings and diagrams that aid one's grasp of concepts covered in the text. I am grateful for not only the nimble fingers but also the care and intelligence of Jane Hedley, who typed some of the initial chapter drafts, and of Linda Froio, who has so cheerfully worked through the additional chapters and all the many revisions.

Archimedes is supposed to have said, "Tell me where to stand and I will move the earth." It is hoped that this book can provide a place where readers can stand and from which they can gain a perspective on the research process that provides leverage for improving the social and behavioral sciences.

Syracuse, New York
March 1985

David R. Krathwohl

Contents

Figures

The Author

David R. Krathwohl is Hannah Hammond Professor of Education at Syracuse University. He received his B.S. degree (1943) in psychology and his M.A. (1947) and Ph.D. (1953) degrees in educational and psychological measurement and evaluation, all from the University of Chicago.

Krathwohl's research and writing were in the field of measurement and educational psychology until he became dean of the School of Education at Syracuse University. After leaving the deanship, he has worked largely in the field of research methods, with some writing in evaluation.

He has written a number of journal articles, but his most cited work is the *Taxonomy of Educational Objectives*. He was one of the authors of the *Cognitive Domain Handbook* (1956), edited by Benjamin S. Bloom, and was senior author, with Bloom and Bertram Masia, of the *Affective Domain Handbook* (1964). The handbooks have been translated into seven languages.

Krathwohl is a former president of the American Education Research Association and currently serves as its editor-at-large. He is also a former president of the Educational Psychology Division of the American Psychological Association.

Social and Behavioral Science Research

A New Framework
for Conceptualizing, Implementing,
and Evaluating Research Studies

Introduction

Summary, Orientation, and Overview

This book starts by examining the question "What is behavioral science knowledge?" As the answer is found to be "The building of a consensus around empirical evidence," the next questions are: How does one build that consensus? What are the criteria by which a study is judged? What are the constraints inherent in the very nature of the process? What additional constraints are imposed by resource limitations and society? These questions lead to an examination of the criteria of good research and a lengthy discussion of each criterion by itself and in relation to the others.

Finally, one comes to the question whether the criteria that fit quantitative research are also appropriate for qualitative and other research methods. This question leads to the development of a typology of behavioral science researchers. One may view the typology either as a set of roles that behavioral scientists play or as a set of basic orientations from which they view their work. Probably, for some who are flexible, they are roles; for others, they are basic orientations. Comparisons of the research criteria emphasized by various types show marked differences.

More specifically, the book makes these major points:

1. "Knowing" is one's personal judgment that a relationship exists. "Knowledge" results when there is a consensus of such judgments (Chapter One).

2. The task of researchers is to create such a consensus with respect to their knowledge claims, and they must do so with the successive audiences who will judge their work. The first audience usually consists of one's immediate peers, who, familiar with the work, make suggestions and encourage one to carry it further. They are the persons most competent to judge the knowledge claim being advanced, typically knowing not only the particular field but also important characteristics of the researcher's technique and research situation. The second is usually composed of those persons whose judgment will facilitate the acceptance of the knowledge claim by a wider audience—for example, other colleagues, convention program committees, journal editors. A network of professionals in audiences, each further removed from the expertise initially required to judge the claim, extends to laypersons and students. If there is a consensus at the more specialized levels, each less specialized audience tends to accept the claim. When professionals fail to agree, it is very confusing to those without the expertise to judge for themselves (Chapter One).

3. The criteria of a good study are derived from determining what is involved in consensus creation through presentations of research (Chapter Two).

4. The search for relationships may be carried out in any way one wishes; it is a creative act that should not be circumscribed. But, in accord with preestablished criteria, those acts must include the gathering of whatever evidence is needed to present the knowledge claim (Chapter Two).

5. It is the presentation of the researcher's knowledge claim as an article, book, film, or speech that is circumscribed by expectations and criteria. The research is presented as a credible chain of reasoning in order to gain a consensus. One must build a chain that will reduce the audience's uncertainty that the projected relationships do indeed exist (Chapter Two).

6. We can describe a prototypical chain of reasoning that encompasses most researches and which can be adapted to others. It begins with a link that relates the findings of previous research to the problem, question, or hypothesis posed in the present study. The next link translates the problem, question, or hypothesis into the study design. The next link joins together the six links of which the design is composed: (a) subjects, (b) situations, (c) observations or measures, (d) treatments or independent variables, (e) basis of comparison by which an effect is sensed, and (f) the procedure that indicates who is observed or measured and when that is done and, if there is a treatment, who receives what treatment and when. The design is linked to data collection, which is linked to the conclusion of the

study. This conclusion, in turn, will link to the problem, question, or hypothesis of a new study as research continues (Chapter Two).

7. Presentations of knowledge claims based on quantitative methods follow closely the deductive order of the chain. Studies that are mainly descriptive and involve qualitative methods may use only the middle portion of the chain, which specifies subjects, situation, and so on. But if an explanation, theory, or generalization is advanced, it is usually inductively reasoned from the description, and the chain is used to relate the explanation to the description. If a qualitatively discovered relationship is validated by showing that it holds in situations beyond that in which it was first observed, or if a study builds on previous research to extend it, the chain of reasoning is followed much as in a quantitative study (Chapter Two).

8. The prototypical chain of reasoning has aspects analogous to a metal chain: A chain is only as strong as its weakest link; each link must be as strong as the others; the strength of the preceding link in the chain determines the necessary characteristics of the next; where two or more links collaborate in joining the preceding link to the next one, the collaborating links share the load of a single link, so one collaborating link may compensate in strength for another's weakness. Along with other characteristics, these help define the criteria of a good study (Chapter Two).

9. Typically research is an attempt to show relationships among variables or phenomena. The *power* of the study to bring about a consensus that the *link* between the phenomena or variables exists would reasonably seem to be called the study's *linking power*. But there is already a closely related term in common use, *internal validity*. To distinguish the newly defined but related term, the old one is modified to *internal validity (linking power)*, or, in abbreviated form, *internal validity (LP)*. In parallel fashion, the *power* of a study to bring about a consensus that the relationship can be *generalized* to other target persons, situations, times, treatment forms, ways of measuring or observing, or study designs or procedures would properly be called its *generalizing power*. But again a term is already in common use, *external validity*, so it will be modified in parallel fashion: *external validity (generalizing power)*, or, more briefly, *external validity (GP)* (Chapter Three).

10. The internal validity (LP) of a study depends on (a) presenting a *credible explanation* of the phenomenon, (b) showing that the explanation can be translated accurately *(translation fidelity)* into the events observed in the study, (c) *demonstrating* through those events that the *relationship* exists (if one is validating a hypothesis, confirmation of the strongest possible prediction of what will occur

is a very convincing demonstration), (d) showing that the demonstration cannot be reasonably accounted for by *rival explanations,* and (e) showing that this demonstration is consistent with previous work and is a *credible result* (Chapter Four).

11. The external validity (GP) of a study depends on (a) setting forth the *generality* of the *explanation,* (b) showing that *generality* has been representatively *translated* into the events of the study, (c) *demonstrating* that the *generality* claimed is represented in those events, (d) showing that the generality of the demonstration is not restricted by *rival explanations* of what occurred, and (e) judging that the *results* of the study are *replicable* in those instances to which generality is to be inferred (Chapter Five).

12. It is difficult to simultaneously maximize internal validity (LP) and external validity (GP) in the same study; researchers must decide how to optimally *weight* each. This decision usually follows from previous research (for example, has the existence of the relationship been established but not its generality?) and the nature of the policy, if any, to be determined by the outcome of the study (for example, the practice sounds reasonable, let us accept it and find out how broadly it holds) (Chapter Five).

13. In addition to optimally weighting internal validity (LP) and external validity (GP), the researcher must optimize four other aspects: (a) the *formulation* of the *question* investigated, (b) gaining *credibility with the audience* so the chain of reasoning is accepted, (c) *information yield* for the study, and (d) the *allocation of resources* to the various research tasks (Chapter Six).

14. Points 7 through 13 describe the conditions that must be met to build a strong chain of reasoning. In addition, these must be met within three limits and constraints:

a.   The *limits on resources* available to the researcher, including his* personal time, available secretarial, consulting, and computing services, journal space, or convention time for presentation of the study. The minimum of resources required for a study that will achieve one's goals is usually sought.

b.   The *ethical standards* of the profession as well as legal constraints and the requirements of human and animal subject protection review boards and privacy legislation.

---

*Rather than use the awkward "he or she" and "him or her" throughout the book, as no inclusive pronoun has been generally adopted, I shall in some instances vary the gender of the pronoun, thus giving approximately equal attention to female and male.

c. The constraints that *institutional procedures and routines* impose on the researcher, especially as institutions try to maintain "business as usual" (Chapter Six).

15. Researchers differ on what they construe to be the nature of a behavioral science. These differences have implications for their research methods and what they value as good research. Therefore, the criteria one must meet to carry out good research vary depending on one's orientation to knowledge and to the methods of research. One's beliefs about the nature of a behavioral science also affect what one does to gain a consensus. The orientation of the audience among whom one seeks a consensus is also important (Chapter Seven).

16. It is possible to cluster orientations to knowledge and methods of research into a *typology* of seven types: pragmatist, analyzer, synthesizer, theorizer, multiperspectivist, humanist, and particularist (Chapter Seven).

17. Researchers are socialized into a type during their graduate training. Some early, many later, find that their work and perspective fit several types, so that for such individuals the orientation may be better perceived as a role. This will probably be truer of mature researchers than of those enthusiastic and zealous individuals who have just been socialized into an orientation (Chapter Seven).

18. The conditions of points 10–16 can be related to the orientations to knowledge and method (the typology) in order to show which are most important for a given orientation and which are less so (Chapter Eight).

19. Some orientations are wedded to viewing relationships as causal. The cause-and-effect model has problems that some researchers perceive as sufficiently serious that they have called for abandoning it. Doing so seems unrealistic; causal analysis is frequently useful. But it is helpful to understand the objections to the causal model, such as the problem that any given cause-and-effect relation focuses attention on only one link in a causal chain. When cause-and-effect thinking is used, complex cause-and-effect models should be considered as well as simple ones (Chapter Nine).

20. The internal validity (LP)/external validity (GP) formulation can be related to the internal and external validity formulations of Cook and Campbell (1979) and Campbell and Stanley (1963) and to Cronbach's "reproducibility" (1982). It is hoped that this formulation has some advantages that will make it useful and will result in stronger behavioral science studies as well as a greater appreciation of the different orientations to behavioral sciences and their potential contributions (Chapter Eleven).

1

What Is Social and Behavioral Science Knowledge?

> We are a scientific civilisation; that means, a civilisation in which knowledge and its integrity are crucial. . . .
>
> Science is a very human form of knowledge. We are always at the brink of the known, we always feel forward for what is to be hoped. Every judgment in science stands on the edge of error and is personal. Science is a tribute to what we can know although we are fallible.
>
> —Jacob Bronowski, 1973, pp. 437, 374

The screen door slams, books and papers drop onto the front hall table, and Jamie comes into that always yummy-smelling kitchen, where he knows he'll be greeted by "Hi, what did you learn today?" If it weren't for the milk and chocolate chip cookies, he'd probably try to avoid the question, but they put him in a good mood. Somewhat against his better judgment, he proceeds to tell how the teacher explained long division. Mother, to whom the method is entirely foreign, and afraid her son is learning it all wrong, protests: "That's not the way to do it at all!" That makes Jamie defensive: "Mrs. Gillogly is right! She knows more about long division than you do, Mom!"

Well, purely aside from the merits of that remark, it is still a rude shock for that mother to realize that the teacher has replaced her as the source of reliable knowledge. But even that incident probably won't start her thinking about the difficulty her child is having in determining how to know when something is true—when something should be accepted as knowledge. It is a problem that he will face all through his life, just as his mother has all through hers. Yet, probably only in those rare times when Jamie or his mother is faced with conflicting opinions of trusted experts will either of them stop to think about how it is that something comes to be accepted as knowledge—and then not for long.

Knowing is something we take for granted; it is rare that we try to determine how we know something. When we do, it is usually to recall who told us or where we read it rather than to directly check the evidence that would help us determine its truth or falsity. For the hard fact is that most of what we know comes from sources other than our own personal observations. That is what makes the assurance that a source of information is trustworthy so important to us. Indeed, our dependence on the judgments of others as a source of reliable knowledge is so great that one of the developmental tasks of maturing involves both learning to trust others and discriminating sources of dependable knowledge from those to question.

The first of these, trust in others as the source of what is true, comes easily for most of us. Indeed, as the preceding vignette illustrates, trust in some sources can be so absolute in small children as to be disturbing. Further, when this trait continues into adulthood, we consider such a person to be naive and to have a "childlike trust." That we consider such trust inappropriate in a mature adult indicates that most of us master this second task as well.

Indeed, Jamie was already showing signs of discriminating his sources, much to the consternation of his mother, who was sure he was making his judgment incorrectly. Ah, there it is, *"making his judgment incorrectly."* Jamie and his mother must make a judgment about the source of the information and also a judgment about whether the source is correct in this instance. It is the judgment that determines for Jamie, for his mother, for you, for me, for anyone, what we will accept as knowledge and what we will not. (Most of the time we do this without consciously thinking about it; see Polanyi, 1958, and his later writing.) It is a personal judgment that we alone must make. We may let others make it in the sense that we trust their judgment and accept it as our own, but we must first make the judgment to accept theirs—*a judgment must be made.* KNOWING IS A PERSONAL JUDGMENT. Here, then, is the first step in determining what is knowledge.

This process can also be viewed as a *reduction in uncertainty* (Cronbach, 1982). The judgment may be considered an estimate of one's uncertainty. When this uncertainty is high, we are unwilling to admit whatever is being judged to the category "knowledge." When evidence of studies or the testimony of authorities reduces our uncertainty sufficiently, however, we are willing to do so.

The concept of uncertainty reduction—or its mirror image, the certainty with which knowledge is held—has the advantage of being able to reflect different levels of certainty. And clearly, although we may have a "knowing" threshold when something is admitted to our store of knowledge so that we will act on it as if it were true, not everything that crosses that threshold is held with the same certainty. We may reluctantly agree to fluoridation but only tentatively accept that it is safe and continue to scan the literature for studies that show the opposite. Or we may accept it but buy bottled spring water for drinking just to be on the safe side. Other items for which the explanations are equally removed from direct sensing, such as the relation of the earth and sun, we accept with quiet certainty, feeling sure the sun will rise tomorrow.

The level of the threshold probably bears a relation to how important the item is to us. Thus we may easily accept as knowledge an item from Ripley's *Believe It or Not!* that means little to us but may have a very high threshold requiring considerable evidence of safety before we are willing to agree our community should fluoridate the drinking water.

In addition, we make that judgment differently for different areas of life. In some instances—religion or law, for example—we may accept traditional authority. But we may reject that same authority in others—for instance, in knowledge about how the universe came to be or about evolution. We often accept the word of those we consider specialists, particularly in areas we know little about or are unable to experience directly. But we may determine to see for ourselves in other instances or to compare the knowledge claim against our own experiences for consistency. Much behavioral science knowledge is tested against our own experiences to see whether it "rings true."

Except as we study philosophy, we are typically not very conscious of this process. Nor can I do much more than somewhat raise your consciousness about it here. But this will be enough to pose some questions that will pave the way for a somewhat different perspective on behavioral science methodology. And that, of course, is my intent.

If, as is suggested in the preceding paragraph, we consider sources differently in making the "knowing" judgment, then perhaps we should examine more carefully what these sources are and how they affect our judgments. We shall turn to that next, but we must note that the discussion to this point still leaves unanswered the important question "When does 'knowing' become 'knowledge'?" We'll get to that.

Sources of Knowledge

Knowledge comes from many sources, and since the source often determines knowledge acceptance, a discussion of sources is important. Obviously, a source of focal interest is science, but it may help in understanding the nature and strengths of science if we first examine the others. Cohen and Nagel (1934) proposed that these other sources are personal observation and experience, authority, intuition, and tradition—a framework I shall use and somewhat further develop. I shall then examine the nature of knowledge before taking up science as a source.

Personal Observation and Experience

Personal experience is the source one most trusts; "Show me" is the cry of skeptics everywhere, not just those who add, "I'm from Missouri." If you can actually experience that emotionally disturbed children are less likely to act up when you, as teacher, move smoothly rather than abruptly from reading to art, then you are likely to be convinced of the validity of the principle that smooth transitions are essential to classroom control (Kounin, 1970).

Experiencing how things move and change is the method first used in childhood to explore the world. If you can't recall your own delight at discovering something new, watch the pleasure an infant shows in her discoveries. This, not incidentally, is the same pleasure a scientist feels on making a discovery. Re-creating that pleasurable sensation is a powerful motivator.

An important characteristic of personal experience is the need for infant and adult alike to find an order, or pattern, to their experiences. Where there are no obvious patterns, humans impose them—for instance, with a mnemonic device like "Every Good Boy Does Fine," which recalls the notes on the lines of the treble clef in music. This mnemonic translates an arbitrary set of letters into a sentence with a pattern of meaning that can be remembered. Judson notes, "Beat of the traffic, pulse of the phone, the long cycles of the angle of the sun in the sky. Patterns, rhythms, we live by patterns. . . . Patterns set up expectations. . . . To perceive a pattern means that we have already formed an idea of what's next" (1980, p. 28). And of course prediction is one of the most important outcomes of knowing, for if one can predict, one has a chance to control, thereby changing the outcome—an exciting possibility.

So personal experience, particularly that which results in the pleasure of discovery and that which can be organized into patterns, is a very important source of knowledge. It is, for that matter, the raw stuff of science, for the personal experience of the scientist is the basis for claims to knowledge discovery in such personally observed cases as experiments, surveys, and field studies. Alternatively, personal experience provides the ideas and hunches about what to study and what will lead to a newly discovered fact or relationship.

In general, we are able to trust our sense impressions, but we have all been exposed to sleight-of-hand magicians and to optical illusions in which these impressions betray us. We must then judge what to accept as true. When one finds that one cannot trust sense impressions, as we learn on succumbing to the lure of carnival funny rooms intended to trick our senses, one can be very upset, even nauseated.

Knowing depends on a personal judgment that one can trust the evidence of one's experiences or observations. Further, one's ability to organize those experiences in meaningful ways helps solve problems and contributes to more effective and efficient actions in one's environment.

Intuition

The category of intuition encompasses those propositions that are so obviously true as to be self-evident; merely stating them is enough for their acceptance. In many instances we infer such propositions from the world around us. The sun appears to revolve around the earth, a self-evident "fact" that was accepted for centuries. Similarly, that the earth was flat was a self-evident proposition long believed. Many beliefs about the inability of women to make decisions, to hold positions of authority, to do certain tasks well, were believed self-evident by men who cited their slighter build and presumed emotional nature.

From these examples, it is self-evident that not all self-evident propositions are true, a matter on which you will have to make a judgment, just as any person accepting a self-evident proposition does. So knowing, for self-evident propositions, involves making a judgment, just as it does with other sources.

It is threatening to have self-evident propositions turn out to be untrustworthy. If a particular proposition does, then how about others? How are we to distinguish the propositions to trust from those not to? There is no easy way! We tend not to question such propositions, for this is a quagmire from which there is no easy exit.

Tradition

The category of tradition includes all those things that "have always been true." The books that undergird various religions, such as the Bible, the Koran, and the Talmud, contain a large body of such knowledge. Interestingly, a variety of such books offer surprisingly similar rules of behavior. The Golden Rule, "Do unto others as you would have others do unto you," appears in some form in various such books. Perhaps experience results in convergence.

The advice passed from generation to generation, from father or mother to son or daughter, is also a part of the body of traditional knowledge. This is a particularly critical source in primitive cultures with fewer avenues to information than modern societies.

Traditional knowledge, especially of the religious kind, tends to be accompanied by authorities who facilitate its application to day-to-day situations. One's acceptance of the tradition is often linked to one's acceptance of the authority. But not always; the Golden Rule seems to be part of the traditional cultural wisdom for middle-class America almost regardless of religion. In some groups, it is converted to "Do unto others before they do it to you," a maxim that may be more practicable in the style of life to which they are exposed.

In either case, "knowing" relies on a personal judgment of whether to accept the tradition. In some instances, one must judge whether to accept, as well, the authoritative source of that knowledge, which gives and interprets it. This point quite naturally leads into the last of the sources other than science, authority.

Authority

Since we can experience personally no more than a small corner of our world, since most propositions are not self-evidently true, and since tradition tends to come with an authority figure, authorities are, without question, the major source of our knowledge. One accepts a fact or proposition as true because it was either presented by or accepted by someone considered an authority. This may be a teacher, a physician, a professor, a minister, a priest, a rabbi, an imam, or any of the variety of persons we accept as more knowledgeable than ourselves about a given area. Many professional persons earn their livings by being authorities. The personal judgment that in direct experience determines acceptance of something as true is now a judgment about the acceptance of the authority, thus preparing one to accept the knowledge the authority endorses as true.

There is a continuum of authorities, from the arbitrary, or dogmatic, kind, who present something as true by reason of their position, or ability to enforce its truth, through authorities who by position, experience, and their rationale are believable, to reasoning authorities who, though starting from a position of acceptance as an authority, nevertheless indicate the basis for their judgment and present a case for you to judge.

Dogmatic Authority. Dogmatic authority is found in some traditions and some religions where, if there was a rationale for a given truth, it has long since disappeared. Moon cycles may at one time have been the best guide for planting so as to avoid losing tender shoots to the frost or for gauging the rhythm of fish travel. One can still find published advice for planting and fishing based on this lore.

In some instances, a dogmatic authority may enforce certain points of view for ideological purity, as the Russians did Lysenkoism, the idea that each animal and plant could genetically pass on to its offspring characteristics that it acquired during its lifetime. In a dictatorship, dogmatic authority can, of course, be enforced.

Most religions offer a combination of authority by position and tradition, lying between the extremes, but many also provide a rationale to support their authority and explain the validity of their dogma. The dogmatic authority tends to be more trusted in matters involving values, in which one sometimes perceives that "right is right" and an appeal to reason leads only to endless discussion and argument. In matters dealing with the facts of existence or consequences of actions, the reasoning authority is especially trusted.

Challenges to dogmatic authority are quite threatening, just as they are to the other sources we have been examining. As with the challenge to intuition or tradition, if one doubts the authority in this instance, where does it stop? How does one discriminate the instances to question from the ones to accept? And perhaps most serious of all, if one disagrees with the authority violently enough or often enough, the veil of authority vanishes. The person loses the credibility that an authority must have to remain one.

Reasoning Authority. At the other end of the authority continuum is the reasoning authority, who is much like the scientist. Indeed, many of the characteristics of the reasoning authority are ones that help make science a source of so much accepted knowledge.

Any authority's past record of success, of being correct, is certainly a factor in engendering confidence. In this respect the reasoning authority figure ideally differs from the scientist, since, according to scientific principles, any scientist's claim to truth is judged solely on the basis of each new case put forward. In this view all scientists are equal when they claim something is true. To enforce this principle, some journals and government agencies remove the author's name before sending articles or research proposals to be judged; they want the article or proposal judged, not the author's reputation. In fact, of course, at conventions, in congressional testimony, and on similar occasions, leading scientists are likely to be thought to have a keener intellect and a better sense of what is true or false than either the less experienced or the run-of-the-mill researcher, and they take on the characteristics of the reasoning authority, including the mantle of authority, by reason of their previous success. Historians of science can cite numerous instances when the course of science was set back because a newcomer's ideas were discounted in the face of lack of acceptance by a leading scientist. The case for the sun revolving around the earth was perpetuated by scientific authorities long after contrary evidence challenged it.

Prime among the characteristics of the reasoning authority approach is the logical force of the arguments put forward in the rationale or explanation. For example, suppose we note that smooth classroom transitions aid in controlling emotionally disturbed children by continuously directing their attention to external stimuli, thus averting attention from internal turmoil that would result in disturbing actions. This argument makes Kounin's (1970) proposition much more convincing and acceptable than the stark assertion that "smooth transitions are correct teacher behavior."

Ideally, such an authority has little to gain by others' acceptance of her statements. In actuality, of course, this is rarely true. For some there may be nothing more than the pleasure of recognition. For others there may be monetary gain, directly or indirectly, that recognition brings. Nevertheless, just as too obvious advertising appeals are counterproductive, so also too much personal gain by an authority raises suspicions that attaining the next reward quickly may become more important than taking extra time to verify accuracy.

An important characteristic of the reasoning expert is integrity, which results in openness about what she does or does not know, willingness to reveal the weaknesses in the case, and a balanced presentation of pros and cons. All this makes it less likely that something is being hidden that might affect the judgment and that if something is missing, it is by intent.

Challenges to reasoning authority may seem less serious than those to dogmatic authority; one may find good reason to disagree with the authority in one instance but still accept that authority in another where her rationale holds. But if the reasoning authority is rejected often enough—or violently enough in a serious instance—then, like the dogmatic authority, she loses her authoritativeness.

Clearly, in the acceptance of the authority in general in the case of dogmatic authority, or in particular instances in the case of a reasoning authority, there is a judgment to be made, a judgment that results in knowing.

Knowing, a Personal Judgment; Knowledge, a Consensus

So far we have seen that each of the potential sources of knowledge requires a decision by the individual whether to accept something as "known." How are such judgments translated into knowledge? Basically by a series of individual judgments arriving at the same conclusion, by a consensus that something is accepted as known. This may be a consensus that the word of some authority (the pope, the president, a dictator) is to be accepted; it may be the result of common experience (we all can see that humans have ten fingers, two eyes, and one nose); it may be the acceptance of something commonly and intuitively obvious (the sun goes around the earth). In any of these instances, it is the common acceptance that allows something to be called knowledge. Knowing involves a personal judgment; knowledge involves a consensus of such judgments.

The fact that a consensus develops around a knowledge claim is typically not apparent or given much thought except in those instances when it doesn't develop. It becomes painfully obvious when authorities we want to trust disagree. In many areas genuine disagreements among experts cause confusion; this is especially obvious in the health field. For many persons, for instance, the evidence is overwhelming that adding a fluoride to drinking water reduces tooth decay with no harmful effects. Yet, hold a public hearing in any community in the country, and vociferous critics, convinced of its harmful effects, will appear to testify against the practice, citing their experts and evidence. Their personal "knowing" convinces them that it is *not* without harm, and they try to build a consensus in the community that their "knowing" should be that of the community as well—that there should be consensus that fluoridation is harmful. In this instance, the majority view that it is harmless commonly prevails, but the process illustrates the consensus problem, especially when particular findings are the basis for political action or policy.

The idea that the formation of knowledge is a social process involving consensus may be interpreted to mean that there need be no correspondence between "knowledge" and "reality" or "truth" (however one wishes to define those terms—a book in itself but not our focus here). This would be a very disturbing point of view that nobody would want to believe. But the fact is that it is true for those phenomena for which there is no way of gathering evidence other than the testimony of other humans. A group *can* believe as true whatever the consensus of the group agrees to, particularly if it seeks no additional confirmation beyond the say-so of others.

One can see an example in religious cults that have unique beliefs. Although the community in which the cult exists may hold no consensus about those beliefs and therefore not accept their truth, the cult members do hold a consensus about those beliefs and accept them.

For most knowledge, however, we seek some confirmation beyond the belief of other persons. Typically we want independent confirmation in the form of some evidence that we personally or someone we trust can interpret. This fact, of course, suggests the role of science.

Scientific knowledge is also formed from a consensus but with three important differences from other sources:

1. The consensus in these instances *is formed around the interpretation of evidence.* (You no doubt recall from your history books that one of the characteristics of the Renaissance—as well as a foundation of science—was dependence on carefully gathered evidence, in contrast to the prevalent prior practice of sitting around thinking about a subject.)
2. The consensus is developed within rules or norms intended to prevent an arbitrary and unwarranted consensus from developing.
3. The evidence around which the consensus is developed must meet certain criteria.

The criteria that the evidence must meet will be the focus of much of this book, so they will be developed in other chapters. Later in this chapter we shall examine the norms or rules within which a consensus in science is developed. These norms were well described by Merton (1968). As you are no doubt realizing by now, this chapter is devoted to laying the groundwork for understanding what knowledge is and the various sources of knowledge, including science. This perspective is necessary if one is to understand the larger picture within which science operates. To obtain a better understanding of science, let us examine in more detail science as a source of knowing and knowledge.

Science

Of all the methods of knowing, science is most closely associated with discovering truth in modern life. Indeed, Descartes thought that any knowledge that can be questioned ought not to be called science (Machlup, 1981). But individuals at the forefront of science always have divided opinions about what is to be accepted as knowledge. So even though Descartes' definition may sound right to the person on the street who thinks all propositions advanced by science are true, that is too limited a definition to encompass the process of scientific knowledge development.

Science as a Social Process of Consensus Building

Much of the content of science is beyond the reach of personal experience for the layperson. Indeed, even scientists themselves do not personally experience most of the findings of science outside their own field of specialization—their personal experience is limited to their own research and the field and laboratory experiences of their training. Rather, they depend on the process of science to judge the evidence presented by the researcher who did the study. Thus science depends on a social process whereby a consensus around the interpretation of evidence is reached and accepted by those not in a position to observe the evidence themselves or, in many instances, to participate substantially in the process. Campbell (1977) has likened the process to a "fishscale"; it might also be likened to the overlapping pattern of shingles on a roof. It consists of a series of individuals each further removed from the study in question, looking over the shoulders of those who have made previous judgments about a knowledge claim. This is one of Merton's (1968) norms, the process of "organized skepticism," at work. (We shall see later Merton's analysis of the other norms of science.)

If we look at the process in more detail, it starts with the individual investigator or investigative team who complete a study intended to establish a knowledge claim. Having, as best they can, designed it to fit the criteria a study must meet in order to be accepted, they judge its results to see whether, as the study was actually carried through, a knowledge claim seems warranted. This is the "knowing" judgment of the researcher that a knowledge claim is valid. His problem then is to present that claim in such a way that he can explain the situation well enough to others to answer whatever questions or doubts they may have so they will arrive at the same "knowing" judgment he did. He will need to show that he is a competent researcher with integrity who sets forth the evidence and its interpretation in such a way that others can judge for themselves and see that the claim is warranted. As we shall see in later chapters, it is from an analysis of what is required to achieve these goals that the criteria of a good study and a broader perspective on research methodology can be developed.

Next, a study report is prepared that presents the evidence and the possible interpretations of it and then presents, as tightly as the evidence will permit, a chain of reasoning for the knowledge claim being advanced. The process is essentially the same whether it is a new discovery, verification of a previous claim, or evidence rejecting a previous claim.

Typically this report is circulated among other scientists working in the same or closely related fields who are in a position to judge the work and who make suggestions and comment on the report and the validity of the claim. If the claim passes this test, it may be presented orally at the convention of a scientific society, again a test with peers who are in a position to judge whether the claim is warranted. If it passes this test (or, failing, if it can be mended satisfactorily), the study is typically submitted for publication. Sometimes the convention presentation step is skipped or occurs while the manuscript has been submitted but not yet published.

Scientists value most highly those journals that use a peer review process to select their articles, since editors, good as they may be, are unlikely to be specialists in all the areas included in their journal. Competent, neutral specialists, chosen by the editor, judge the acceptability of each article and give their opinion on whether it is ready, possibly with revisions, for publication. Such judgments are rendered as a service to the profession without compensation. Many journals remove information identifying the author to ensure that the merit of the article, not the author's reputation, is the determining factor.

Occasionally researchers in the same or related fields, on reading the report, may try to replicate the study. Though quite common in the natural sciences, this is a rare response in the behavioral sciences. More likely, if the work seems to have validity in their judgment, they will develop a study that, by extending or otherwise building on it, tests it. Their acceptance (or rejection) of the work is, in turn, noted by others less closely related to the expertise required in the initial study, often by broader specialists assembling a review of work in an area. The expertise of these others overlaps that of those in the initial area, but they are not typically specialists in it. Their summarization and review of this initial piece of work and of those building on it will be integrated into the larger body of research in the area. Such reviews are most helpful to those writing texts or preparing encyclopedia and handbook entries on the subject. The authors screen such reviews for material well enough accepted to be included in these compendiums of established knowledge. Thus the work of professionals with overlapping specialties, each watching over the work in her area of expertise and in a sense policing it, results in judgments that are scrutinized and passed on to those with less specialized expertise. These eventually find their way to laypersons in communications that are accepted as authoritative because the preceding process requires both careful screening and consensus building.

Science as Uncertainty Reduction

Earlier we saw that the process of knowing can be interpreted as the reduction in uncertainty about the interpretation of evidence to the point where it crosses the individual's threshold, that level of certainty where it becomes, for that individual, knowledge. So also the process of consensus building that results in others' accepting a researcher's claim as knowledge can be interpreted as the lowering of the level of uncertainty among those who form the consensus. Since the consensus is made up of "knowing" judgments, and since the level to which uncertainty must be reduced probably differs somewhat from individual to individual, the task of developing the case for one's peers may, for some persons, mean setting a higher standard than they themselves might observe. Thus the threshold level of uncertainty for something to be considered knowledge is not fixed. Indeed, we operate with various levels of certainty (or amounts of reduction in uncertainty) in different spheres.

The level of certainty that I require before I will design a new study built on the last one I performed may be lower or higher for me than for others. The level required for publication will be that established by the reviewers and clearly varies with the reputation of the journal. The level of certainty required if the published article is to be included in a review of the research of an area is at least as high as, and perhaps slightly higher than, that at which the article was accepted for its first publication in a journal. The level of certainty for acceptance into a text is probably still higher and requires a broader and deeper consensus among those working in the area. The level for admittance to a handbook or encyclopedia that represents itself as summarizing the established knowledge in an area is probably higher still. Thus we can see that the level used for continuation of research in an area is probably lower than that for transmission to the layperson as established knowledge. Yet, at all levels, there is a reduction of uncertainty judged sufficient for the intended use of the knowledge. That seems to be the guiding factor.

The Process of Science and Its Norms

It should be clear by now that for science to produce accepted knowledge requires a functioning social system and any social system requires norms and rules to maintain the system and facilitate its work and, in particular, to help ensure that any consensus that develops is warranted. Merton (1968) described these norms, one of which, organized skepticism, was referred to earlier. The others—universalism, communism, and disinterestedness—do not as clearly indicate by their titles what is meant. Let us, therefore, look at each more closely.

Universal Standards for Knowledge Claims (Universalism)

Knowledge claims, whatever their source, are to be judged by preestablished criteria that are common across all such claims. The reason is to prevent a consensus from developing around one study by applying special criteria not used for comparable studies. One doesn't apply a different set of criteria to those just beginning to do research than to senior researchers; nor should nationality, race, religion, and so forth make a difference. It is the quality of the work itself rather than the characteristics of the research, the financial supporter, or the sponsoring institution that should be the focus of judgment.

Common Ownership of Information (Communism)

Scientific norms reduce proprietary rights to the minimum. Information is to be open to others; indeed, there is an obligation to communicate findings. Individuals like Lord Cavendish, whose experiments demonstrated the presence of oxygen but who did not publish them, are viewed as having misplaced modesty. The communal character of science, Merton notes, is exemplified by Newton's remark "If I have seen farther, it is by standing on the shoulders of giants." Many universities have regulations limiting or banning research that cannot be freely published because of a sponsor's conditions.

Integrity in Gathering and Interpreting Data (Disinterestedness)

That the scientist can be trusted to gather data and to interpret it without regard to her personal predilections about what it should be or what it should show is, of course, essential to the integrity of the process. Occasionally newspapers will give considerable space to, for example, an investigator who faked data to make the results come out right, and there have even been congressional hearings over fraudulent science (Broad, 1981a, 1981b). Campbell (1979), caricaturing the scientific position, suggests that instead of science being groups policing one another, one can view it as "self-perpetuating mutual admiration societies whose social systems prevent reality testing, stifle innovation as heresy, suppress disconfirming evidence" (p. 181). Presumably these groups could call anything true knowledge that they agreed on. (For example, the president, the secretary, and presumably the members of the International Flat Earth Research Society believe the world is "a flat disc floating on primordial waters, with the North Pole at its center and Antarctica around its circumference" [Gates and Smith, 1984, p. 12]. They have developed a consensus around their evidence that is quite different from the one most of the rest of us accept.) Indeed, since a major intent is to convince the consumer of the truth of the researcher's knowledge claim, then any method of advertising, propaganda, or persuasion that would be effective in this process seems fair. Feyerabend (1975), who sees research as a hurly-burly of claims and counterclaims, presents Galileo as a case study in point. He shows that Galileo's famous sketches of the moon were so inaccurate that simple observation would have exposed them. Moreover, Galileo advertised his successes and hid his mistakes, and he wrote in persuasively styled Italian rather than the academic Latin. Feyerabend considers him a propagandist as well as a scientist.

Some scientists may seem to act as manipulators of public opinion in instances such as the argument over when human life begins, a central factor in the case against legal abortion, and can be accused of being propagandists for what they believe. Further, there are undoubtedly instances when researchers have so much of their lives invested in a particular theory or viewpoint that discussions of competing theories become passionately fought battles in which no technique of convincing others is barred. These are exceptions that, although they contribute little to the integrity of science, nevertheless enliven the scientific scene.

Feyerabend may see such instances as the stuff of normal science, but most researchers and philosophers of science do not. Their perception comes from watching the peer review process at work wherever one seeks to communicate a knowledge claim: in journals, at a convention or meeting, or in publishing a book. Each of these ways of setting forth a knowledge claim is monitored by gatekeepers who apply agreed-on criteria. Further, except when scientists are dealing directly with the lay public and when, if bent in that direction, they could exploit the public's credulity, ignorance, and dependence, they are normally dealing with equally well-trained and capable peers. Thus the potential for successful scientific fraud is small and the chances of detection great. Considering the large number of research studies, by almost any standard the amount of dishonesty is small. But any at all is more than the system allows, and the authority of all science is reduced by indiscretions of any one of its practicing members.

Organized Skepticism

Organized skepticism is a basic norm that makes science a unique source of knowledge. It is the responsibility of the community of scientists to be skeptical of each new knowledge claim, to test it, and to try to think of reasons that the claim might be false—to think of alternative explanations that might be as plausible as the one advanced. This challenge to new knowledge is *sought* in science rather than avoided as it is in other methods such as authority and intuition. It helps assure the validity of the new knowledge.

Sir Karl Popper (1959) and his followers would argue that it is by the acting out of this skepticism, by actively trying to disconfirm knowledge claims, that science proceeds (more on this in "How Science Logically Proceeds," in Chapter Three). But, as we have seen, once a knowing judgment is made, individuals act on the basis of the knowledge as if it had some certainty—in some instances tentatively, as with the fluoridation decision; in others with considerable certainty. Instead of building tests to disconfirm findings advanced as true, people are more likely to build on them, to try to advance our understanding, and to try to find the breadth of generality of the proposition and its strength under varying circumstances. (Popper and his followers would view the latter as disconfirmation tests— finding where the proposition does not hold.)

Popper's description of science may be somewhat more descriptive of the physical sciences than the behavioral. But hardly any proposition in either the behavioral or the physical sciences holds regardless of circumstances. In the behavioral sciences, people are so different and are so affected by the variety of circumstances in which they find themselves that there are nearly always situations in which a proposition would not be expected to hold. There are so many such unexplained variations that we expect them. Although, like physical scientists, we would like to explain the aberrations, we are less prone to see them as contradicting the main proposition than physical scientists. For the physicist, for instance, all electrons behave alike; similarly protons, positrons, and so on. Should a generalization applying to one of these kinds of matter be disconfirmed by a study, the disconfirmation would be expected to apply to all particles of the same kind. But in the behavioral sciences, we have yet to develop a typology tight enough that we can predict behavior in particular situations from it. We can forecast tendencies and increase the odds of predicting what might occur, but we do not yet have the predictive power of the physical scientist. We do not have the equivalent of electrons that are all alike, positrons, and so on.

Thus, although Popper's ideas apply in theory to the behavioral sciences, they seem less descriptive of the norm of operation than in the physical sciences. The behavioral sciences have a norm of organized skepticism of the same kind as exists in the physical sciences that operates in the critique of studies before and after publication. But there are fewer attempts to replicate studies exactly, and the likelihood is greater that accepted new findings will be built on in further study of the phenomenon, thus examining and confirming the finding in a new way. Gradually the uncertainty about a finding is reduced as these studies accumulate, and a broader and deeper consensus develops among the members of a discipline about the nature of the phenomenon.

The practice of organized skepticism depends on the support of the previous three norms: universal standards, common ownership of information, and integrity, or disinterestedness. The use of common criteria for all knowledge claims of the same kind is essential to the fair judgment of each one; we can't be skeptical about the claims of one study on the basis of one set of criteria and of a similar study on a different set. Common ownership, the openness of information for critique, is essential if scientists are to have an adequate basis for applying and judging the knowledge claim. Finally, the integrity with which data are collected and interpreted, not allowing personal biases to intrude, is essential to having trustworthy evidence on which to base a "knowing" judgment. Thus, all the norms work together to support organized skepticism in such a way that science can explain away uncertainty and achieve consensus around knowledge claims.

Additional Characteristics That Enhance Consensus Building and Knowledge Acceptance

Characteristics of science additional to the norms just described contribute to making it a trusted method for knowing and knowledge building: (1) the perceived *objective* nature of its methods, above the dictates and biases of any one scientist, (2) the *replicability* of findings, which ensures that it was neither the particular circumstances nor a chance circumstance that resulted in a finding, (3) the insistence on *empirical* demonstrations to validate whatever theoretical and speculative work has been advanced, and (4) the *self-correcting* nature of science wherein findings are held as tentative until they are replaced by better-established knowledge claims. Each of these characteristics contributes to the consensus-making power of science. Add to these the logical persuasiveness of science spokespersons as they prepare carefully built chains of reasoning to present their claims to knowledge, and one can understand how, as a consequence, science is accorded the status and prestige of authority, a status that in itself is conducive to consensus building. These characteristics derive largely from the perception of science as a natural science.

To what extent does the mantle of science as a prestigious and trusted source of knowing extend to the behavioral sciences? Clearly, not to a great extent. Although objectivity, replicability, empiricism, and self-correction are also present in the behavioral sciences, there are differences that reflect on the behavioral sciences' consensus-building capacity. Let us examine the characteristics and note the differences.

Objectivity

A more descriptive name than *objectivity* is *intersubjective testability;* that is, phenomena observed by the researcher would be seen in the same way by another observer. A particular concern here is that the findings are not influenced by the researcher's emotions, biases, or predilections. Clearly that is easier when one is dealing with springs or beams of light that everyone can see or touch than with human perceptions. Psychologists in particular have made great efforts to find ways of observing and measuring phenomena that are as objective as they can make them. In doing so, however, they have been accused of studying only phenomena that lend themselves to such "clean" measurement and thereby missing really important variables and holistic views of problems.

By contrast, sociologists and anthropologists, who do *not* confine their observations to things that can be measured objectively, seek holistic views and whatever the important variables in them may be. But there is then always the concern that what they consider important and the way they view it may flow from their own biases and predilections, sometimes built into them by their culture and expectations. We like to imagine that we objectively observe whatever is present, but even what we see may be influenced by our expectations. As Ferris (1981, p. 66) notes, physiologists think of the eye as delivering television pictures to be observed. But "psychologists disagree. The eye, they say, is part of the brain and delivers not television pictures . . . but processed information, much of it . . . hypothesis. . . . And in the dialogue between the eye and the rest of the brain, what we see can become what we expect to see. A field mouse is transformed into a snake to the thinker who fears snakes." Animated conversation can become an argument to those expecting it.

One can avoid this problem with tests, scales, attitude measures—so-called objective measures, with which the decisions about what to observe, how to observe it, and how to evaluate it are all agreed on in advance. But in doing so, one often pays the price of forgoing natural observation—one gives up the chance to observe what is important in *this* situation and evaluate it in terms of what it means there. The problem thus becomes one of trade-offs, one of many I shall be pointing out; science, behavioral science especially, is full of them. Objectivity may not be easily achieved in the behavioral sciences, and when it is, there may be trade-offs that can weaken the research; sometimes objectivity exacts too high a toll.

Replicability

Findings resulting from scientific methods should be replicable. Someone else should be able to duplicate the procedure or the experiment and observe the same results. Indeed, as findings are successfully replicated, they gain credence with other scientists. If replications by interested others are to be possible, two conditions are necessary: (1) public procedures so the descriptions are available (the norm of common ownership of information) and (2) precise descriptions of what was done or observed.

These conditions are generally observed in the behavioral sciences, so they are not the problem. Yet, as we have already seen, exact replications are considerably less frequent in the behavioral sciences.

It is difficult to explain the general lack of replications, although one may speculate about the reasons. One reason may be the greater desire among behavioral scientists to do a study that is their own. Whereas the tradition in the physical sciences is to do a dissertation suggested by one's major professor, often a needed part of a larger research project conceived by someone else, behavioral science students are much more likely to be encouraged to do a dissertation of their own invention. Thus, whereas natural scientists from the start accept the fact that good science means doing studies invented by someone else, behavioral scientists are more oriented toward going off in their own directions and devising their own research designs.

Another possible reason has already been observed in the difficulty of replicating, especially in a different context. As noted earlier, electrons, springs, and liquids of the same kind behave alike. Perhaps even more important, they behave the same way outside the laboratory as in it. Unlike humans, they do not sense that there is a difference. In the behavioral sciences, however, a laboratory study may not replicate under field conditions. The behavioral scientist is therefore denied the careful control of conditions available in the natural sciences. Further, even replication in the same subjects may be dubious, because every experience changes a person slightly, so that even experiencing the identical situation a second time may elicit a different response from the first. Add to these factors the variability in feelings of power and powerlessness, of exhilaration and depression, of eagerness and withdrawal that different subjects experience toward a study and will allow, to varying degrees, to affect their behavior during a study, so that two sets of subjects may not respond similarly. It is not hard to understand why replicability is more of a problem for the behavioral than for the natural sciences.

Empiricism

As we saw earlier, empiricism is one of the main discriminators between science as a source of knowledge and other sources. Other methods than science also require a consensus of knowing judgments, but in science it is a consensus about the *appropriate interpretation of evidence,* an essential difference. Science depends not on sheer armchair speculation but on actually trying things out: observing actual instances (getting empirical data) to see whether and how something works. Speculation is very useful in suggesting ideas, but it is the confirmation or disconfirmation of speculations empirically that provides the basis for scientific consensus building about their truth or falsity.

The behavioral and natural sciences are more alike in this respect than in some others, but the behavioral sciences have a special problem. To empirically gather data on a characteristic, one must be able to translate it into something that can be sensed—seen, smelled, felt, heard, or tasted. Unfortunately, many of the characteristics we wish to study or the behaviors we wish to record are internal to human beings. They are apparent only if and as they affect observable physiological characteristics or overt behavior. Interpreting the meaning of data therefore requires accurately inferring which external manifestations match the internal ones we want to study. Empirical "measures" are at least one inference removed from the behaviors or characteristics themselves. Even though we use empirical methods, inferences from those measures to internal behaviors or states are less than certain.

Self-Correction

The norm of organized skepticism, discussed earlier, clearly supports the self-correcting nature of science. Scientists, by holding that all knowledge is only tentatively true until replaced by new and more substantively established knowledge, see the best of two worlds. On the one hand, self-correction permits the accretion of a solid knowledge base through proper skepticism and challenge of old findings. On the other hand, it allows asserting the truth of what is accepted as knowledge with enough certainty for those who need to use it to do so with some assurance that they will not be too far in error. But the fact that there is always the tentative aspect warns the user, particularly on the fringes of knowledge, to make provision for instances when a tentatively accepted consensus may have erred.

Note that I describe science as "asserting the truth of what is accepted as knowledge *with enough certainty.*" This is consistent with viewing the function of research studies as reducing the uncertainty about the nature of a relationship or phenomenon. I have already noted that there are different levels of uncertainty (amounts of reduction of uncertainty) for initial publication, research reviews, handbooks, encyclopedias, and so on. But in science, if knowledge is always to be held as tentative, the uncertainty is never reduced to zero; there is always the possibility, although it grows progressively smaller with the accumulation of evidence, that new evidence will call for a reinterpretation of knowledge considered established. Although we realize the truth of this assertion if we think about it, in practice we act, in the main, as if the uncertainty were reduced to zero. This makes a practical difference in behavior only when a new knowledge claim confronts us that challenges what we thought we knew.

Scientists, for example, tend to be scornful of "mind over matter" claims. When transcendental meditation (TM) was advanced as a cure for some of the world's ills, especially reaction to stress, many dismissed it out of hand. But these were largely scientists acting toward a field outside their own field of knowledge as laypersons might. Those whose area the claim touched took it seriously, and a recent review of research on TM shows that it apparently has no greater ability to reduce stress than resting (Holmes, 1984). So it turns out that those who were scornful were correct in rejecting the claim, but only those who entertained it seriously and subjected it to test were acting in proper scientific tradition.

Knowledge Versus Truth—an Example

Finally, smoldering underneath much of the chapter is the question whether knowledge and truth are the same thing. One hopes that they are, intends them to be, and generally believes they are. But the argument that knowing rests on a personal judgment and knowledge on a social consensus seems to suggest uncomfortably that knowledge could be a relative concept that depends in part on the society in which one lives. A story may help to illuminate the relationship, some points in the chapter, and the role of science.

Dr. Lincoln Moses, dean of the graduate school at Stanford, likes to make this point with a story of the Peace Corps volunteers who were sent to a Caribbean island to teach the natives new methods of agriculture. When the natives found out how ignorant these volunteers were about the facts of growing things, they decided they could properly ignore fertilizers and the rest of the volunteers' advice. The volunteers did not even know that stones grow over the year! Every spring when one plants a crop, one takes the big stones out of the field, but of course it is too much trouble to remove all the little ones. Next year there is always a new crop of big stones! Anyone who has worked on a garden, especially one in stony soil, cannot help having some sympathy for these natives.

Here is an instance in which, to us, knowledge and truth are *not* the same thing. Knowledge is shown to be relative to what the group believes. In this instance, to the islanders, it was true knowledge that stones grew.

The source of that knowledge—personal experience, tradition, intuitive self-evidence, or an authority—is not clear; it could have been any of these. Whichever it was, not only did it mislead the islanders, but so firmly was the knowledge held that it led them to distrust science—to us, a more reliable source of knowledge. Note that once the authorities (the volunteers) were proved wrong, they ceased to be authoritative.

The source of that knowledge could not have been science. Even if, from careless observation, the proposition that stones grew had been advanced, it would in time have been replaced by the fruits of more careful observation. With the self-correcting norm of science operating, new knowledge would have replaced old. And because of the norm of holding all knowledge as tentatively true, the islanders would not have so firmly held to the appealing falsehood.

Careful scientific observation of the rocks in a sample of plots throughout the year would have shown that they did not grow; rather, large ones worked their way up and emerged. Out of the interpretation of carefully gathered observations, one could not have attained a consensus for the proposition that rocks grow. The value of empirical evidence as a basis for achieving consensus in science differentiates it from other knowledge that also might achieve consensus, such as a religious teaching.

Presumably, had the volunteers adopted the methods of science and showed the fruits of their knowledge from careful observation, they might have won the islanders over both to the agricultural practices they wished to demonstrate and to science. Science, by its track record, by the maintenance of its norms, and because of the characteristics of its methods, is a very convincing, and therefore successful, way of adding to knowledge. The fact that it is self-critical and holds all truths as tentative is not entirely understood by the public, especially when reversals of previously held "truths" occur. Nevertheless, even this characteristic gives it an integrity that most sources of authority lack.

Had the volunteers been trying to convince the islanders of behavioral science principles, they might have had a tougher time of it. Although behavioral scientists have adopted the norms of science, they are not as successful in demonstrating characteristics such as objectivity, empiricism, and replicability that make the natural sciences so convincing. Further, had those behavioral science principles been counterintuitive, as rejection of the idea that rocks grew was to the islanders, the problems would have been even greater. Behavioral science findings, when they deal with things in which people have had experience (and most behavioral science findings do), rarely find ready acceptance if they are counterintuitive (Lindblom and Cohen, 1979). Behavioral science has its greatest impact where it reinforces intuitively (and experientially) acceptable positions. And as Prewitt (1980) notes, "The social sciences seldom get credit for their counterintuitive findings, as legion as they are, because people quickly rearrange their belief systems, claiming that they 'knew it all along'" (p. xxiv). This is especially true where several positions can be rationalized as common sense and research delineates one of these as the accurate one.

Finally, the contrast between the volunteers, for whom science was a trusted source of knowledge, and the islanders, for whom it was not, shows that acceptance of science is itself, in part at least, a cultural phenomenon. Is our society, with its emphasis on science, closer to making truth and knowledge synonymous? Clearly we believe so. And the self-correcting character of science suggests that, in the long run at least, it is a reliable method of finding truth.

Andrejs Ozolins, a very insightful student in one of my classes, described very well a relaxed view of how science proceeds (in response to a take-home examination, January 12, 1983):

> The purpose of science is the generation of knowledge; but what a researcher can hope to do is no more than to come up with a plausible story to tell about the world, an account which helps us feel at home but which inevitably breaks down at some point into a fresh mystery. In time, parts of various stories or accounts coalesce into what everyone agrees is knowledge without consulting epistemologists. And, sometimes, everyone has to agree that what they agreed to was not so; someone has come up with a more plausible story.
>
> I don't think this view diminishes or denigrates science. The criteria for plausibility are very stringent, and they can be articulated far more precisely than the grander notion of knowledge. This view does not offer to make a Prometheus of every researcher, but the emotions of gods may not be the best preparation for endeavors which, well done, can be the highest achievement of human beings.

2

From Discovery to Confirmation

Building the Chain of Reasoning

> In each period there is a general form of the forms
> of thought; and like the air we breathe, such a form is
> so translucent and so pervading, and so seemingly neces-
> sary, that only by extreme effort can we become aware of
> it.
>
> —Alfred North Whitehead, 1933, p. 12

Were Whitehead living today, he would probably agree that the pervading form of thought is science, and the effort to understand that process, though in some aspects as difficult as the quotation indicates, is very important. The previous chapter has given some indication of this form; the next chapters pin down more explicitly what occurs and the criteria by which one can judge it.

This chapter makes two points:

1. During the discovery phase of a study, when one is seeking patterns of related variables or trying to make sense out of a mass of apparently random detail, one may do anything that helps to find a pattern. In the words of a philosopher of science, Feyerabend (1975), "Anything goes."

2. Believing that one has found a pattern or relationship, one now seeks to interpret for others the evidence that the pattern or relationship exists and that, in contrast to plausible alternatives, the explanation being advanced is the best one. This is the confirmation phase; one has a claim one wishes to be considered true, to be fact, to be knowledge. There are conventions and expectations about how such a knowledge claim is made. One expectation is that as closely reasoned an argument as possible will be presented, including an examination of the cases for the strongest alternative explanations and the cases against them.

These two points make good intuitive sense. It stands to reason that "anything goes" in the discovery phase. We don't know the routes to discovery; if we did, everyone would be pursuing them; knowledge growth would be much faster and would be routine rather than unexpected. Of all phases of research, discovery is the least routine; one never knows when or where a breakthrough will occur. In fact, it is the unexpectedness of the discovery phase that gives a special fascination and excitement—just as in watching sports on live television, where one never knows what is going to happen next.

Similarly, the confirmation phase makes intuitive sense. In convincing someone of the existence of a pattern or relationship, it is clear that one presents a closely reasoned case with examples. So does the researcher! That there should be common patterns for the presentation of such knowledge claims is sensible too: It simplifies the task of making judgments. Note how the articles in most research journals follow the same format. Only as a pattern is established that allows one to apply certain criteria quickly and determine the fit can so many claims be processed and assimilated or discarded.

Accordingly, not much solid advice about the discovery phase of research can be given; it is a creative art. Therefore, although the material that follows will briefly discuss the discovery phase, most of the chapter concerns the confirmation chain of reasoning. Succeeding chapters will take up the criteria for judging knowledge claims.

The Discovery Phase

What picture comes to your mind when you visualize a working researcher? Most likely it is an organized person engaged in goal-directed activity who knows exactly what to seek, what background material to study, what steps to take next, which data to collect when, and what to do with them. If so, you are visualizing the stereotype conveyed by research reports intended to explain to readers why a knowledge claim is valid. They read as straightforward accounts of highly organized activity.

Some research is like that; the discovery phase involves choice of a problem, and this is sometimes routine. Perhaps one is even given the problem to work on; perhaps the route to the present study was made unequivocally clear by previous work.

But discovering one's own problem usually follows a period in which one's work is typically unsettled—leads are followed, explored, discarded, new ones tried, old ones gone back to, and so forth. When one is not sure what one is looking for, the discovery phase can be very disorganized. Observing a culture for the first time, one isn't sure which of the various behaviors define that culture and are the really significant ones as viewed by its members. New teacher education students sent to observe classrooms are likely to find methods of classroom control the most fascinating issue—who misbehaves and how the teacher responds. It is only later that the significant aspects of teacher behavior more directly related to the learning process can be discerned. Actually the term *discovery* is a little colorful for this phase, which may or may not yield new discoveries but which definitely consists of exploratory activity.

On occasion that exploratory activity isn't disorganized at all but is a straightforward trial of the various candidates for a solution, as in the search for a drug that will cure a disease. Thomas A. Edison was noted for such searches. He is said to have systematically tried hundreds of substances in experiments costing more than $40,000, a very large sum in the 1870s, in seeking a filament that would give light as it conducted electricity in his incandescent lamp bulb. Some exploratory efforts have a logic and pattern to the investigator, but other efforts may be close to an associational chain rather than conforming to formal logical rules. Although some would argue that this chain has a logic of its own, its logic may be very difficult for others to discern.

There are some common ways of discerning new relationships. Using classroom control as an example: (1) Finding out first what others have learned about classroom control is one of the most helpful, since it tells where to look and what to look for. By going into the classroom, one can, for example, (2) observe the contrast between teacher behavior in rooms where teachers control behavior and those where they don't, (3) formulate ideas about what might cause children to misbehave and then check them out to see whether those ideas appear to work, and (4) watch a teacher to see when he has control of classroom behavior and when it is lost to see what has changed. These are only a few of many ways of finding patterns. It is very hard to tell what is going to work.

vonOech (1983) uses the term *germinal phase* for the discovery phase. "In the germinal phase, ideas are generated and manipulated; . . . it sprouts the new ideas" that are harvested in what he calls the "practical phase," where ideas are evaluated and executed (p. 31). vonOech contrasts the modes of thinking that dominate the two phases as soft and hard. In the germinal phase, soft thinking plays an important role; in the practical phase, hard thinking is more appropriate. The two kinds of thinking can be characterized by these contrasting lists (adapted from vonOech, 1983, p. 30):

Soft	*Hard*
metaphor	logic
dream	reason
humor	precision
ambiguity	consistency
play	work
approximate	exact
fantasy	reality
paradox	direct
diffuse	focused
hunch	analysis
child	adult

In the discovery phase, one often plays with ideas as a child might; one is comfortable with ambiguity, even with things that may not make sense, that are humorous, dreamlike, fantasylike, esthetic; one follows hunches and intuition; one often uses metaphors and analogies.

Feyerabend's statement "Anything goes," quoted earlier, is a paraphrase of this full sentence: "All methodologies have their limitations and the only 'rule' that survives is 'anything goes'" (1975, p. 296). Indeed, methods do have strengths and weaknesses, and the problem is to find the particular method that works in your particular situation, with your outlook and with your skills of observation, manipulation, and analysis.

The work of discovery is rarely reported in journals, either in the natural or in the behavioral sciences. Mainly in the reminiscences of famous researchers or the occasional recounting of a famous discovery, such as the story of DNA as told by James Watson (1968) in *The Double Helix* or by Judson (1979) in *The Eighth Day of Creation,* does one get a glimpse of the excitement that attaches to such work in the natural sciences and the "anything goes" nature of the process. Similar accounts in the behavioral sciences are equally fascinating. Golden (1976) gives the text of an original research report and then an account by the author of how the research came to be or some interesting aspect of it. Siegel and Zeigler (1976) similarly give the background behind research and include interesting chapters by Harry Harlow and B. F. Skinner. *Sociologists at Work* (Hammond, 1964) is a similar book focusing on sociological research.

One such account is Whyte's appendix to *Street Corner Society* (1955), in which the author tells of the problems of being so close to the situation that it is difficult to sort out what is significant from the mass of data. At one point, he is asking, were there two social groups in the Italian Community Club? How could he be sure? He maps the movements as the members socialize in the evenings. Who stands near whom when they are voting on an issue? Observations, questioning, mapping—it is a blend of methods.

An important part of the work of research is learning what to focus on, finding something significant to study. One researcher defined "basic research" as "what I do when I don't know what I am doing." He meant by this that his work was not so much goal-directed as it was a matter of "following his nose" into whatever looked interesting, not knowing what would be found there or its significance, if any, or even what to pay attention to as potentially significant. More important, the discovery phase of research is a matter of becoming familiar with a situation or phenomenon and learning what to look for, distinguishing pattern from background, "following one's nose."

Have you noticed how a word you have just learned suddenly seems to occur frequently in whatever you read or in the conversations around you? Probably there all the time, it was ignored before as part of the background. Now it is meaningful and the focus of attention. That is what happens when a researcher finds a pattern.

Finding such patterns is not confined to the discovery phase. In fact, Feyerabend (1975) argues that the distinction between the phases of discovery and confirmation (or "justification," as Reichenbach originally called it) is false and arbitrary. Certainly one doesn't stop "discovering" in the confirmation phase, nor are confirmation efforts necessarily absent from the discovery phase. These two processes are frequently intermingled: One often doesn't realize where discovery leaves off and confirmation begins—*except* when one stops to present one's knowledge claim. Then the work is typically written up as a confirmation claim with data that look as though they were, from the start, designed and carried through as a confirmation research study.

The mix of discovery and confirmation activities is illustrated by a research project engaged in by Norman Kagan, William Farquhar, and me that attempted to discern how videotaping could be useful in studying the counseling process. Initially we used Bloom's process of stimulated recall (1953), which we named "Interpersonal Process Recall" (IPR), to study how the counseling process proceeded. We videotaped the counselor and client during the counseling process. After the session, the tape was replayed to them and stopped at what we considered key points in the dialogue to allow them to recall what they had been thinking at that time. We soon realized that this recall facilitated the counseling process. Moreover, the client could find the significant spots at which to stop the tape better than we could, so control of the videotape playback was transferred to the client. Together, counselor and client could analyze what was going on in the sessions, viewing the tape objectively and discussing thoughts that lay behind the statements. Then the recall session itself was tape-recorded and used as a basis for counselor and client discussion to see whether discussion of that would facilitate things even further. As this process proceeded, it became the basis of a series of articles describing it and its effectiveness (Kagan, 1972; Kagan, Krathwohl, and Miller, 1963; Kagan and others, 1965, 1967, 1969).

Wondering whether we could get through the layers of defense more rapidly, we considered the use of hypnosis in addition to IPR. We experimented with it in an exploratory fashion, finding a method that we thought was useful. This, in turn, became the subject of an article suggesting the efficacy of the combination of methods for therapy (Woody and others, 1965).

The parallel of therapy to the learning process suggested that IPR might have some use as a method of studying instruction. We accordingly videotaped teacher and pupil and played them back to see what was going on. New insights resulted (Kagan and others, 1965).

In this example, one can see cycles of exploration, confirmation, and reporting that concretize efforts to make IPR more effective, try it with new problems, and to get through to another layer of client self-analysis. As the method is extended to new problems, each researcher reaches some reasonably firm basis for "knowing" and either designs a study to show what seemed to be discerned during the exploratory studies or assembles the data from the exploratory studies in a confirmatory chain of reasoning. Thus the alternation from discovery to confirmation and the distinction between these phases in real research is not as clear as might be inferred from descriptions of them as research phases. Yet, it is clear that when the confirmatory write-up is started, this phase conforms to the expectation established by the research community for such reports. It has the characteristics of vonOech's "hard" thinking.

The pattern of exploration, confirmation, exploration, confirmation in this example is not particularly disorganized. One reason is that our study was done before half-inch portable videotape equipment was available, and we had to use a television studio and personnel that cost nearly $400 per hour—we couldn't be frivolous. Another reason is that this was a sponsored study, and few sponsors will allow free exploration. At a minimum, sponsors expect it to be kept within certain bounds. In fact, most require in the funding proposal a complete description of all proposed activities with a time schedule showing what will get done when. This means, inevitably, that much of the discovery phase is done with thought experiments, in which one simulates in one's mind what might happen, rather than with actual manipulation. Pilot testing can also be used.

There is no method, formula, or set of techniques that will guarantee success in this task. "Anything goes!" One can find clues in the work of successful researchers; for instance, successful researchers tend to read further back into the seminal literature than less successful ones. However, there is a lot of "mucking around" in order to find patterns; being organized may help, but being flexible probably helps more.

The Confirmation Phase

The *presentation* of a knowledge claim that a particular pattern or relationship exists is typically constrained to a special format and judged by certain criteria. The word *presentation* is emphasized because it is the presentation of that work, rather than the work itself, that is necessarily highly organized and goal-directed. It is the presentation that is woven into a tight argument in support of the claim. The work itself may have been spread over a period of time, started and stopped, immersed in a larger investigation of which it is a part and may itself not present a very organized picture. It may have been a part of the discovery phase. But by selectively pulling together relevant fragments, one can imbue the presentation with an integrity and unity of focus not present in the work itself.

The work itself may be done in any pattern that best suits the researcher's style of life, capabilities, ways of looking at things, and so on. Many times, of course, it is actually as straightforward as the presentation makes it appear to be. Clearly, as before, some techniques seem more facilitative than others; straightforward ways of working seem more efficient. One has to learn what one can and cannot do, what works in the particular situation in which one finds oneself. First preparing an outline for one's essay was touted by one's English teacher as *the* way to write! Yet, it may not work for some people. Similarly, straightforward descriptions of research methods are efficient if followed as textbooks present them, but that isn't always the most effective way to use them for everyone. Even for those for whom a straightforward approach is a "natural" way to work, the behind-the-scenes accounts suggest that things are rarely as straightforward as they are presented. But one puts on the "straightforward" approach for whatever presentation of knowledge claims one asserts.

I have used terms like a *tight* argument in support of a claim, a *tight* chain of reasoning, and a *straightforward* approach to suggest how a scientist presents the knowledge claim. Let us look at this aspect more closely to discern the criteria of a strong argument, approaching it first from a common-sense layperson's point of view and then from the scientific point of view, which, it turns out, distinctly parallels the layperson's!

Research as a Layperson Might Do It

Suppose that the day's newspaper headlines tell of yet another prison riot, with prisoners protesting their treatment by guards. You may be tempted to put it aside with a "well, the prisoners probably deserved it anyway" attitude. But for some reason the situation starts to bother you, and you find yourself wondering whether there is more here than meets the eye. Your pastor, from his experiences in prison visits, ventures that the guards seem to be different persons when he meets them outside prison walls. You wonder where other instances of such transformations might be observed. You recall sayings such as "Power corrupts." You remember the mousy schoolmate who, on being given responsibility as a hall monitor, was intolerably authoritarian in that role. Is it the person? Is it the situation? Or is it the combination?

You might build up a file of experience by talking to friends, strangers—anyone who will discuss the issue. Suppose that in time you come to a belief that the prison system is so structured as to be destructive of relationships among persons. You seek to convince others of this situation, using the reasons you have discovered, such as the expectations of the other guards, the fear of what will happen if a guard appears "soft," and the corrupting effect of power. You illustrate with instances that bear as powerfully as possible on the point of view being advanced.

Let us consider what has happened. During the discovery and formulation stage, a problem became formulated. The experience of others was gathered, and one came gradually to focus on the prison situation itself as the strongest force determining prisoner/guard relationships. One formed a point of view and began to marshal evidence toward this view. The work had been moving toward the confirmation phase; it is difficult to know when it crossed that artificial line, but at the point when one began to present the case as "fact" to others, one was presenting a knowledge claim. One presented it not as a story of how it was discovered and formulated but as a view of the truth. The case was bolstered by what others had observed, organized into as strong a rationale or explanation as one could muster, and illustrated with examples that both brought the problem to life and helped convince others of the "truth" of the view being advanced. Alternative explanations such as the disposition of the individual to be authoritarian were undercut by contrasting the guard's behavior outside the prison with that in the role as guard. The argument was shown to be consistent with what others had learned about role behavior, and the argument as a whole was shown to be credible.

These steps, which one follows in ordinary problem solving as well as in the development and communication of explanations of phenomena, are very similar to those a researcher would go through in examining the same problem. Reread the foregoing account; then turn to Figure 2 (p. 42), which describes the researcher's steps in setting forth a knowledge claim, and compare the steps in the account with the headings in the figure. There is considerable similarity, isn't there?

Research as Behavioral Scientists Did It

Now let us see how some researchers, Haney, Banks, and Zimbardo (1973), who were also concerned with this problem, worked with it. In research such as Milgram's experiment (1963), they had examples of the extreme behaviors that individuals could be induced to exhibit. In that study, subjects, in an experimental setting that seemed to legitimize such behavior, gave what they had every reason to believe were strong, painful, and possibly dangerous electrical shocks to "fellow subjects." It therefore seemed to Haney, Banks, and Zimbardo that the prisons themselves might be a strong factor in legitimizing authoritarian behavior. They contrasted this idea with an alternative explanation, the "dispositional hypothesis," that those who take such jobs as prison guard are disposed to seek situations where they can be authoritarian in their relations with others—in this instance, the prisoners—and that prisoners, with their flawed, antisocial personalities, are underdeveloped and weaker individuals. Haney and associates felt that this explanation both was less satisfactory and held little hope for change. To them, the problem seemed more "bad soil" than "bad seed." They believed they could show the effect of the prison situation and at the same time eliminate the "bad seed" alternative explanation by introducing psychologically healthy individuals into "bad soil," a simulated prison. They rejected the natural setting because it would prohibit controlling the two influences in such a way as to separate their effects.

Accordingly, they advertised for paid subjects to volunteer for a two-week study of "prison life." From the seventy-five college males home for the summer who responded, the twenty-two most physically and mentally stable were selected to participate. Half were randomly assigned as guards, half as prisoners. A very realistic simulation, including the use of regular police officers to arrest and book the prisoners, was enacted, and extensive observation, testing, and recording took place. The simulation was prematurely terminated after the sixth day; five prisoners of this healthy, stable group had to be released because of extreme depression, rage, or anxiety. The guards, by contrast, appeared to be enjoying the power and control and were reluctant to give it up. But the interaction both between guards and prisoners and among the prisoners themselves was becoming increasingly negative. Harassment by the guards escalated overall as the experiment wore on, and prisoners became more passive. In private prisoner-to-prisoner talk, which one would have expected to be about girlfriends, college life, and vacation, 90 percent was about prison conditions. Further, prisoners began to accept the guards' negative attitude toward them, so that 85 percent of their statements about fellow prisoners were uncomplimentary and deprecating.

The researchers were distressed both by how easily sadistic behavior could be elicited from individuals who were not sadistic types and by the frequency of emotional breakdowns in persons selected for their emotional stability. In their conclusions the researchers discuss the pathology of power and the "prisoner syndrome," conditions that occurred even though this was a simulated situation with none of the possibilities of involuntary homosexuality, no racism (subjects were all white males), and no beatings or threats to life. Further, the maximum sentence was the two weeks for which the subjects were employed for the study!

It is interesting, apropos of the discussion about science as a means of explaining to individuals the truth of knowledge claims, that Haney (1976), in discussing the prison study, compares this experimental research to teaching, also a technique for explaining knowledge claims. He says, "At its very best, research is an act of teaching, an attempt at instructive communication. Through its unusual perspective or 'angle' it seeks to isolate from the buzz of experience [those] patterns and relationships that the complexities of everyday life may have masked or rendered imperceptible" (p. 178).

An Analysis of the Two Phases

The Discovery Phase

Let us look at Figures 1 and 2, which respectively describe the processes of discovery and confirmation in general terms, and then relate them to the process that Haney, Banks, and Zimbardo went through in this study. As is typical of such reports, theirs says very little about the discovery and formulation phase. We do know that they examined the research of Milgram and others bearing on the problem. A distinctive feature of the study is the way the simulation cleanly controls for the "dispositional," or "bad seed," explanation of prison conditions by assigning normal, stable individuals randomly as guards and prisoners. This clever aspect may have been a starting point, especially since Milgram had difficulty eliminating challenges that the effect he found was a function of the university milieu (he repeated his study off campus), and that may have made Haney and his associates think about this aspect. Further, Milgram's study, like Haney's, was a simulation. Of course, it does not appear in the write-up that this control was a starting point, but that is often how research proceeds.

Figure 1 conveys this "start where you wish," "anything goes" attitude by the placement of the items, so that one may start reading anywhere on the page, just as there are a variety of points of entry to any problem. Further, although one can see parallels between certain aspects of the discovery and the confirmation phases (compare Figures 1 and 2), an important difference is the sequential chain of steps in the confirmation phase. The discovery aspects are not sequenced in any way. Indeed, they could be listed in any order, since researchers can start with any one of them and then develop others. As the researcher works through more and more of the discovery aspects, it becomes increasingly clear how the confirmation phase can be carried out. In field studies, sometimes the important variables emerge only after all the data have been collected and are being analyzed.

Just when material is selected and organized for the confirmation presentation varies from study to study. In some studies, what is to be done is clear from the initial formulation of the problem, and the study is a straightforward matter of carrying out the steps and then

Figure 1. Discovery and Formulation Phase: Anything Goes.

•Take an area of concern or interest, a new technique, a suggestive study, available data that can be analyzed in new ways, suggested next studies in past ones, and so on.

•Find a metaphor or analogy that fits the situation of interest.

•Try to identify and clearly state the central problem.

•Link an idea or hunch to past experience, to build forward from past literature, to profit from past mistakes.

•Play with the various aspects of the situation, link them up in different combinations to see what, if anything, reasonable becomes apparent. Doodle with it.

•Follow one's hunches to look at interesting, unusual, esthetically pleasing, or humorous aspects of the situation.

•Discern a pattern, explanation, rationale, theory, or point of view.

•Formulate questions, hypotheses, predictions, and models.

•Formulate a way to approach the problem, if possible, an unusual perspective or angle that highlights an aspect that was previously imperceptible or masked.

•Fill one's mind with all one can learn about the situation and then do something else; work "off center" and see what emerges from one's unconscious.

•Do pilot studies, thought experiments, trials with a few cases; in field studies actual data collection; exploratory data analysis.

Figure 2. Confirmation Phase: The Chain of Reasoning.

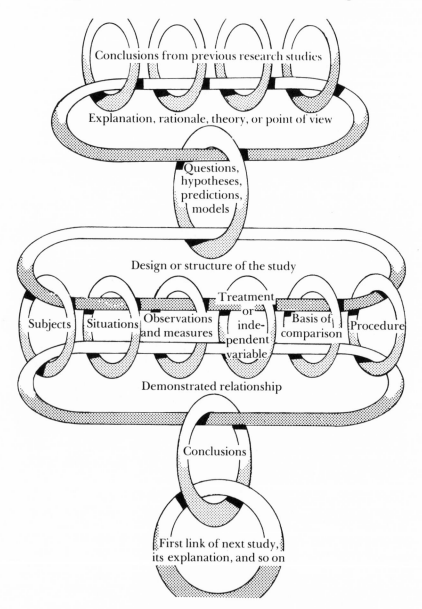

describing what was done and interpreting it. But more often the discovery phase lasts longer, and there are shifts back and forth between the confirmation phase and the discovery phase. For example, if the data do not come out as planned, one may shift back into the discovery mode to collect more data and try to discern whether the particular study design was poor, whether there was something wrong with the initial formulation of the problem, or both.

Since the Haney, Banks, and Zimbardo study is presented in a straightforward manner, as though it were designed that way from the outset (as it may have been), we don't know how much of this exploration occurred. The only evident surprise was that the study had to be cut short because the effect was more powerful than had been expected.

The Confirmation Phase

The logic of the write-up proceeds as a chain of reasoning in accordance with the expectations laid down for the confirmation phase. The links and their order are shown in Figures 3, 4, and 5, which are the top, middle, and bottom sections of Figure 2 with the specific aspects of the prison simulation study imposed on them. We can see the general steps reflected in the specific ones of the prison study. The chain begins in Figure 3 by showing that the study was tied to previous findings. The researchers discussed the problem of "bad soil" versus "bad seed" and indicated how the simulation might help to decide this issue. Next they took up the question of what would happen to stable, normal young men assigned to guard and prisoner roles in a prison situation, with a general hypothesis that assignment to guard and to prisoner treatment would result in significantly different reactions on measures of interpersonal interaction, mood, and so on. Descriptions of the design follow in Figure 4: It links the subjects (selected volunteer college students), the simulation situation, the measures and observations, the treatment—the roles that the guards and prisoners were to play—and the procedure, reporting what happened to whom and when. As shown in Figure 5, the researchers presented and discussed the findings of the study, showing the relationship between the roles played and changes in behavior, mood, self-concept, and other measures. Finally, conclusions were drawn about the nature of this relationship, showing how the data support an expanded explanation and better understanding of the situation. A hope is expressed that this study would move others to consider the psychic costs "exacted from real prisoners and guards in their struggle to adjust to an environment far harsher than any we could have simulated" (Haney, 1976, p. 176).

Figure 3. The Chain of Reasoning in the Prison Simulation Study:
Linkages to Previous Research and Selection of a Research Question.

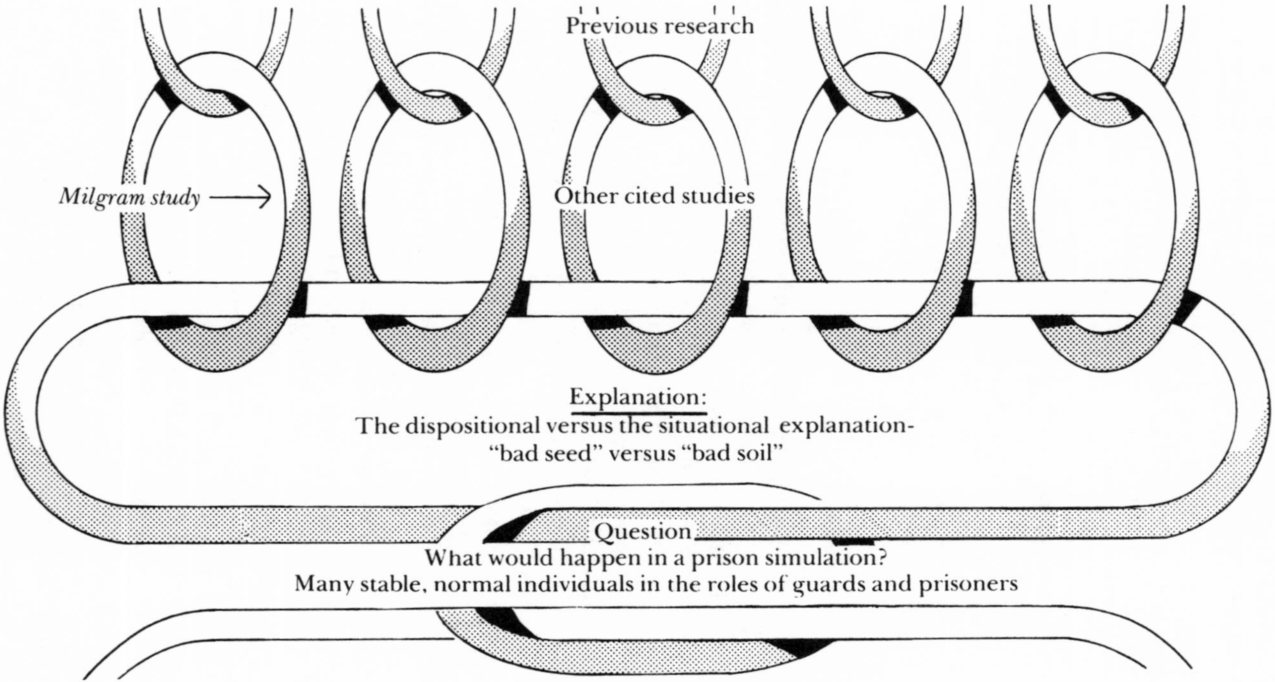

Milgram study →

Previous research

Other cited studies

Explanation:
The dispositional versus the situational explanation-
"bad seed" versus "bad soil"

Question
What would happen in a prison simulation?
Many stable, normal individuals in the roles of guards and prisoners

Figure 4. The Chain of Reasoning in the Prison Simulation Study: Design of the Study.

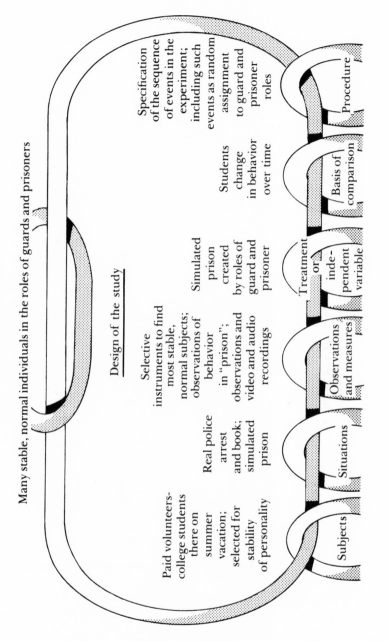

Figure 5. The Chain of Reasoning in the Prison Simulation Study: Conclusion and Linkages to Further Research.

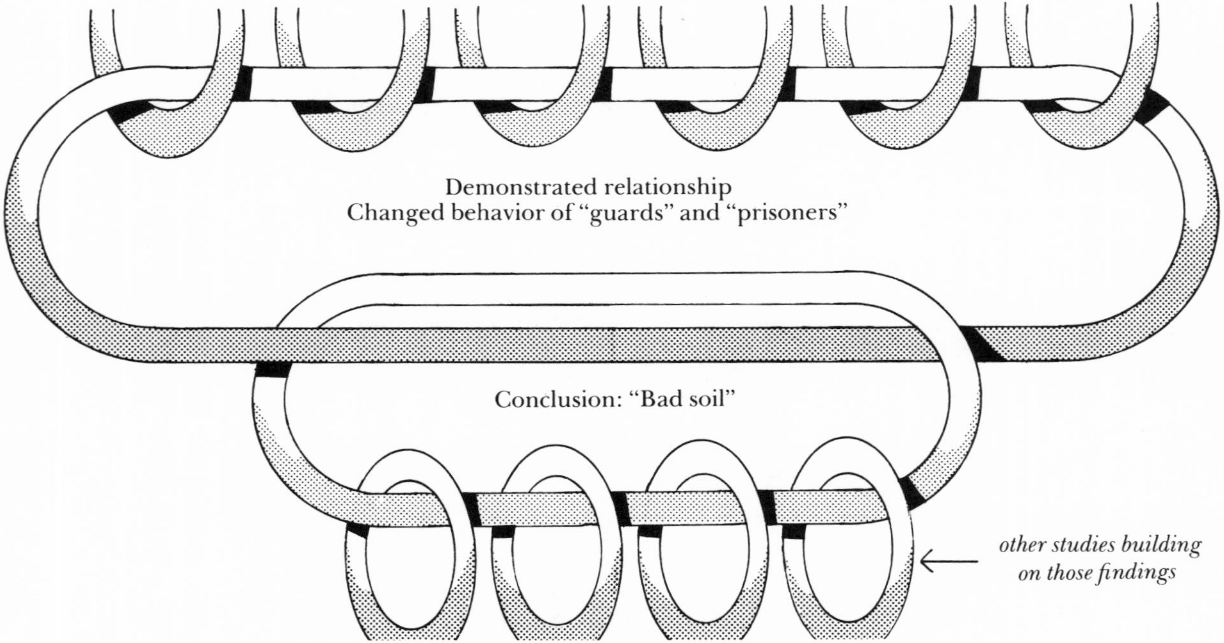

Demonstrated relationship
Changed behavior of "guards" and "prisoners"

Conclusion: "Bad soil"

other studies building
on those findings

A Chain of Reasoning—A General Model

The chain-of-reasoning model in Figure 2 can be used as a model of the presentation of any quantitative study. Generally such studies are presented in sequential order of the links from top to bottom. The problem of the study is tied to previous work in the field and, in turn, leads to a question, a hypothesis or prediction, a model, or a theory, depending on how well established the previous work in the field is. If it is well established, one may be working out various parts of a theory. If one is just starting, one may have only questions and no hypothesis or prediction. That step is a critical one, for it is translated into the operations that form the study itself. The six facets of the study design—subjects, situation, observations, treatments or independent variables, basis of comparison, and procedure—constitute the areas in which decisions must be made to form the study design, whether the study is qualitative or quantitative.

The subjects link describes the units with which the study is concerned. Usually they are persons, hence the name *subjects*. But they may be organizational units—for example, businesses in a study of a new management style, classrooms in a study of classroom control. Usually the units—persons, businesses, classrooms—are sampled. Occasionally the whole population is used when it is small enough—for example, all the Vietnamese students in a typical small-city school.

Qualitative researchers may object to the use of the name *subjects* for this facet of the design. The cartoon in which one mouse tells the other, "Watch how I've got this guy trained; every time I step on this lever, he gives me a piece of cheese!," is helpful in understanding their point of view. It illustrates vividly the difference between the experimenter's perspective and that of the subject being studied; the latter is the domain of most qualitative researchers. They prefer words like *informant* or *host* that suggest equality or even deference to those who help them understand how situations look to them. By contrast, the term *subject* implies control by the researcher. It is hoped that researchers sensitive to the term will automatically substitute *informants* or whatever comes naturally and forgive the assignment of a brief title in order to simplify already complex terminology.

The situations link describes the situation in which the subjects are studied. The situation may be determined by the choice of subjects, as when a business or classroom is the subject, but it may be independent, as it was in the simulated prison study, in which choice of students to play guard and prisoner roles was independent of the simulated prison situation.

The observations link describes whatever measures or observations are made in the study. In the prison simulation study, measures were used to choose the most stable subjects, and observations were used to determine what happened to them in the simulated situation. Measures are often used to determine what happened to the subjects during an experiment. Those measurements are compared with similar measures taken before the study started or measures of a comparable group taken at the same time.

The treatment or independent variable link describes whatever is to be related to the effect or, in noncausal relationships, the variables to be related. In the prison simulation study, the simulated prison situation was the treatment. *Independent variable* can be used as a name for treatment, but it is more often applied to variables which cannot be manipulated or administered as a treatment can but which are related to the effect being studied—socioeconomic class or basal metabolism of subjects, location or size of a business. The effect being studied is called the "dependent variable," since in a causal relationship presumably its state is determined, at least in part, by the independent variable. The changed behavior of the prisoners was an effect, their mood one of several dependent variables observed. In a study of classroom achievement, intellectual ability might be the independent variable and achievement the dependent variable.

The basis-of-comparison link describes the means by which one shows that a change occurred as a result of a treatment or that certain characteristics vary together. In the prison simulation study, comparison of pre with post states is the basis of comparison that shows the effect of the treatment. In a study of businesses with different levels of implementation of a particular management style, employee morale as related to extent of implementation might provide the basis of comparison that showed that these characteristics varied together.

The procedure link includes a schedule that indicates who gets what measures or treatment when, who is assigned where, and how assignments are made. It is like the DNA in a cell that contains the directions for cell reproduction. In the simulation study, the procedure called for pretesting to find the most stable candidates, their selection, random assignment to guard and prisoner roles, the "arrest and booking" of the "prisoners," and so on.

From the data collected, the next link in the chain, the final link, develops—namely, the conclusions. For quantitative studies, those that deal with measures, tests, observation counts, and other numerical data, the link labeled "demonstrated relationship" can be shown in more detail. It consists of several links, as shown in Figure 6, involving gathering data, summarizing them, determining the

Figure 6. Lower Links of the Chain in a Quantitative Study.

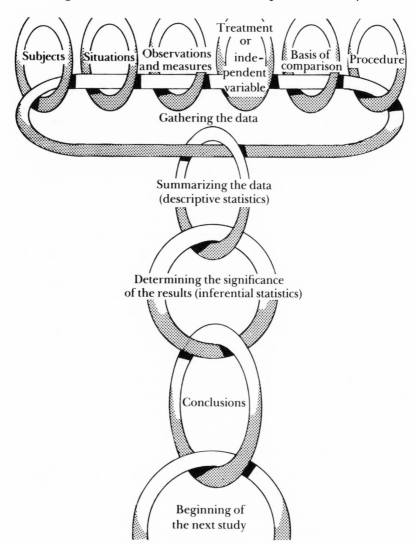

Subjects Situations Observations and measures Treatment or independent variable Basis of comparison Procedure

Gathering the data

Summarizing the data
(descriptive statistics)

Determining the significance
of the results (inferential statistics)

Conclusions

Beginning of
the next study

significance of results, and drawing conclusions. In the prison simulation study, the data gathered were self-report measures, observations
of interactions, and audio- and videotape readings. Summarizing the
data involves reducing the detail in some way so one can grasp its
central meaning. This may be done by such descriptive statistics as the
mean or a correlation coefficient. It may also be done with pictures by
plotting the data on graphs. Many times, the difference between
groups, such as the difference between prisoners and guards, is small.
Then one doesn't know whether the difference is a chance one,
resulting from the normal variability from group to group, or whether
there was a real difference between the groups as a result of the roles.
Here, as we shall see in later chapters, inferential statistics helps one
to determine which differences to call chance variability and which to
call the result of the treatment under study. In the prison experiment,
the differences are between the guards' and the prisoners' measures.
For example, in thirty-two incidents in which a verbal threat was
issued, twenty-seven involved a guard threatening a prisoner and only
five vice versa. Intuitively this finding seems overwhelmingly to
support the differentiation of the guard role in the direction one might
expect; inferential statistics provide additional assurance.

It should be noted that the links in Figure 6 are dependent in
a hierarchal way, just as those in Figure 2 are. Thus the nature and
structure of the data to be gathered are determined by the design. The
appropriate descriptive statistics or graphs are determined by what
data were gathered, as are the inferential statistics. And finally, the
conclusion flows from the results of the statistical analysis, plus such
other data as help one to interpret the results.

The Lack of an Exact Correspondence
Between the Research Write-Up and the Chain of Reasoning

Those familiar with research reports may be bothered because
many *do not* resemble the chain of reasoning, and even those that do
fail to label their sections according to the chain. This is a valid concern, so let us clarify the relation between the chain and the research
write-up.

The chain of reasoning describes the *logical flow* of the
knowledge claim. The literal flow of the write-up may or may not
correspond exactly with this. Indeed, how each author presents this
logic is a function of many things, such as the traditions in one's
discipline, the particular journal in which the report appears, the kind
of research being reported, what the author emphasizes, the point or
goal of the research, and the author's preferences for how to communicate most effectively.

As will be noted in Chapter Ten, which presents and analyzes two studies using this book's framework, the logical chain exists, though the flow of the presentation is designed to communicate what the author thinks is critical. For instance, the first study, a typical case, begins with material that sets the problem in context and then discusses previous research, the first link in the chain. Similarly, the study does not stop after the conclusions as the chain suggests, but continues to defend the knowledge claim against possible objections through the last sentence. Many studies end with forecasts of the next link; that is, the research that could or ought to follow.

Some journals label sections with terms closely approximating those in the chain, but even in these instances there is usually a single section labeled "procedure" that describes all the links of the chain involving the research design and the design choices. Sometimes within the procedure section one may find subheadings that correspond to chain headings such as subjects or treatment, but rarely basis of comparison. However, the flow of logic is present in the headings even though the same terms are not used.

It is the logical rather than the literal presentation of the knowledge claim that we describe in the chain of reasoning; they may correspond exactly, but most often do not.

The Application of the Chain to Qualitative Studies

Many qualitative studies and an occasional quantitative study are purely descriptive, and the chain-of-reasoning concept is not relevant. The chain of reasoning applies where one is trying to establish a relationship and provide understanding; the latter is the heart of science. Purely descriptive studies are *not* unimportant; the major criterion is accuracy of representation. The same criteria underlie the problems of translation of concepts and constructs and of measures and observations. We shall deal with these in the course of trying to discern the criteria of a study that helps us understand relationships. Purely descriptive studies are usually the earliest phases of studies of relationships that build on them; consequently, discussing the latter includes the criteria appropriate to the former.

Qualitative studies in particular are often largely descriptive. A study of a primitive culture, for instance, may simply describe the culture without drawing generalizations or drawing out principles. But when principles are described or a generalization is drawn, then the chain of reasoning becomes relevant. The parts of the chain will be present, although the case will probably be made more by examples drawn from the field than by tying the generalization to previous research. Further, the parts of the logic chain may be scattered throughout the case description. In comparison with a quantitative study, they may be much less evident, as demonstrated by the qualitative example in Chapter Ten. In the case of a description that embodies several generalizations within the same article or chapter, the chains for each may be intertwined or presented sequentially. Nonetheless, as we shall see in later chapters, the concept of a chain of reasoning and the criteria that it leads to are relevant for both quantitative and qualitative studies.

Usefulness of the Chain-of-Reasoning Analogy

The analogy of a chain of reasoning for the presentation of a knowledge claim seems apt, because there are at least four characteristics of a real chain that usefully apply to a chain of reasoning as well:

1.   A chain is only as strong as its weakest link.
2.   All links in a chain should be built to about the same strength.
3.   As the work load is picked up by the first link and passed to successive links, the work load—and therefore the nature of each link—is determined by the previous links.
4.   Where several links together join those above and below them, there may be trade-offs to compensate for weaknesses.

Although these propositions may seem self-evident, their application to the chain of reasoning deserves close examination.

1. *A chain is only as strong as its weakest link.* The chain of reasoning is basically an argument for a knowledge claim. To the extent that any part of that argument can be faulted (for instance, the explanation or theory does not seem reasonable, the sample of subjects is inappropriate, the observations or measures do not measure the right things, the analysis was not done correctly or was inappropriate), the chain is weakened and one is less likely to accept the knowledge claim. If the fault is serious enough, the link fails and the knowledge claim is rejected.

In the prison simulation, had there not been careful screening and random assignment of the subjects to roles, one might have faulted the study for possibly including individuals who were "bad seed." One would then have an alternative explanation for what occurred, and it would not be clear what the contribution of the "bad soil" was. It is only as one trusts the screening procedures that the "subjects" link holds. If one believes the procedures might have been inadequate, that "link" fails and the conclusions must be rejected.

2. *All links in the chain should be built to about the same strength.* This follows from and is really a logical corollary of the first principle rather than a new proposition, but it is worth emphasizing. It makes little sense to have one link in a metal chain as thick as an ocean liner's anchor chain and others as thin as sewing thread. There is no point in putting resources into a link that is already sufficiently strong and burly when those resources could be used to strengthen a weak link. To do so is mismanagement of the project's resources and produces a weaker chain than need be. For instance, why work hard on the simulation aspects of a prison, enlisting the aid of the Palo Alto police to make it realistic, if the measures and techniques that will be used to observe the effects are not up to the job? Some of the resources otherwise devoted to the simulation might be better used to strengthen the observations and measures.

In whose judgment should the links be of equal strength? The judgment of strength is subjective. The important point to remember is that *one's audience* makes the final judgment. One is seeking to build a consensus in that audience for one's interpretation of the study. One must live with oneself and be personally convinced before presenting the findings to others. But those findings will be reasonable to others only if *their* criteria are satisfied also. Further, predicting the perception of the audience of a future report is not easy. But one cannot avoid doing so if one is to forge chains of reasoning that adequately support the knowledge claims. Where personal priorities and those one attributes to one's audience differ, one has a problem to resolve that involves trade-offs—a problem I will come back to in later chapters.

3. *As the work load is picked up by the first link and passed to successive links, the work load—and therefore the nature of each link—is determined by the previous links.* By the way a step advances the argument for the knowledge claim, it sets boundaries for the next; each step is shaped by the argument to that point. The argument for the knowledge claim should flow smoothly down the chain from outset to conclusion, each step carrying its load in turn. Thus the chain of reasoning starts by linking the present study to previous work that must be recognized in whatever hypothesis, question, or theory the study sets out to investigate. The nature of the hypothesis link determines where one looks for evidence, at whom, with what measures, when, and how one does it. These are matters determined by the design links of the chain. The evidence turned up by the design determines the conclusions that can be drawn, which is the final link in this study but is picked up by the next study that builds on this one.

One can see this plan of logic in the prison simulation study. It starts by linking the new study to previous work, builds on that work, and goes beyond it. For example, Haney and associates, working with the situational and the dispositional points of view, chose to test these explanations, believing the former the more powerful one. This step led to the general hypothesis that the behavior of stable, normal individuals would be differentially affected by serving as a "guard" or "prisoner." That link flows out of the analyses of previous work and thought about the prison situation as the findings of previous work (such as Milgram's study) apply to it.

The design of the study is implicit in what has gone before and calls for a translation of the terms of the hypothesis or proposition being confirmed into actions to be taken in the study. The accuracy of this translation, its *translation fidelity*, is critical to one's ability to infer something from the study about the proposition of concern. The translation of terms into action or operation has been called an "operational definition." For instance, the way the guards were told to act was an operational definition of the guard's role and what it meant to be a guard in the simulated prison. Similarly, tests are operational definitions of characteristics. The meaning of "most mentally and physically stable subjects" was embodied in the judgments of responses to a background questionnaire and to an interview by one of two experimenters. Thus the process of selecting "stable, normal" subjects translated the hypothesis into the "subjects" link of the design. The random assignment of subjects to guard and prisoner roles provided a comparable base for later comparison as their behavior differentiated in the simulation exercise. This was the "basis of comparison" link. The simulated prison, which was constructed in the basement of an academic building, defined the "situation," the roles of "guard" and "prisoner," the "treatment," the various measures, video and audio recordings, the "observations." And so the hypothesis was translated into each link in the design.

The procedure link of the design contains the directions for carrying out the study, operationalizing the logic for random assignment that lies behind the basis of comparison of groups of individuals, and operationalizing as well treatment, measurement, and observation so that these are done appropriately as called for in the explanation and its translation into the design.

Finally, as the study is carried out, the demonstration must be interpreted and conclusions drawn, the nature of the design determining what demonstration occurs and what interpretation can be drawn. So the nature of each link is determined by prior links in the chain, and the presentation of the explanation flows down the chain, building a case that is internally consistent with what has gone before.

4. *Where several links together join those above and below them, as they do between the design and the demonstrated relationship link, there may be trade-offs among the several links to compensate for weaknesses in one or another of them.* The six facets that specify the design—subjects, situation, observations, treatment, basis of comparison, and procedure—connect the design link to the demonstrated relationship link. Thus they "share the load" between these two latter links. Consider it a real chain attached to a 1,200-pound load. The load exerts a 1,200-pound pull on each joint in the chain, including that between design and demonstrated relationship, and, of course, the six links that join them are subject to this strain as well. But since they share that load, if they are equal in strength, each has to bear only 200 pounds of it to keep the load suspended. But they need not carry the load equally so long as the total carried equals 1,200 pounds. For example, the subject link might carry 400 pounds to compensate for the observation and treatment links, which carry only 100 pounds apiece.

In the same way, the six facets of the design chain may compensate for one another. For instance, suppose that a treatment results in only a very weak effect. To compensate, one could strengthen any or a combination of several links. The easiest remedy, and the one usually chosen, is to increase the size of the sample so that the study will be more sensitive to a small effect. Further, particular characteristics that might inadvertently dominate with a small sample (for example, with three guards and three prisoners, the guards might all happen to be tall and the prisoners short) will average out over a larger group. Alternatively, one might make one's observations as sensitive as possible by defining ahead of time all possible manifestations of authoritarian behavior, even the weakest ones. Still another possibility would be to adjust the basis of comparison. Thus, if one suspected that the prison environment might be strong enough to affect stable individuals only marginally but would definitely affect unstable ones, then one might set up four experimental conditions: the one that was carried out with stable individuals in both roles, one with unstable individuals in the guard role, a third with unstable individuals in the prisoner role, and a fourth with unstable individuals in both roles. If one's hunch is correct, the pathological behavior ought to be greatest in the last, least in the first, and in between in the other two. Yet another way would be to increase the strength of the treatment link by prolonging treatment or by making it more severe. One could make one or several of these adjustments.

So, where some links of the design are weak, one may be able to compensate by strengthening other links. But there may be trade-offs to be considered, and it therefore needs to be done thoughtfully. For instance, extra subjects will require extra resources and may also have other effects; if morale in a prison is affected by the size of its population, increasing the sample size might yield different results than using the smaller-sample design.

Christine Murray, a student in one of my classes, suggested a fifth implication of the chain analogy: "Like a metal chain, a chain of reasoning that is tied in knots is very difficult to straighten out." So true!

3

Two Key Criteria
of Research Studies

Internal Validity (Linking Power) and
External Validity (Generalizing Power)

With the exception of studies that are entirely descriptive, researchers are universally trying to find the linkage of one thing to another—traits of persons to their performance, characteristics of classrooms to learning, conditions in business organizations to profit, inflation to recession, features of cultures to presumed consequences. In the prison simulation study discussed in the last chapter, the linkage sought was of the prison situation to the abnormal behavior of those who took the roles of "guard" and "prisoner." That study was very persuasive that the abnormal behavior was indeed *linked* to the conditions established by the prison situation. It seems natural that this *power* of a study to demonstrate the *linkage* between variables might be called the *linking power* of a study.

The linking power of a study is its capacity of its chain of reasoning to explain a relationship in such a way that one comes to believe that the author's interpretation of the evidence is the only proper one. This definition is similar, though not identical, to the way many researchers use the term *internal validity*. To indicate the similarity, let us call linking power by the already existing term, *internal validity,* but to keep its distinctiveness clear, modify it: *internal validity (linking power)* or, more simply, *internal validity (LP).*

57

Internal validity (linking power) is the judged validity with which a statement can be made that the relationship thought to link the variables is the only appropriate interpretation of the evidence. Put more simply, it is the judged reasonableness that the variables were indeed linked in this instance as proposed. Or again, in terms of the definition of knowledge we have been using, it is the judged power of a study to build a consensus around that interpretation.

The term *internal validity* was developed by Campbell and Stanley (1963) to mean the appropriateness of the judgment that the experimental treatment as implemented had an impact on the measures of effect in this particular instance. Cook and Campbell (1979, p. 38) refer to it as the "validity with which statements can be made about whether there is a causal relationship from one variable to another in the form in which the variables were manipulated or measured." Among other differences, this emphasis on the "form in which the variables were manipulated or measured" rather than the variables that the measures are intended to represent is an important distinction between internal validity and the construct of internal validity (LP). The latter is defined in terms of the relationship between variables. Indeed, many books interpret internal validity as the relationship between the variables rather than between their measures: Best (1981), Chadwick, Bahr, and Albrecht (1984), Cozby (1981), Denzin (1978), Lin (1976), McMillan and Schumacher (1984), Mouly (1978), Orenstein and Phillips (1978), Sax (1979), Simon (1978), Slavin (1984), and Williamson and others (1982) are all consistent with this interpretation of internal validity (LP).

Although a study may be designed to demonstrate that the linkage exists in a particular instance, it is not that particular one that is usually of concern. That instance is considered an example of a larger class of instances to which this relationship should generalize. To what extent, for example, could one generalize to new subjects and situations or to another point in time? Would new studies show the same results with other instruments purporting to measure the same characteristics?

The power with which the chain of reasoning of a study shows that the relationship *generalizes* beyond the instance in which it was demonstrated is therefore also a key characteristic. In parallel fashion we could call it the *generalizing power* of a study. The generalizing power of a study is the judged validity with which statements can be made that the generality claimed for the relationship is the only appropriate interpretation of the evidence. Put in terms of the definition of knowledge we have been using, it is the power of a study to build a consensus accepting that generality.

But, as before, there is a term in common use, *external validity*, with a closely associated meaning. Therefore, as with *internal validity (LP)*, I shall use the modified term *external validity (generalizing power)* or, more simply, *external validity (GP)* to differentiate it from the older term.

Campbell and Stanley's original definition of *external validity* might actually serve as the definition of *external validity (GP)*: "External validity asks the question of *generalizability: To what populations, setting, treatment variables, and measurement variables can this effect be generalized?*" But Cook and Campbell (1979) changed the definition while continuing to use the same term. Further, external validity (GP) is broken down into a series of judgments similar to those for internal validity (LP). Therefore, it seems best to distinguish *external validity (GP)* from *external validity,* using the modifying *(GP)* for generalizing power, parallel to the modifier used for *internal validity (LP)*.

One can see both internal validity (LP) and external validity (GP) in the Haney, Banks, Zimbardo prison simulation. The intent was to link very firmly the negative self-reference feelings of the "prisoners" and the hostile behavior of the "guards" with the creation of these feelings and behaviors by the prison situation. The researchers ruled out the alternative explanation that such feelings result more from the kinds of persons that prisoners and guards are to begin with by randomly assigning subjects to guard and prisoner roles. That the study firmly associated the behavior and the prison environment quite successfully and dramatically is a tribute to its internal validity (LP). Further, especially for a simulation study, in contrast to a field study of the real situation, one comes away with the feeling that prison conditions could shape such behavior not only in comparable simulations but in real situations as well—a tribute to its external validity (GP).

So internal validity (LP) and external validity (GP) are two key characteristics of any study. The stronger the internal validity (LP), the greater the validity of statements that the relationship proposed as linking variables is the only appropriate interpretation of the evidence. The greater the external validity (GP), the wider the scope of applicability of the relationship to new situations beyond the circumstances in which it was demonstrated.

Although writers on internal and external validity such as those cited have described "threats to validity," a thorough and systematic explanation of what contributes to internal and external validity, especially as defined here, will be very useful. If we can determine what contributes to internal validity (LP) and external validity (GP), then we may be able to design studies so as to strengthen these key factors.

I shall begin that process in this chapter, laying the basic framework. In the following chapters I shall explore these terms in considerably greater detail and then put them in the larger perspective of the other decisions to be made in designing a study.

Internal Validity (LP)

One way of describing internal validity (LP) is as the ability of a study to reduce uncertainty that a relationship exists (see Cronbach, 1982). The audience comes to the study with a high level of uncertainty: Its members are not convinced that the relationship exists; it has not yet been admitted to the body of facts they term "knowledge." Internal validity (LP) is the capacity of the study to decrease that uncertainty. As noted earlier, the level of uncertainty required to cross the knowledge "threshold" is a personal decision. Judgments that cross the threshold result in an individual's "knowing"; "knowledge" results from a consensus of such "knowing judgments."

How Science Logically Proceeds

With strong enough internal validity (LP) and a sufficient consensus, can one ever "prove" a proposition is true? Popper (1959) and others have pointed out that one never proves a proposition; the proposition merely escapes disconfirmation. There are multiple ways to test any proposition, such as different samples and different ways of measuring. Any single test does not prove the proposition is true—it merely adds one more piece of evidence that the proposition has not yet been disconfirmed. Although theoretically the process of escaping disconfirmation is never-ending, in effect what is happening is that each piece of evidence lowers the uncertainty about the relationship until it crosses the knowledge threshold. The amount of evidence required is a personal decision. Even after the relationship has crossed that threshold, there might still be some as yet untested instance in which it would be disconfirmed. That is why all scientific knowledge is held as tentatively true.

In contrast to the never-ending process of escaping disconfirmation, however, *one actual disconfirmation* is enough to disprove the proposition as it was formulated. If only one disconfirming result from a good study is found and the proposition was to apply in that instance, then there are at least some limiting conditions under which it is not true. In addition, it is likely that it will also not be true in other, similar circumstances, and if this is the first test of the proposition and there is no prior affirming evidence, then it may prove to be entirely false. Therefore, a dependable disconfirmation at best limits the proposition and at worst rejects it as untrue, but a positive result does not prove a proposition, which only escapes disconfirmation with each test. This is the *logical* way in which science proceeds; it is the logic typically taught in statistics classes.

How Science Seems to Proceed

But that appears not to be the way behavioral science seems, subjectively, to work. When we have an idea about a possible new relationship, we do not pick the instance in which it is least likely to work to try to disconfirm it. Rather, we seek to confirm it where it is most likely to work; we seek to increase our certainty that the proposition is true. Only after it is reasonably well confirmed do we typically seek out the limits within which it holds and the places where it might not hold. Although certainty and uncertainty are arithmetically complementary, most of our emphasis seems to be on increasing the certainty with which the proposition is held. And if in our discussions we mention our uncertainty when the idea is new, we are much more likely to concentrate on certainty as we approach and cross the knowledge threshold. Not all knowledge is held with the same certainty; even after crossing the threshold, certainty continues to grow or erode as evidence accumulates. Not only is knowledge that has crossed the threshold held at different levels of certainty, but as discussed under "Science as Uncertainty Reduction," in Chapter One, it is a mistake to think of the threshold at which we accept a finding as knowledge as being at a constant level.

In a practical sense, the test of whether something has crossed the threshold into knowledge is whether an individual is willing to guide her actions as if the findings were true knowledge. And certainly here there are different levels of certainty requirements, depending on consequences. One might be willing to submit something for publication as a possibly true finding to be confirmed by further research but not be willing to act on it where one would be hurt if it were not true. We want to be very, very certain of knowledge that may have life-threatening consequences. We may be willing to advance findings as true that are just barely across the threshold if the negative consequences of our doing so are minimal or absent.

The Bayesian statistical position expresses very nicely the apparent process. It argues that one comes to each study with a level of uncertainty about the truth of the knowledge claim to be tested, a level that might be expressed in the odds one would give in a bet on the expected outcome of the study. The results of the study modify those odds either positively or negatively, depending both on the outcome *and* on the judged internal validity (LP) of the study. As a result, the next study of that proposition is approached with either increased or lessened certainty, and the process continues until there is a level of certainty that crosses the knowledge threshold (or, having failed over a series of studies, we discard the proposition as not true).

Characteristics of a Successful Study

Each study, therefore, affects the odds expressing our certainty about a relationship. Some very successful studies, such as the prison simulation one, may affect the odds dramatically. What is it about a study that can change the odds in this manner, that can make us feel sure that a relationship does indeed exist? We can use the prison simulation study as an example from which to tease out these characteristics.

The first thing the study did was to advance a *credible explanation* of why behavior in prisons was a function of the situation. In the studies of Milgram (1963), individuals were led to administer what they believed were extremely painful electrical shocks to other experimental subjects in a situation where they perceived that doing so was legitimated. This finding suggests that individuals will behave in ways one would not expect them to if they believe that the behavior is legitimated by the role that they are expected to play. Thus "prison guards" might be expected to be brutal and authoritarian, especially considering the nature of the convicts with whom they must deal. This credible explanation undergirds the study and makes the possibility, indeed the likelihood, of positive results seem reasonable.

The next step was to translate this hypothetical idea into reality. But the actual prison situation was not used; there would be too many uncontrolled variables that might lead to reasonable explanations other than the situational one with which the study was concerned. The prison situation was simulated as realistically as possible, however. Thus the second step was to *translate* the idea of the study into the choice of subjects, a situation, set of observations, a treatment, a basis of comparison for showing that change occurred as the subjects were observed daily, and a time schedule and procedure for running the study.

Third, the researchers *demonstrated* that the expected *changes in behavior did occur*. In this instance, the change was dramatic, and the observations clearly showed changes in behavior in the predicted direction.

In many behavioral science studies, however, change is small enough that one is not sure whether whatever change occurred is the change one was looking for or merely the result of the variability from person to person and of measurement from one point in time to another that shows up as the random error of any study. Consequently, inferential statistics are used to identify those changes that are too large to be likely due to error and thus more likely due to treatment. This is a fourth important aspect of the study, the *elimination of all reasonable alternative explanations*—in this instance, the confusion of a real change with that attributable to random variation.

Another reasonable alternative explanation the study recognized was that the characteristics of individuals who take the jobs of guards, especially in interaction with the deviant and unstable personalities of prisoners, might have created the abnormal behavior. The researchers eliminated this explanation, you will recall, by selecting only the most normal and stable of the volunteer subjects and randomly assigning them to the roles of guard and prisoner.

Fifth, together with a judgment of this study's consistency with previous evidence in the area, all aspects described above go to make up a final judgment of the *credibility* of the study.

Characteristics of Internal Validity (LP)

The steps just described seem to be those that go into making a judgment of a study's internal validity (LP). Let us see whether we can formulate them as general characteristics of a study. The internal validity (LP) of a study is the combination of five judgments:

1. *Explanation credibility*—is the relationship to be demonstrated at least plausible and its rationale or explanation credible?
2. *Translation fidelity*—is the demonstration a true example of the relationship? (Is the operational translation of the proposition acceptable?)
3. *Demonstrated relationship*—was the demonstration successful in showing that the indicated relationship held in this instance?
4. *Rival explanations eliminated*—is there no way that the result can be accounted for by other reasonable explanations?
5. *Credible result*—is this finding credible in view of past research and the previous four judgments?

The judgments form a multiple hurdle array. That is, each judgment affects the next, a positive judgment making the next one easier, a negative one making it harder or even nearly irrelevant. For example, if one rejects the author's explanation, the rest of the study is probably irrelevant. Typically, the reader will examine it to find all its weak spots to rationalize his initial judgment. (Of course, should that search not prove adequately successful, he will be forced to start over and reassess his initial position.) If the explanation is accepted but the study is not an accurate translation of the explanation, the study is irrelevant to the extent that the translation is poor. Each decision affects the next.

In contrast to internal validity, which is directed toward validating cause-and-effect relationships in the context of experimental studies, internal validity (LP) is intended to apply to any kind of relationship. The projected relationship, or "link" between variables, may be one of any type: cause and effect (time on task leads to greater learning) or symbiotic (familiarity with a musical piece leads to greater liking of it, to seeking more encounters with it and thus greater familiarity; that leads to even greater liking, and so on) or any of the seemingly very large variety of patterns. Some of these are explored in Chapter Nine.

The projected relationship may be one that was looked for or predicted as a result of an explanation or theory, or it may be one that appeared in the data so that an explanation was concocted after it showed up. As we shall see, the internal validity (LP) of a study for the latter situation is considerably less than for the former. Sometimes, of course, the researcher tries a whole series of variables to determine which successfully predict, with very little or no explanation or rationale for the variables or for delineating those that work from those that do not. The study may still have internal validity (LP), but the internal validity (LP) judgment will be weakened by the lack of a credible explanation.

Further, whereas the development of Campbell and Stanley's (1963) and Cook and Campbell's (1979) concept of internal validity occurred almost entirely in the context of the experimental method, internal validity (LP) is intended to apply broadly to any study that advances a generalization or proposition, regardless of the method used—experimental, quantitative, or qualitative. It is intended to describe the criteria by which the knowledge claim may be judged.

Relation of Internal Validity (LP) to the Chain of Reasoning

Figure 7 shows the relation of the parts of internal validity (LP) to the chain of reasoning discussed in the previous chapter. The five judgments that compose internal validity (LP) are indicated at the links to which they are most closely related. Just how these judgments relate to particular links can be demonstrated by following through another example.

Figure 7. Internal Validity (LP) and the Chain of Reasoning.

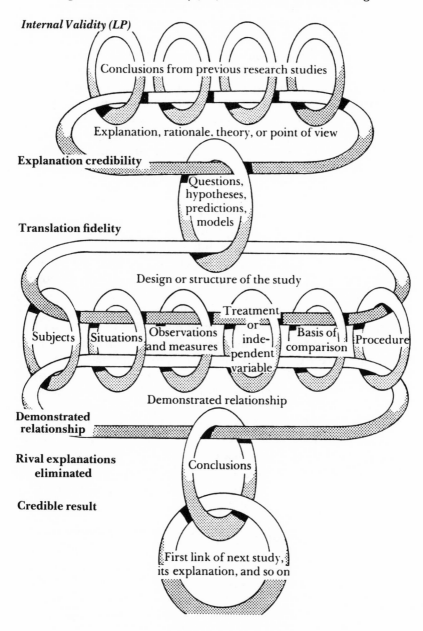

Internal Validity (LP)

Conclusions from previous research studies

Explanation, rationale, theory, or point of view

Explanation credibility

Questions, hypotheses, predictions, models

Translation fidelity

Design or structure of the study

Treatment or independent variable

Subjects Situations Observations and measures Basis of comparison Procedure

Demonstrated relationship

Demonstrated relationship

Rival explanations eliminated

Conclusions

Credible result

First link of next study, its explanation, and so on

Suppose that we are interested in how individuals' behavior is affected by the situation in which they find themselves, as in the simulated prison study, but in this instance, let us pick a more familiar environment, the classroom, in which all of us have, at least at an early time, spent a good part of our lives. Consider where a student is seated in the classroom in relation to learning. If we examine previous research studies, we will find one by Wulf (1977) and one by Becker and others (1973) that indicate that most achieving students prefer to be seated in the front and center in the classroom. Further, there appear to be action zones in the classroom, and those who sit front and center interact more often with one another and with the instructor (Hare and Bates, 1963). One can argue that being directly under the instructor's gaze, in the middle of the discussion rather than on its periphery, and so forth ought to have an effect on one's attending to the instruction and hence on achievement.

Figures 8, 9, and 10 adapt the general model of the chain of reasoning in relation to internal validity (LP) of Figure 7 to show how it applies to a projected study of the effect of seating placement on achievement. The previous findings, explanation, hypothesis, possible design alternatives, and design chosen are shown superimposed on their corresponding links in Figures 8, 9, and 10. For example, a brief statement of the explanation appears in Figure 8 in the first large link. This explanation leads to a hypothesis in the link that joins it to the design link. At the design link, the hypothesis is translated into design alternatives (Figure 9), from among which one set of alternatives is chosen to demonstrate the relationship, and that is shown superimposed on the next link.

How would one go about judging the internal validity (LP) of this study? The first judgment, explanation credibility, is whether this hypothesis and its explanation are credible for the audience. Does the research hypothesis logically follow from the explanation and previous findings? In this instance, previous research appears to provide a reasonably credible explanation that is plausible enough to permit one to expect positive results.

The second judgment, translation fidelity (Figure 9), concerns how one can logically and practically translate the research hypothesis into a study. There are many ways of operationalizing it, and alternative possibilities are suggested under the headings "Subjects and situations," "Observations," and so forth imposed over the links at the design level of the chain. The question for translation fidelity is whether the design chosen is among those that would accurately translate the hypothesis into operational terms. More specifically, the judgment is whether the study described in the statement at the

Figure 8. Internal Validity (LP) Judgments in Relation to the Chain of Reasoning in the Classroom Seating Placement Study: Explanation Credibility.

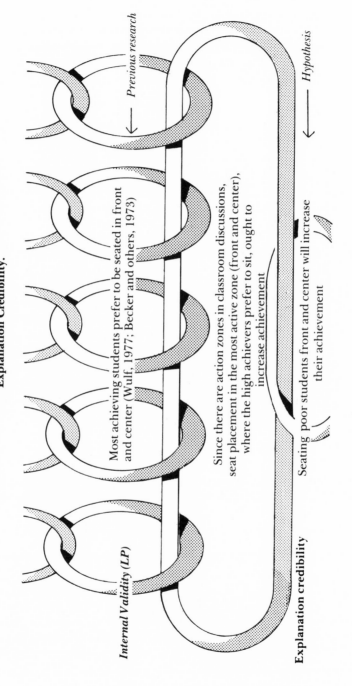

Previous research

Hypothesis

Most achieving students prefer to be seated in front and center (Wulf, 1977; Becker and others, 1973)

Since there are action zones in classroom discussions, seat placement in the most active zone (front and center), where the high achievers prefer to sit, ought to increase achievement

Seating poor students front and center will increase their achievement

Internal Validity (LP)

Explanation credibility

**Figure 9. Internal Validity (LP) Judgments in Relation to the
Chain of Reasoning in the Classroom Seating Placement Study:
Translation Fidelity.**

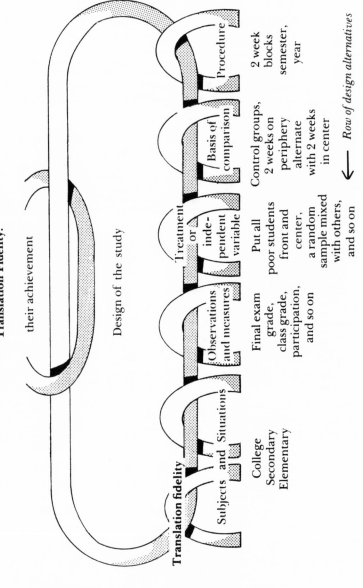

Figure 10. Internal Validity (LP) Judgments in Relation to the Chain of Reasoning in the Classroom Seating Placement Study: Demonstrated Relationship, Rival Explanations Eliminated, and Credible Result.

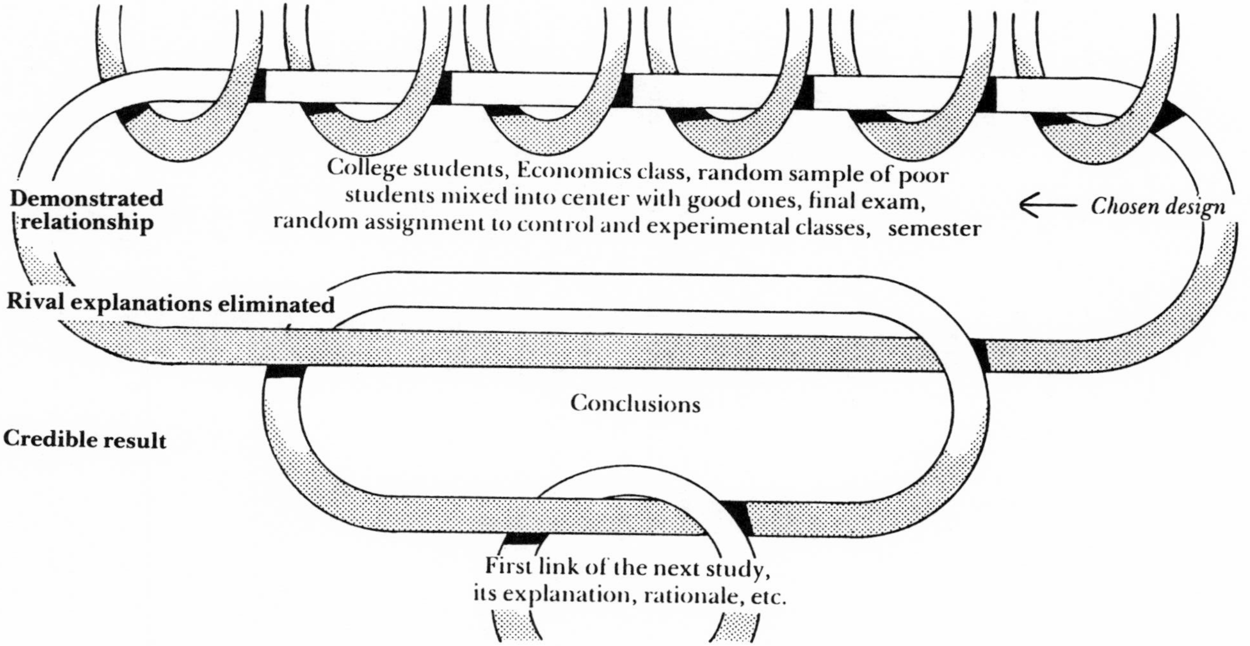

Chosen design

Demonstrated relationship

Rival explanations eliminated

Credible result

College students, Economics class, random sample of poor students mixed into center with good ones, final exam, random assignment to control and experimental classes, semester

Conclusions

First link of the next study, its explanation, rationale, etc.

"demonstrated relationship" level is a satisfactory translation of the proposition "Seating poor students front and center will increase their achievement."

As the features in the design description just below the design alternatives indicates, choices from among the suggested possibilities used college students who were randomly assigned to experimental and control sections (same instructor) of a second-level economics class. Students in the experimental section with low grades in the introductory course were mixed in with students with high grades, in a ratio of three of the former to one of the latter, and assigned to center front seats. In the other section, comparable low-grade students were assigned to seats around the periphery of the classroom. (Note the possible ethical question raised by the potentially harmful treatment of the low-grade students.) The course grade was the measure of the effect, all grading being done by an outsider who did not know which student was in which group.

The third judgment, demonstrated relationship, portrayed in Figure 9, asks whether, as carried out, the design was a successful demonstration of the relationship. Was the instigating condition (center seat placement) present before the effect occurred? Was there an effect? Did it match closely what was expected? Were the data congruent with the hypothesis and theory? We would need actual data for this step, and this is only a projected study here. The questions convey the kind of information needed for this judgment.

The fourth judgment, rival explanations eliminated, asks whether there is a way to reasonably explain the effect other than the theory or proposition already advanced as its explanation. For instance, one might question whether the instructor who did the grading for the class might also have taught the introductory class and therefore already have had established opinions about each person. If he used these impressions in assigning grades, rather than noting the improvement of the low-grade students, he might ignore it and thus cause a finding of no experimental effect for these students. Thus prior knowledge is a possible uneliminated alternative explanation of any effect. One must decide whether that explanation is reasonable.

The fifth judgment, result credibility, is a thought experiment about whether the result is credible or whether this is likely to have been a highly unusual result. How does this result compare with one's expectations based on other studies and one's personal research experience? Is the result credible in that light, or does it strongly contradict it? If the latter, is the chain of reasoning tight enough to overcome one's doubts about credibility?

Internal validity (LP) is the judgment subsuming all the previous ones. Suppose that one believes that the hypothesis is plausible and the explanation reasonably credible. The translation is accurate. The data demonstrated support for the hypothesis and seemed credible. But the possibility that the grading instructor knew the students might have affected his grading, and so it is a potential rival explanation. Internal validity (LP) as a whole might be reduced by this alternative explanation.

In this instance, to evaluate overall internal validity (LP), one must judge the plausibility of the alternative explanation. If the study were done in a small college where prior knowledge of the students is likely to be high, the rival explanation would be plausible, and internal validity (LP) might be impaired seriously. Conversely, if the study were done in a large university where the likelihood of such knowledge is almost chance, the explanation would be much less plausible and might not be judged to lower internal validity (LP) seriously.

External Validity (GP)

External validity (GP) is important because it shows that a relationship that exists (that has linking power) applies beyond the instance in which it was demonstrated. The value of a proposition or explanation is that, having demonstrated it in one instance, one can now use it in others. Judging generality is the matter of determining which "others."

Alternative Ways of Thinking of Generality

One may also think of generality as robustness (Rossi and Berk, 1980; Wimsatt, 1981). A robust treatment will produce the same results under varying circumstances, with a variety of subjects, with different operators, when observed with different relevant instruments, and at different times.

A third way of thinking about generality is in terms of replicability. Generality as replicability asks whether the phenomenon could be replicated under different circumstances and then proceeds to consider how broadly and how greatly the circumstances could be varied and the phenomenon still replicate. Cronbach (1982) discusses this concept as "reproducibility." (See Chapter Eleven.)

Only if one were studying the whole population in which a relationship might have any significance would one *not* care about external validity (GP). It is difficult to think of such instances.

Presumably the U.S. census might be such a case, but even there, a relationship in the United States between marriage pattern and income, for instance, might be generalized to other countries as well. Since studies of complete populations are rare, we are almost always concerned with generality and therefore with external validity (GP). Even in applied work intended to be of value only to a particular institution, the sponsoring institution is always concerned with other subjects: the next group of applicants for admission, the next group of clients, and so on.

Determining External Validity (GP)

Assessing the external validity (GP) of a study is basically parallel to judging the internal validity (LP), but in this instance one is asking broader questions—for example, not about the credibility of the explanation but about the generality claimed for that explanation. Similarly, one asks about generality for each of the five decisions made in internal validity (LP). Therefore, external validity (GP) is also a sequential set of five judgments, and as in internal validity (LP), the fifth judgment, "replicable result," which is parallel to "credible result" in internal validity (LP), contributes strongly to the overall generality assessment.

Figure 11 adds the five judgments of external validity (GP) to Figure 7, which showed the relation of internal validity (LP) to the chain of reasoning. An examination of Figure 11 shows the strong parallel between the judgments involved in internal validity (LP) and external validity (GP). Further, as the figure shows, the judgments are related to the same links of the chain of reasoning.

More explicitly, the five judgments are these:

1. *Explanation generality*—what is the level of generality stated or implied in the proposition, explanation, or theory being advanced? Is it reasonable?
2. *Translation generality*—is that level of generality accurately translated into the design of the study so that the subjects, situations, observations, treatments, and so forth are chosen so as to represent the persons, situations, measures, forms of treatment, and so forth to which generality is intended to be extended?
3. *"Demonstrated generality"*—does the level of generality being claimed extend at least to this instance? (*Demonstrated generality* is in quotation marks because, as in Popper's discussion of "proving" a proposition, cited in connection with internal valid-

**Figure 11. Internal Validity (LP), External Validity (GP),
and the Chain of Reasoning.**

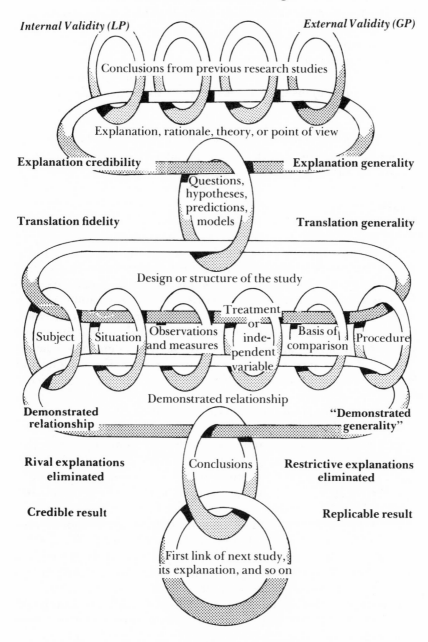

Internal Validity (LP)   External Validity (GP)

Conclusions from previous research studies

Explanation, rationale, theory, or point of view

Explanation credibility   **Explanation generality**

Questions,
hypotheses,
predictions,
models

Translation fidelity   **Translation generality**

Design or structure of the study

Treatment
or
inde-
pendent
variable

Subject | Situation | Observations and measures | Basis of comparison | Procedure

Demonstrated relationship

**Demonstrated
relationship**   **"Demonstrated
generality"**

**Rival explanations
eliminated**   Conclusions   **Restrictive explanations
eliminated**

Credible result   **Replicable result**

First link of next study,
its explanation, and so on

ity (LP), generality cannot be conclusively demonstrated; one can only show there were positive results in this instance.)

4. *Restrictive explanations eliminated*—are there alternative explanations of the phenomenon that would limit or restrict its generality from that claimed?

5. *Replicable result*—would this demonstration replicate with other subjects, other situations, other instruments or observational techniques intended to assess the same variables, other forms of the same treatment, other times, and other procedures?

Just as with internal validity (LP), the judgments form an array of multiple hurdles. Each judgment affects the next, a positive judgment making the next one easier, a negative one making it possibly irrelevant. For example, if no generality is expressed or implied for the phenomenon, there is no explanation generality to judge. Or if the generality claimed is unreasonable, then just as with explanation credibility, the reader is likely to be critical of the study to justify that original judgment of unreasonableness. The translation fidelity judgment is dependent on the generality claimed or inferred in the first judgment. If the translation is deemed inappropriate, then even if the study results are positive, the demonstration will be irrelevant so far as supporting the claimed generality is concerned. Only if the results are both relevant and positive can one proceed to a possible positive stance in the last of the five judgments—whether this evidence suggests that the relationship generalizes beyond this instance. External validity (GP) is the totality of these judgments, largely summarized in the last of them.

In examining the external validity (GP) of the Haney study, we start with explanation generality, the authors' claimed or our inferred generality from their research report. It is clear from their report that they intend the study to generalize to real prisons. They begin by looking at the failure of prisons to rehabilitate prisoners and suggest that there may be more to the problem of prison conditions and "bad soil" than to the usual dispositional, or "bad seed," explanation.

When looking at translation generality, we are, of course, faced with the problem of a simulation versus the real thing. The authors themselves point out that the simulation was not nearly as rough as the real prison, with rife involuntary homosexuality, racism, physical beatings, and threats to life by both prisoners and guards. So they believe that the real situation is far harsher. Further, the simulation included things that would not occur in a prison: The prisoner "uniform" resembled a smock or dress that, when worn without underclothes, forced prisoners to sit in unfamiliar, feminine postures.

Use of a homogeneous middle-range sample may have resulted in "softer" individuals unused to the vicissitudes of life, and their weaknesses may have encouraged whatever sadistic tendencies were latent in the guards. Might the guards have been rougher because they knew the prisoners were unlikely to strike back? In short, it is very difficult to devise a simulation about which no doubts can be raised. The seriousness of the question is a matter of judgment, but the one thing clear is that the experimenters tried to make the differences between the real and simulated situation such that if they could show the effect in the simulated situation, the inference to the real situation would be that much easier. That is a very good practice in a simulation.

The judgment of "demonstration generality" involves asking whether the effect showed in the study situations where it should have, and of course it did. But the extent to which the effect is generalizable to real prisons depends on the judgment of translation generality.

In terms of eliminating explanations, explanations that would limit or restrict the generality, Haney and associates did a good job of eliminating most of the usual problems affecting external validity (GP). But one may wonder about the effect of the students' knowing it was an experimental situation. Did they exaggerate their role playing on purpose to please the investigators? There were extensive debriefing sessions, and reactivity was not mentioned in the report as a topic.

Finally, how about "replicable result"? It would seem that a replication of the exact study might well yield the same results. But when one considers a replication with more realistic subjects, situation, and treatment, then the doubts about the fact that this is a simulation, not a real prison, return. One wonders whether an actual replication of the study with real guards and real but the most stable prisoners and, in another group, real guards but the least stable prisoners would show the effect in both instances. What would happen in these two situations if the treatment were benign and warm? These questions are the kind one would ask in considering whether this is a "replicable result" with the intended generality. It is clear there are some real concerns about overall external validity (GP) and generality to the intended target, real prisons.

The Gradual Limiting of "Universal" Propositions

The generality of a proposition or explanation is frequently considered after the fact. One often is so delighted to find a regularity or pattern that there is a tendency, at first, to think of it as universal. It is only after a bit of thought, and sometimes a disappointing study as well, that one begins to reduce the scope of generality and establish boundary conditions within which the relationship applies.

Initially thought experiments, mentally trying unusual applications such as other cultures or handicapped individuals, are used to restrict the area to which the relationship applies. Such considerations bracket the limits, leaving for empirical work the refinement of the boundaries where thought experiments leave doubt about the outcome. And exploration of why those boundaries exist leads to new understanding of the phenomenon—new boundaries, new explorations, and so forth.

In practice, then, generality is a matter of continually refining the boundaries of applicability: setting expectancies, modifying them in terms of empirical studies or thought experiments—contracting here, expanding there: a "cut and fit" process with replicability (the assurance that a boundary has been correctly established), greater understanding, and new questions expanding the knowledge network.

In a discussion of the failure of behavioral science results to replicate, Cronbach (1975, p. 121) notes: "The aim of social and behavioral science, since Comte, has been to establish lawful relations comparable to those of the . . . natural sciences. The program has not been without success, else it would not have commanded loyalty for so long." He qualifies this statement by adding: "We need to reflect on what it means to establish empirical generalizations in a world in which most effects are interactive." Cronbach's answer is "to assess local events accurately, to improve short-run control." This is a matter of finding generalizations that are good only within certain prescribed boundaries, or as he puts it, to find the "boundary conditions of the generalizations" (p. 126). Actually Cronbach's answer is twofold. In addition to finding generalizations good only within certain prescribed boundaries, such as inner-city schools, test-anxious children, profit-sharing businesses, or voluntary organizations, he notes: "The other reasonable aspiration is to develop explanatory concepts that will help people use their heads" (p. 126). This is like the "cognitive map" approach, which will be explored in later chapters dealing with a typology of behavioral scientists. One of the types builds studies that will enrich people's "cognitive maps" (see Chapter Seven).

Clearly, Cronbach's advice is good; so far as I am able to determine, all generalizations fail to replicate under some circumstances. From the standpoint of theory testing, one can view a lack of replicability as a refutation of the theory or explanation on which the study was based. Typically, however, we don't do this, as Kuhn (1962,

1970) notes. We patch the theory or otherwise try to find ways of interpreting past experience so that the aberration can be explained.

In still another sense, however, such aberrations are to be sought, for they provide us with instances where only by an extension of our knowledge about how the phenomenon works can we include the nonconforming finding. They teach us the limits of our knowledge and, when those limits can be pushed back, lead to new knowledge.

For instance, under most conditions, a well-organized, businesslike teacher best produces achievement. But with children of low socioeconomic status, it appears that a warm, accepting teacher produces achievement (Medley, 1977). This discrepancy can be viewed as a conflict in findings so basic as to suggest that we really don't know what kind of teacher produces achievement, a refutation of developing theory; or as a boundary condition that indicates where the businesslike teacher is effective; or as an important opportunity to try to understand why the two situations differ and how the pupil/teacher relationship furthers pupil learning. This last interpretation provides new understanding of the teaching/learning relationship.

Studies designed to emphasize external validity (GP) are less frequent than those emphasizing internal validity (LP). But when done, such studies are usually aimed at answering a policy question such as "Will the treatment work if adopted in these situations?" Such studies usually examine one or more "representative" or "typical" situations with the expectation that results from them will have generality. Studies of Head Start, for instance, left the determination of the treatment—the Head Start curriculum for underprivileged preschools—almost entirely to the local school. The question was "Does Head Start as a program have generality?"—that is, "Does it work wherever and however put in place?," a policy question. Internal validity (LP) would have been concerned with the relation of particular curricula or curriculum elements to the children's program.

Inference, Extrapolation, and Generality

Generality is always an inference. Bracht and Glass (1968) point out that establishing external validity is a two-stage process—first defining the target population to which the generality is to be demonstrated and then sampling that population. No matter how carefully the sampling is done, it is always a leap of faith to generalize from sample results to the population of which the sample is presumed to be representative. However, when one uses random sampling or some form of probability sampling, one has statistical estimates that help one gauge, with certain odds, the boundaries within which the population value lies. One then has some basis for judgment of generality. But it is worth noting that such careful sampling is usually only to subjects. Such formal sampling is only occasionally applied to situations (unless situation and subjects are sampled together) and more rarely still to treatments.

With nonrandom or nonprobability samples—the commonly used convenience, or "grab," samples, for instance—such indexes are not available, and it is simply a judgment of whether the circumstances of the study sufficiently resemble another situation to which we hope to generalize that the inference may be made.

Thus the determination of generality is always an inference, an extrapolation from a situation that was studied to one that was not. At best it is a matter of inferring where, as a result of careful sampling, the study's design permits inference to a larger population of subjects, of situations, of times, of treatments, and of measures. At worst, we can only make a guess about the similarity of some other set of circumstances to the one studied in order to judge the likelihood that the study results generalize to it.

At this point, readers who skipped the introduction are referred to the overview of the book summarized on pages 1-4. Other readers may wish to review that discussion before continuing with the following chapters.

4

Reformulating the Concept of Internal Validity (Linking Power)

Internal validity (LP) is the judged validity with which statements can be made about a study that the relationship proposed as linking the variables is the only appropriate interpretation of the evidence. The major characteristics that contribute to internal validity (LP) have been described and its relation to external validity (GP) noted. Now we need to look at these characteristics in detail so we can better design studies with the desired internal validity (LP). In addition, we will find that one of the judgments, demonstrated relationship, consists of several separate subjudgments, listed in this chapter as separate subheadings. The major judgments that contribute to internal validity (LP) are recapitulated in Figure 12, together with the subheadings to be described under "Demonstrated Relationship."

Explanation Credibility

Is the relationship to be demonstrated, at least plausible, and its rationale or explanation credible? Very strong linking power is developed by the combination of a theory, rationale, explanation, or point of view supporting a proposition that is highly plausible—believable to the point of being persuasive. The terms *explanation, rationale,* and *theory* all refer to explanations of phenomena. Rationales and especially theories are more formal than mere explanations

Figure 12. Judgments Contributing to Internal Validity (LP).

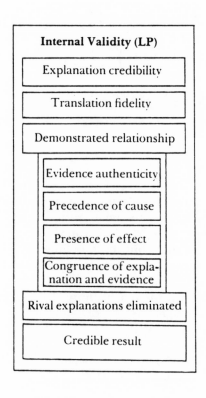

but serve the same function. A point of view would typically come from a qualitative study in which the participants' perception of the situation provides new insights that explain behavior. The intent here is to be inclusive of the different kinds of explanation statements.

It is possible to advance a proposition without an explanation, but to do so risks its being dismissed as a coincidence. For example, every U.S. president since 1840 who was elected in a year ending in zero has died in office or been the victim of an assassination attempt: Harrison, Lincoln, Garfield, McKinley, Harding, Roosevelt, Kennedy, and Reagan. Only in Reagan's case was the attempt unsuccessful. This is an amazing regularity spanning more than a century. But as a cause-and-effect relationship, without a rationale for why there should be such a relationship, it is not convincing. It seems more a prank of chance; a coin shouldn't come up heads ten times in a row, but once in every 1,024 times, on the average, it does. A theory, rationale, or explanation is especially important in getting an audience to consider an otherwise implausible relational possibility.

A credible explanation prepares the audience to accept supportive research findings; indeed, if sufficiently compelling, it may even cause individuals to seek holes in a negative study in order to maintain the belief the rationale created. Conversely, if the explanation is doubted to begin with, readers are likely to seek out and emphasize the study's weaknesses.

At first glance, this process may hardly seem like objective science. But we can look at it another way: Science proceeds both at the theoretical and at the empirical level; one wants to be sure the evidence is trustworthy before discarding a reasonable explanation in which, perhaps, much previous work is invested. Such caution causes a second look at studies where perhaps real weakness did not exist and to have discarded theory because of those results would have been an error. Kuhn (1962) says we hang onto our explanations, patching them up as long as we can, until someone comes along with a new view that revolutionizes how we look at things.

There have been instances in which clinging to an explanation has done considerable disservice; the prolonged rejection of the Copernican theory is a well-known one. The researcher and audience stand most in danger when the explanation is very persuasive and confirming results tend to dull critical tendencies. It remains to those less enamored of the explanation, or those more able to be objective, to supply the balance.

Qualitative researchers may propose theories to explain their data but often, instead, use the points of view of the participants. Antagonisms between supervisor and employee, for instance, may become quite understandable when their perceptions of the job situation reveal widely divergent expectations. Thus points of view often serve as very credible explanations in qualitative studies.

Characteristics of a Credible Explanation

What makes an explanation credible? As we shall see later in examining ways of building credibility with the audience, there is much overlap between that topic and this. I can usefully specify some important characteristics here, however.

1. *Credible explanations build on already accepted knowledge.* A believable explanation uses tight logic to build on well-accepted knowledge, the kind of truths people instantly recognize and identify with. New knowledge that connects with and builds on accepted knowledge is more likely to be recognized and accepted. My friend Gus Root put it well: "You are lighting a candle at the boundary; knowledge is the illumination of lots of small candles." Stent (1972) investigated what made a study premature. He noted that Avery's 1944 work on DNA antedated related work by twenty-three years but was not built on. Mendel's 1865 principles of heredity were "rediscovered" after thirty-five years. Stent concluded that "a discovery is premature if its implications cannot be connected by a series of simple logical steps to . . . generally accepted knowledge" (p. 84). As noted earlier (under "Knowledge Versus Truth," in Chapter One), behavioral science has the most impact when it reinforces intuitively acceptable positions.

But what about counterintuitive studies? They are often the most interesting and important kind. They are important because they correct prevailing impressions that lead to inappropriate behavior. The fact that they are counterintuitive provides a special fascination (Davis, 1971). Such studies have special value in making clear the role of the behavioral sciences in contributing to our knowledge of behavior beyond what could be understood from common sense.

Often the researcher is able to gain acceptance by disarming the reader, explaining, at the outset, how relations that appear to be counterintuitive really are not and then proceeding to make a strong case for them. Consider, for example, Becker's (1963) assertion in *Outsiders* that the unusual behavior of individuals labeled as deviants is in reality caused by other people's labeling them deviants (Davis, 1971). Becker convinces us that the usual way of viewing the situation is more properly turned around.

For many individuals, personal experience is the basis for accepting or rejecting behavioral science explanations: Does the explanation "ring true" for those situations I have personally experienced? If it doesn't, the evidence either will have to be solid and persuasive to overcome the resulting negative set or will have to provide some basis for believing that my experiences were atypical.

2. *Credible explanations are formulated before their demonstrations—they are not rationalizations made up to fit the data.* Explanations should precede the gathering and analysis of data; in that respect they are predictions of what one will find. When they are constructed after the fact, they appear to be rationalizations of why the data came out as they did, rather than credible explanations. When an explanation has been concocted to fit data derived from a particular situation, one is never sure whether it is unique to that situation or has any generality. It is only as one is able to show generality through new demonstrations with new data that the explanation becomes convincing.

This is a problem that individuals doing case studies must contend with. They are likely to find which are the important variables only as the study progresses; they then develop an explanation to fit the circumstances studied. Unless they have data that were not involved in the development of the explanation with which they can show the explanation also works, the explanation is likely to be perceived as applicable primarily to the instance studied.

3. *Credible explanations permit prediction.* Depending on the state of knowledge in a field, the explanation may be very global and general or may be specific and detailed. In either event, it points to what to observe. This is important, for in any situation there are more than enough things to attend to. Knowing, for instance, how long after the cause to expect the effect is very important where it is long delayed, as in the effect of education on the quality of adult life.

Further, the power of the explanation to predict the effect with precision markedly strengthens the case for a relationship. Consider the greater certainty with which variables are linked that is provided by successively stronger predictions (assuming that they are accurate):

- *When to expect the effect.* One is predicting not what to expect but merely when the effect will appear. Usually the effect is immediate, so it is a minimal prediction. Learning, for instance, usually shows immediately after instruction. Timing may be important with measures of retention, however. The timing of the measurement of retention where the learning curve drops very rapidly, as it does shortly after most learning takes place (if there is no intervening practice to strengthen recall), can be critical in determining the amount of retention found. Depending on when one measures, one may be measuring a steeply changing function. Only after it plateaus or at least gets less steep, as most forgetting curves tend to do, does timing become less critical.

Timing may also be important with delayed effects. It considerably strengthens one's confidence in an explanation if accurate predictions are made of when an effect will appear. Developmental phenomena such as those Piaget propounded are good examples. Much of the testing of Piaget's explanations has taken the form of trying to show that his predictions are not time-dependent, that children can be trained to show various capacities before, from a Piagetian point of view, they are developmentally ready.

• *Direction of the effect.* Usually when there is an explanation of the phenomenon, the direction of the effect can be predicted—for example, if one is expecting an improved method of instruction to increase learning. It is mainly in exploratory instances that one cannot predict direction. With a new treatment, one may not be able to predict definitely whether individuals will improve or grow worse, be more or less motivated, and so on. Being able to predict the direction of effect is the basis for choosing one-tailed over two-tailed tests of statistics in a study, a choice that significantly increases sensitivity to small effects.

• *Size and nature of the changes.* The more precisely one can predict the changes that are to take place, the greater grasp one shows of the working of the phenomenon; with greater understanding, the more likely the explanation is to be accepted and the higher the internal validity (LP). If the explanation permits one to describe the qualitative changes that will result from a particular treatment and their size, this is very strong evidence for the basis of prediction. Predicting size in the behavioral sciences is very difficult unless one is dealing with time, such as that the person's reaction time will be halved, or some physical effect that is measured on a scale with a real zero point and meaningful units. Most behavioral science measures use scales with no meaningful zero point and with units that are meaningful only for comparing individuals on that particular scale. Without a real zero point—what is zero intelligence?—one cannot say that a person with an IQ of 120 is twice as bright as one with an IQ of 60. Further, even with our best efforts to make comparable scales, a person's IQ will vary substantially from test to test. So meaningful predictions of size involving measures of constructs—characteristics one cannot physically measure—are likely to be limited unless one can predict changes within a given scale: "Students will gain 5 IQ points on the Stanford-Binet or half a grade from their current average of 2.5 on the California Achievement Test."

Predicting qualitatively described changes may be easier when they involve mainly direction: The individual will grow happier, more motivated, less anxious, more active, and so on. Such predictions may often even be tied to measures rather than observation scales, making the evidence, for most individuals, even more acceptable.

- *Size and nature of the effect not just at one value or level of treatment but over the range of values the treatment, cause, or variable can assume.* This is the most complete prediction, of course, and is the kind that one makes from a theory, especially when one has a mathematical function that describes the behavior. Economists strive for this kind of prediction in their estimates of what will occur in the economy under a range of conditions. If the predictions are accurate, the evidence is very strong that the variables are linked as the explanation indicates, and the contribution of explanation credibility to internal validity (LP) is very high. The stronger the explanation, the stronger the prediction, and the more successful the study is likely to be in building a consensus.

Explanations as Protection Against Misinterpretation

The weaker the design of the study, the heavier is the burden of interpretation that rests on the explanation or theory that under-girds the study (Magidson and Sörbom, 1982). When a design is weak, one may have a variety of alternative explanations to eliminate. The more precisely the effect is targeted, and the more accurately one can anticipate what should *not* happen as well, the more satisfactorily the evidence can be interpreted. Where one can specify the nature, size, and timing of the effect, one can often delineate the observed effect from that which would be expected under alternative explanations. Thus a strong explanation can compensate, to some extent, for a weak design. (For further discussion, see Abt and Magidson, 1980.)

Along these same lines, a strong explanation helps to reduce what are known in statistics as Type I and Type II errors. A Type I error is made when the statistics lead one to believe there is an effect too large to be accounted for by the random error in the study, when indeed this is one of those very rare instances, such as when a coin does happen to come up heads ten times in a row, when the random error does happen to be that large; there is no real effect. A Type II error occurs when the statistics used to describe the effect lead one to believe there is nothing in the results but random error, when there is a real effect but the study is not sensitive enough to sense it; it is buried by the size of the random error.

Where there is a strong explanation, one might disbelieve results that indicate that there is nothing but random error. Assuming that the experiment was, perhaps, not sensitive enough to sense the effect, considering it a Type II error might be a more satisfactory decision than discarding the treatment. One might be missing a good possibility for further study.

Similarly, where an effect appeared and there is no reasonable explanation, there is a strong suspicion that a Type I error might have been made. If the effect disappears when one tries to replicate the study, this explanation is reinforced.

Thus explanation credibility helps to identify situations that are prone to Type I and Type II errors, and it is the major tool we have for that purpose short of actual replication of the study.

Translation Fidelity

The explanation, depending on its strength, leads to a question, a prediction or hypothesis, or a theory or model. If there basically is little explanation, then perhaps one is simply setting forth a question that specifies when to look for something interesting: "What happens when a counselor feeds back an insight to a client?" With greater understanding of what is going on, one can make a prediction or hypothesis: "Clients who are ready will accept the insight; others will reject it." With still greater understanding, the workings of the client can be modeled, or a theory of how therapy proceeds can be posited in such a way that it can be tested: "As therapy proceeds, the client's feelings of self-abnegation and anxiety decline; counselor insights, especially those that explain negative behavior, tend to raise them. Clients are ready to accept such insights when the insights do not reraise their self-abnegation and anxiety levels above the discomfort level they are accustomed to handling well."

Depending on the completeness of explanation advanced by the study, translation fidelity examines whether the study is focused on the right target area and the proper level. If the hypothesis or prediction level is used, it examines the translation of terms like *ready, accept,* and *insight* into definitions that guide the researcher in carrying out the study. At the model or theory level it examines the translation of additional terms such as *self-abnegation, anxiety levels,* and *discomfort level they can handle well.*

Translation fidelity asks, for a study that tests a hypothesis or model, "Has this research hypothesis or model been appropriately translated into operational procedures?" Attention is usually focused first on the measures and observation procedures and, if there is one, the treatment, since these are places where problems are likely to arise. Particularly where constructs are involved—happiness, intelligence, anxiety—the measures may or may not be on target. Therefore, one examines whether the measures or observations of the study and the way they were used are congruent with the terms of the research hypothesis. For example, were the actions of the guards in the simulated prison study congruent with the actions guards normally perform?

Similarly, one examines the treatment, if there is one, for fidelity of translation. The term *treatment* is used to describe a cause or the active agent that results in change. In the prison simulation, the treatment was the simulated situation combined with the roles the prisoners and guards were to play. In the classroom seating example, it is the placement of the students front and center. Treatment fidelity asks whether the treatment, as it is translated into actions or conditions in the study, is congruent with what was intended in the proposition being tested and its explanation. Such congruence is frequently a problem, as when a subject-matter curriculum is effective only if used a certain way; it may require training the teachers to use it.

Finally, of course, there is the translation of the proposition or explanation into choices of subjects, situation, basis of comparison (to show that a change occurred), and procedure—who gets observed and treated and when—and descriptive or inferential statistics (to show the relationship exists). Were these choices congruent with the research hypothesis? Problems may exist with each of these, and in the research planning stage there are usually many choices to consider. Figure 9 illustrates the problem of translation. The various choices for each aspect of the design are superimposed on the design link. For instance, in the "subjects and situations" link, the possible choices are college, high school, and elementary school students. College students were chosen for the design, as is quite appropriate. However, this choice raises a concern that might be less of a problem had either secondary or elementary school been chosen: Some college professors do nothing but lecture. The explanation from previous research, however, suggests there are action zones in the classroom based on student-to-student and student-to-instructor interaction. Such interaction would not be present in straight lecture-style instruction; accurate translation would require that it be. Therefore, assurance of translation fidelity would require that one determine that this economics class did include class discussion. It requires ensuring that the treatment is appropriately operationalized—translated into the proper action—consistent with the explanation and its derivative question, hypothesis, or model.

One choice often has implications for another. In the classroom seating study, the choices of subjects, treatment, and situation are interdependent. Quite frequently the choice of situation will determine the subjects that are to be used, as when a school or business is selected; alternatively, when individuals in them are chosen, that choice designates their organization or place of employment as a research site.

The most serious translation fidelity problem for the behavioral sciences is one only recently encountered by the physical sciences—namely, having to infer the presence of a variable that cannot be directly sensed from its effects on other phenomena that can. In the physical sciences one can determine whether an unseen particle was present by what it did to other particles as it went through a cloud chamber or left an image on a piece of photographic film. Similarly, behavioral scientists are continually trying to assess constructs and concepts that cannot be seen or otherwise directly sensed inside the person but must be inferred from external manifestations such as the person's behavior, how the person reports he feels, his physiological state, or how he perceives the world around him. The definition of anxiety as an internal state must be appropriately matched with its operational definition—the test, observations, scale, or other set of operations that defines what one does to assess the external manifestations (behavior, observation, self-report, physiological changes, perceptions). For example, whether a person is anxious, an internal state, can be determined only by his behavior with respect to a situation, perhaps his responses to a questionnaire or even by physiological measures. The latter is a characteristic of anxiety not present for most constructs. We do not, for instance, despite brain-wave research, have any reliable physiological measure of intelligence. An important question for translation fidelity is how accurately the responses on the questionnaire reflect the internal state. Can they be taken as an adequate index of what is internally present?

But there are even further complications; even a construct like anxiety is often further differentiated. For example, it can be considered as state anxiety, whether an individual is anxious at a given point in time, or trait anxiety, a kind of pervasive anxiety that is characteristic of the person. The task in translation fidelity is to determine what is meant by the term *anxiety*, whether state or trait anxiety (or possibly even another definition), and then ensure that the measures or observations are consistent with it—there are different measures for state anxiety and trait anxiety, two different operational definitions. Thus checking the ways in which constructs and concepts are translated—operationalized—into subjects, situations, observations, and treatments is a prime task in translation fidelity.

This concern with translating constructs is, of course, a central problem of the field of measurement. The extensive discussions of how one determines test reliability and validity all bear on translation fidelity; measures must be valid and, to be so, must also be reliable.

Since most readers are already aware of this literature, attention is called to its relevance without the extensive discussion that would be necessary to cover it adequately.

So, given that there are a number of ways in which the research hypothesis can be translated into a study, translation fidelity reduces to the question whether the set chosen is a genuine instance of what was to be demonstrated. Of course, if there are reservations on this point, the linking power of the study will be lessened in proportion to their severity.

In studies where one does not start with expectations, as in many field studies, what does translation fidelity mean? Basically the same thing, but the direction, instead of proceeding from abstract concept to concrete instances, is reversed. For example, in developing "grounded theory" (Glaser and Strauss, 1967), one is inductively constructing explanations (abstract concepts) that are grounded in the phenomena, the concrete instances one has been observing. Translation fidelity in this instance means that the explanations one develops are fully consistent with the observations they are to account for.

Translation fidelity must be at least reasonably acceptable to proceed to the next question, since if the translation is unacceptable, it is not relevant to ask whether the demonstration is convincing. Let us assume that the translation is acceptable, however, and proceed.

Demonstrated Relationship

Was the demonstration successful in showing that the indicated relationship held in this instance? Answering this, the third question, requires examining the demonstration itself to see whether, in this particular instance, the case has been made that the relationship was demonstrated. This task typically calls for four kinds of evidence:

- Evidence authenticity
- Precedence of cause
- Presence of effect, change, or covariation
- Prediction (or explanation) congruence

As has been pointed out and is discussed further in Chapter Nine, cause-and-effect terminology is not applicable to all relations. Where it is not, evidence authenticity and presence of change or covariation are the relevant sources of evidence for demonstrated relationships. For the many situations in which *cause* and *effect* are appropriate terms, precedence of cause and prediction congruence are important as well.

Evidence Authenticity

At issue in evidence authenticity is whether the evidence is what it purports to be. We generally take it for granted that the researcher was honest. Science functions on trust, and evidence of cheating is rare. But even so famous a researcher as the late Sir Cyril Burt apparently fabricated data (Hearnshaw, 1979); so the concern cannot be dismissed. Occasionally pressures cause people to falsify data. When the score on an examination is particularly important, individuals have been known to have others take the test for them. Interviewers have made up responses in order to make their quotas. In general, however, since investigators either gather their own data or closely supervise its collection, this is not a serious problem.

Authenticity is the most serious problem for historians. They are especially concerned that their evidence is authentic and go to great lengths to establish the authenticity of diaries, letters, and other cirumstantial evidence on which their interpretations of past events depend.

Precedence of Cause

Precedence of cause means that whatever is considered the cause, or instigating condition, was present before the effect, or consequent condition. As the saying goes, "What's done is done!" and whatever comes after an effect can hardly change the effect itself. Therefore, for cause-and-effect relations, precedence of cause is a necessary part of internal validity (LP).

In experiments in which the researcher has control of the treatment, precedence is not a problem, since it can be assured. But in field studies it can be an important piece of evidence that is not always easy to obtain. In the context of rapidly occurring events, the presence of the instigating factor may be difficult to spot and record. In the initial stages of a participant observation study, the important phenomena may not yet be clear, so only a fuzzy delineation of cause may be possible—or perhaps the wrong aspects are attended to and the cause is recorded only tangentially, incompletely, or not at all.

In historical studies or in others such as some sample surveys, where the cause has already occurred, establishing precedence may be based on less-than-solid evidence. The imperfect recollections of individuals (Was the individual nervous before smoking started, or did that occur after?) or circumstantial evidence (The records are otherwise apparently authentic, but we have to estimate the date!) may leave questions about precedence.

In some instances, it is important to determine not only that the cause was present but also that it was reacted to. This is the difference between "nominally" present and "effectively" present stimuli. Precedence in the case of a curriculum may mean not only that the instructional materials were present in a classroom (nominally present) but also that the students perceived or encountered the curriculum in ways consistent with expectations about its use (effectively present).

Presence of Effect

The criterion here is whether the effect appeared—whether there was a change, a covariation, a difference between means, or whatever effect was to appear. If the effect is large, identifying change is no problem. But in many behavioral science studies, there is often a problem in deciding whether there was an effect at all. In these instances we most commonly turn to inferential statistics (*t* tests, chi square, analysis of variance, and so forth) to help determine whether what appeared was just random error of sampling, measurement, and the like or whether it lies beyond the normal range of such error. Inferential statistics give us an estimate of that normal range. Perhaps the most likely problem with small effects is designing a study with insufficient sensitivity to show an effect or change even if it were present. This need not be a problem, however, if one has pilot studies or if there is previous work in the area. Tables (Cohen, 1970) and other sources of aid in statistics books help one estimate whether the study was designed with sufficient sensitivity.

If there is a prediction, it tells where, and possibly when, to look for an effect. Sometimes, however, peculiar unpredicted results appear. In those instances, the same literature that helped one formulate a prediction is also helpful in disentangling those results and properly attributing them to relevant variables.

Where the effect or change is qualitative and cannot be categorized, ordered, or quantified, one relies on verbal descriptions. The descriptions of abnormal behavior in the prison simulation study were of this kind. One needed no instrument to see that the "guards" were becoming abusive and the "prisoners" abject. Good qualitative researchers have no trouble describing effects, change, and covariation well enough that the audience is satisfied without numbers, especially when the effect is clear. The biggest problem for the qualitative researcher is to describe how closely variables covary when the covariation is far from perfect, when instances in which they covary together are mixed with those in which they do not. If it is possible to explain what determines whether and when they vary together, such explanation is welcomed as new knowledge. When it is mixed with random variation, it is more difficult to describe adequately without numbers.

Congruence of Explanation and Evidence

If one really understands a phenomenon, the evidence will support that understanding: What the explanation leads one to expect will be congruent with what the evidence itself shows. In studies developing grounded theory, the theory is matched to the data to show that the theory is sufficiently inclusive to explain the data and the match is a good one. In quantitative studies there will usually be a prediction, and one looks for congruence of the prediction and the data.

Even when the effect and its presumed instigating condition are both present and the effect followed that condition, there is still the problem of linking the two. How to do this? We have already noted parts of this process: the importance of a plausible proposition, explanation, theory, or rationale, its accurate translation, and precedence of an instigating condition. Now we add some of the most persuasive evidence, the ability to predict and, possibly, to control. If one can predict effects following certain instigating conditions, create those conditions, and then show that the effect appears, the linkage is very believable. This, of course, is the heart of the experimental method, and there are those for whom no other evidence is adequately convincing.

What about the prediction creates credibility of linking? Although these assumptions may not hold in some instances, credibility of linking is related to—

1. The impressiveness of the predictive feat. The more detail one can supply about the expected relationship, the more impressive the prediction. If one's successful prediction includes the most precise detail, one apparently knows what one is about.
2. The size of the effect. A huge effect certainly helps! That nearly half the "prisoners" developed psychological distress symptoms in the prison simulation study was impressive.
3. Being able to show that the effect prevails even in the face of countervailing circumstances or forces. The fact that the simulated prison situation created this dramatic effect in the face of

countervailing forces—these were the most stable of the subjects available—makes it more convincing.

4. Being able to show that the effect follows exactly the pattern of an intentionally varied cause. The more complex the causal pattern, if the effect follows it, the stronger the evidence for association. Unless some other variable follows that same complex pattern, this demonstration very effectively solves the next problem, eliminating alternative explanations.

Why, if internal validity (LP) is applicable to any relationship, not just those stated in causal terms, are some of the foregoing conditions stated in those terms? Because there is no denying that the experimental method, which involves the manipulation of a cause and the demonstration of a predicted effect, is one of the most powerful techniques we have for demonstrating a relationship. Hence one cannot describe the ways of strengthening internal validity (LP) without including the characteristics of that technique. This is equally true of the eight rules to which we turn next. These embody the principles in detailed advice that may be more helpful than the principles in pointing to practical applications in the design of studies. Remember, internal validity (LP) is defined as the judged validity with which statements can be made that the relationship proposed as linking the variables is the only appropriate interpretation of the evidence, and it includes the judged power of the study to build a consensus around that interpretation. In general, then, internal validity (LP) is greater—

1. With controlled application of the cause, treatment, or instigating condition.
2. With stronger and more detailed predictions.
3. When a change in the cause or instigating condition is followed by large changes in effect.
4. When the effect reverses a prevailing tendency than when change is in the same direction.
5. The more a complexly patterned cause is predictably mirrored by the effect.
6. If the instigating condition or cause can be controlled at will, producing a pattern of cause on demand.
7. The greater the range of instigating conditions over which the predictions can be shown to hold.
8. The more time elapses between the instigating condition and the effect, assuming one can accurately predict the time of appearance of the effect.

Let us examine each of these in detail to see how and why it works.

1. *Internal validity (LP) is greater with controlled application of the cause, treatment, or instigating condition.* When the instigating condition is in the past or is not controlled, observation of things that vary together can be very misleading. Historians are quite fond of noting that, in the early days of this country, growth in the number of churches followed quite well growth in size of the rum trade.

2. *Internal validity (LP) is greater the stronger the prediction.* This was discussed under the topic of explanation credibility and flows from it; a strong explanation can lead to more precise and detailed predictions—direction, size, qualitative changes, related conditions. As noted earlier, indicating simply when the effect will occur is the weakest prediction. A stronger prediction adds the direction of the effect, a still stronger one the size and nature of the change. The strongest gives such predictions over the possible range of values of the cause or instigating condition.

For example, suppose that one thinks anxiety is related to paper-and-pencil test performance but doesn't know whether it will raise or lower performance. That is the lowest level of prediction. Suppose that, as a result of understanding that the effect of anxiety is to reduce breadth of perception and flexibility, one predicts that it will lower performance on creative tasks but increase it on routine tasks. Especially when combined with an explanation, this is a more precise and satisfying prediction; it gives both direction and qualifying conditions.

The next three principles might be thought of as corollaries of this one.

3. *Internal validity (LP) is greater when a change in the cause or instigating condition is followed by large changes in effect.* An effect that does not need inferential statistics to show it is there is especially persuasive. As a physician once told me, "I don't need statistics to know penicillin works."

Again, this was one of the strong points of the simulated prison study and of the Milgram study that preceded it. In the former, the abnormal behavior was readily apparent. In Milgram's study, most subjects turned the handle controlling the strength of the supposed shocks to a reading of "XXX," indicating the maximum shock level. These results speak for themselves. Unfortunately, although strong effects characterize some of the more successful studies, they are the exception rather than the rule.

4. *Internal validity (LP) is greater when the effect reverses a prevailing tendency than when the change is in the same direction.*

Reversing a child's dislike of reading so she is motivated to read is more of a feat than increasing the motivation of a child who already likes to read. Unless one has prior measures of rate of changes and knows that the rate will not change, it is difficult to disentangle the contributions of the two influences that combine to change an effect in the same direction. In successfully bucking the prevailing tendency, a researcher shows that one overcame another, the prevailing tendency. When forces oppose each other and one dominates, their comparative strength is clearer.

5. *Internal validity (LP) is greater the more a complexly patterned cause is predictably mirrored by the effect.* For example, a preset pattern of treatment such as (1) a short, strong treatment, followed by (2) a long period of no treatment, followed by (3) a weak, short treatment, is mirrored by (1) a brief, dramatic drop in aberrant behavior, (2) its recurrence, and then (3) a slight reduction in it. The effect replicates the pattern of the cause. In the absence of an alternative explanation (the fourth judgment, rival explanations eliminated), this is almost as strong evidence of linkage as one can get. The only stronger evidence is described in the next principle.

It is important to note that once a change has occurred, not all phenomena are reversible; indeed, if reversals occur with the removal of therapy that is intended to build in some lasting change in behavior, one would consider the treatment a failure. In addition, induced reversal would be ethically untenable. We do not cure a person only to make her ill again. Thus, it is by no means always possible to demonstrate a reversal of direction. This fact, of course, denies to us one of the most convincing demonstrations for many important phenomena where we would like the strongest possible evidence.

6. *Internal validity (LP) is greater if the instigating condition or cause can be controlled at will, producing a pattern of cause on demand.* For example, in a series of treatment applications, whether to apply the treatment may be determined by the flip of a coin. If improvement follows such a randomly produced pattern of on-and-off treatment, the linkage is extremely convincing. The pattern must be without suspicion of being related to any other condition that might be considered an alternative cause.

Of course, many causative conditions cannot be controlled by the researcher. As a substitute in field studies, if the pattern of the instigating condition can be shown to be random and unpredictable and an effect follows it, one may have a "natural" experiment. For instance, one might be able to show that the morale of a business unit depends strongly on the use of a particular kind of supervision by relating the occasional use of that pattern to changes in morale. Such evidence can be very convincing if one can legitimately arrest the fears that something else that was not observed happened to covary with the presumed cause and therefore might be either the basic cause or a part of the instigating conditions. Clearly the latter is a very difficult task, especially if someone is antagonistic to the study and is looking for weaknesses or alternative explanations.

7. *Internal validity (LP) is greater the greater the range of instigating conditions over which the predictions can be shown to hold.* It is probably true that the strongest linkages are shown in very specific conditions, but at the same time, the logic of this principle is that if one is able to show that the effect holds over a variety of situations, a very strong and pervasive relationship must be at work. That is impressive and convincing. For example, if a set of instructional principles is effective in producing student achievement no matter how poor the teacher appears to be by other criteria, the principles would be very powerful. This same logic applies as well to principle 8.

Prediction over the widest range of conditions is another way of making the strongest prediction—if possible, over the complete range of values that the cause or instigating condition could assume.

The next principle is really a corollary of number 7.

8. *Internal validity (LP) is greater the more time elapses between the instigating condition and the appearance of the effect, assuming one can accurately predict the time of appearance of the effect.* We are so used to prediction of the appearance of short-range or immediate effects that the prediction of long-range ones, especially when the time that the effect will appear is predicted, can be very convincing. The stages of grief following the death of a loved one give persuasive evidence that the superiority of long-range predictions is beginning to be understood. There can be problems in any long-delayed prediction, however, since the longer the intervening time, the greater the probability that other factors than the one being advanced may have been the real causes of the effect, as the longer time permits a variety of other events to occur.

Combinations of Conditions. The linking power of combinations of these eight principles is difficult to anticipate, and each new situation has to be judged individually. For example, is a detailed and precise prediction of an immediate effect more or less convincing than a less detailed and precise prediction of a long-range effect? It depends a great deal on such matters as what phenomenon is involved and the accuracy of the prediction. Although the principles are helpful guides in comparing conditions to determine which gives stronger support to internal validity (LP), considerable judgment may still be needed in making that decision.

Multiple Causation. The preceding discussion concerned only simple cause-and-effect conditions. I have, however, purposely used the phrase *instigating conditions*. Why does that extra phrase clutter up the discussion? For a very important reason. Sometimes, perhaps often, causes are multiple, or combinations of causes are limited to certain situations. For purposes of discussion, we may focus on one condition as a cause, but in fact it is always part of a chain of conditions—a person's drug use was caused by depression, the depression was brought on by persistent unemployment, the unemployment had persisted because job training programs were eliminated, and so on and on. Whether we study depression or unemployment or the elimination of job training programs in relation to drug use depends on where we enter the causal chain. And since elimination of job training does not inevitably lead to unemployment and depression, there is a sense in which all three constitute a complex of predisposing conditions for drug use. So events can always be viewed as being caused by a complex of conditions, or, depending on our focus, we may simplify the situation to look at particular conditions. The term *instigating conditions* is used to describe such complex sets of conditions rather than detailing them in a discussion that is already complicated. The matter of causal chains and different conditions of causation is discussed further in Chapter Nine.

One should not, however, mistake this topic as unimportant. Our world increasingly seems more complex than simple. Variables are effective for only a portion of their potential range or only under certain conditions, and multiple causes are increasingly discovered. Complex patterns of causation are more prevalent than the simple ones we would prefer to seek that have been the prime targets of past research. As our methods are increasingly able to handle multiple causation, we must prepare to handle the variety of causative possibilities we are likely to encounter.

Rival Explanations Eliminated

If there is a plausible alternative explanation to that being advanced by the researcher, then the chain of reasoning is considerably weakened. In the simulated prison study, a potentially very strong alternative explanation, the "bad seed" one, was ruled out by selecting only individuals who were very stable to begin with. Eliminating alternative explanations is one of the major functions of the design of a study. This topic received special study by Campbell and Stanley

(1963) and Cook and Campbell (1979), who developed categories of rival hypotheses, or "threats to validity," as these alternative explanations were called. These categories, to which the authors gave such names as *history, testing, maturation, mortality,* and *selection,* are a very important set of alternative explanations one must guard against. They cover the alternatives most commonly encountered. Though devised in the context of experimentation, they apply to other methods as well. Cook and Campbell (1979) revised and improved some of the Campbell and Stanley (1963) definitions and made useful differentiations. A summary of the rival explanations that have been suggested follows.

History. The effect might be due to an event that took place before the posttest rather than to the experimental treatment. For example, a researcher evaluating the effectiveness of a new history curriculum on the Civil War finds her subjects have been watching a TV miniseries, *The Life of General Robert E. Lee.*

Testing. Because repeated testing of subjects causes them to react differently to second and later testings than to the first one, the effect might be created by repeated measurement. For example, the researcher gives each student an individual oral pretest on the Civil War. Later, to measure achievement, she repeats the procedure. The students are much more relaxed and comfortable at the second testing, a factor that undoubtedly helps them do better on the test.

Instrumentation. As one gains experience in using a measuring instrument, the way it is used may change, so that measures taken at one point in the study differ from those at another point. This difference, rather than the treatment, may cause the effect to appear.

Statistical Regression. When a cutting score on a measure with less than perfect reliability (and that includes them all!) is used to identify a group of subjects, on retest the mean score for that group will be found to move toward the mean of the total group from which they were selected. This is most often a problem where remedial groups are selected by a cutting score on a test, which is then used to measure gains. Any apparent improvement actually may be all or largely statistical regression. Conversely, students chosen to receive an enrichment program because they were unusually advanced may appear to lose over the course of the program if their gain is not greater than the statistical regression. Even if they show a gain, it will be underestimated because it will be reduced by the amount of statistical regression.

Selection. An effect may be due to selection of individuals into different groups on different bases. For example, the volunteers are all put into the experimental group, and the remainder constitute the control group.

Mortality. An effect may be due to the differences in those who dropped out of one group in contrast to those who dropped out of another. If respondents to a questionnaire give different responses than nonrespondents would, then the results do not represent the entire group to whom the questionnaire was mailed, because of the "mortality" of the nonrespondents.

Maturation. Members of one group may change during the study at a different rate than members of another group. This may be due to different growth rates, as the name implies, but it also may be due to any other changes during the study, such as, in a long study, growing tired or bored.

Selection Interactions. Selection may combine with another rival explanation to create an interaction of the two that gives a result that could be mistaken for the effect of the treatment. For instance, a combined effect of selection and maturation may occur when different groups change at different rates during the study because of selection factors. Similarly, selection may combine with instrumentation when different groups, because of their different characteristics, receive different measures. For example, groups of students at different grade levels receive either the intermediate or the advanced form of the same test. These tests might be too easy or too hard for them, leading to ceiling or floor effects because their scores cannot improve or cannot decline.

Researcher Expectancy Effect. The effect that the researcher expects may be communicated to the subjects so that they produce it. Alternatively, the researcher, expecting certain effects, perceives that they do occur or gives the subjects every possible opportunity for them to occur.

Diffusion. The treatment may be communicated to other groups, so that they become treatment groups rather than the control groups they were intended to be.

Reactive Effects. A variety of reactive effects (identified by Campbell and Stanley, 1963, and Cook and Campbell, 1979) may result from subjects' realization that the situation created by the study has changed conditions from normal to atypical. Various reactive effects result from different perceptions of the special conditions. Here are some perceptions and their reactive effects:

1. "We're special." This perception enhances the treatment. Often called the Hawthorne effect, it is named after an experiment at the Western Electric Hawthorne plant. It was concluded that, as a result of the extra attention given by those conducting the study, workers on the assembly line produced more because they perceived

they were special, even when the quality of working conditions was decreased.

2. "I don't want to be a guinea pig." This perception is prevalent in laboratory schools where students have been exposed to too much experimentation; it decreases the effect.

3. "I want *my* child to get that special treatment!" This complaint causes problems for the institution's administrator, who may then try to provide compensatory treatment. Compensation will decrease the difference between treated and untreated but now compensated groups, thereby making the treatment look less effective than otherwise.

4. "I don't want my group to be disadvantaged just because it wasn't chosen for special treatment!" This is a determination by those responsible for the control group that their children are going to do just as well as or better than those "special kids." It is a frequent response of control-group teachers who work harder than usual to compensate for their "nonspecial" status. It is sometimes called the "John Henry" effect after the legendary black railroad worker who pitted his skill against a steam railroad spike driver. As in the previous instance, the treatment is made to appear less effective.

5. "That's new and interesting. I think I'd like that." This is the novelty effect; anything that is new is, at least at first, perceived as more fun and good. It may enhance the treatment effect the first time the treatment is applied, but it wears off. Adapting a new curriculum to one's needs is fun, but once the curriculum becomes routine, enthusiasm for teaching—and hence effectiveness—decreases.

6. "We can't compete with that group—it's getting all that special help. Why try? Let's quit." Low morale and feelings of dismay may cause the comparison group to be less effective than it would otherwise be, making the treatment look better than it is.

These effects, which result because special measures are taken, because the experimenter or other individuals enter the group as strangers, because a treatment is out of character for the situation, or because some other event signals the situation is not normal, can be reduced if one can lower the obtrusiveness of the study. One way is to have the institutional staff, with which subjects would normally come in contact, administer the treatment and possibly even the measures. Alternatively for the latter, one may find ways to make the unobtrusive observations; Webb and others (1970) suggested ways of doing so that are especially appreciated in this regard.

But in addition to these common alternatives, every study may have uncommon and sometimes unique alternative explanations to be guarded against. For example, learning a unit from a text of randomly scrambled sentences was found not to be significantly different from learning the unit with sentences in proper order (Krathwohl, Gordon, and Payne, 1967). An alternative explanation is that breaking the material into scrambled parts created a puzzle that forced the individual into an active learning process rather than merely reading passively. Subjects therefore had to rehearse the parts as they were fitted together and analyze the organization of the material to place it in proper sequence. All this facilitated learning. This explanation lies outside the published categories of alternatives and yet is obvious once suggested. It is the kind of question a bright graduate student asks of the researcher after the study has been concluded. Every researcher tries to protect against such oversights, but "the tightest of designs on Saturday has holes on Monday."

Rival alternative explanations are *additional* explanations *not* being advanced by the researcher. They must be ruled out by the study, or they weaken the researcher's case for the one or more explanations being proposed. The more plausible the rival explanations that cannot be eliminated, the weaker the case for the proposed explanation of the association of variables.

Credible Result

The fifth decision, "Is this a credible result?," builds on the previous four. It considers the study results in the light of previous experience in the area to come to an overall judgment of internal validity (LP). In the set of five sequential and cumulative decisions, credible result is the capstone that determines the internal validity (LP) of the study.

The sequential process began with a decision about explanation credibility. If this decision suggested that the study seemed to have a reasonable base, one examined its translation into operational terms. If the translation was satisfactory and the study yielded positive results with no reasonable alternative explanations, then one came to the fifth decision. Credible result asks whether the preceding seems credible in the light of previous experience with studies as similar to this as one can recall. Credible result is a thought experiment. One asks oneself whether, on the basis of previous experience and the previous decisions, the result is credible, is reasonable to expect, given everything that has gone before, or whether it is a fluke, an anomaly, an aberration, an accident, a random shot, a stroke of luck. If all of the prior four judgments are positive and the result seems credible considering prior work in the area, then the study has strong internal validity (LP).

Some studies will emerge from this judgment process with strong internal validity (LP), but most will be somewhere in the middle. A few that somehow slipped through the peer judgment screen used by most behavioral science journals will have low internal validity (LP). But strong internal validity (LP) assumes that there were positive results and that most of the four prior judgments were reasonably positive. This is not, of course, necessarily true: (1) The results may be positive or negative. Qualitative case studies typically will not have negative results, since the generalizations they advance were developed from—grounded in—the data gathered, but studies using experimental, survey, and most other methods may. (2) Previous judgments may lead one to expect that the data will support or negate the relationship being advanced. These possibilities result in a four-fold table, Table 1.

Table 1. Relation of Results to What Was Hypothesized.

		Data support hypothesis	Data negate hypothesis
Expectations of data created by prior judgments	Data will support relationship to be demonstrated	1. Congruence	2. Dashed hopes
	Data will negate relationship to be demonstrated	3. Surprised expectations	4. Congruence

The results may support one's expectations that the relationship would appear. This is cell 1, congruence. Conversely, the evidence may yield no support for the relationship; if one were critical of the study and had negative expectations, and the relationship did not appear, that also, as shown in cell 4, is congruence. Alternatively, there may be a mismatch of expectations and results. If one expected the relationship to be demonstrated and the data were not supportive, one has dashed hopes, cell 2. The critic who didn't expect the data to support the relationship and finds that they did, cell 3, has surprised expectations. Whichever cell the results fall in, one must justify the credibility of the result and determine whether to trust it or term it an anomaly.

Congruence and Internal Validity (LP)

As previously indicated, where the four previous judgments— explanation credibility, translation fidelity, demonstrated result, and rival explanations eliminated—are positive and the results are consistent with prior work in the field, then one makes a positive judgment of internal validity (LP), and the study falls in cell 1. In most cases that is the end of it; one simply makes a judgment of credible result and strong internal validity (LP).

There are instances, however, in which one has partial but not complete congruence. The following example may make clear both the problem and the solution in such an instance. I was once sent a study that showed the National Teacher Examination (NTE) to be a very significant predictor of how well a teacher's class could read (Summers and Wolfe, 1975). Past results would have led one to expect a very low, positive correlation, since the teacher's characteristics are only one of many factors determining student learning. Indeed, there was a positive correlation, so it was consistent with the direction of the expected result. But the NTE had been combined with other factors to make the prediction, and the multiple correlation was very high. Indeed, it was so high and the NTE such an important factor in the combination of variables used to make the prediction, that I just couldn't believe the result. Although I was uncomfortable with some of the assumptions of the study, I saw no obvious flaw. Had one accepted the result, however, it would have legitimized uses of the NTE that, on the basis of previous evidence from which it differed substantially, would have been entirely inappropriate. I had to argue, therefore, that the result was an anomaly. The key here was holding this study up against previous comparable work and judging the relative quality of previous studies as well as this study. This study failed the credible result judgment, and internal validity (LP) for this result, as accurately reflecting the true nature of the relationship, was judged low. This judgment was later substantiated by statisticians who pointed out several problems with the analysis and assumptions made by the study.

Dashed Hopes, Surprised Expectations, and Congruent but Not Credible Results

What if one's hopes for positive results are dashed, one is surprised by positive results, or the expected results are not consistent with past work in the field? In these instances the judgment of credibility of results is likely to be especially carefully scrutinized. How could one's expectations be so wrong? Why are these results inconsistent with past ones?

Probably the most common explanation for a mismatch between expectations and results is one or more incorrect judgments among those prior to credible result. In the case of dashed hopes, one may have overlooked a problem severe enough to prevent the expected results from appearing, and internal validity (LP) is lower than initially judged. In the case of surprising results, one was inappropriately critical—something that one judged to be a serious limitation of the study turned out not to be. Perhaps the explanation one judged weak was more appropriate than one thought. Accordingly, internal validity (LP) is higher than one expected.

Besides errors in judgment, a second and a third explanation can be proposed. The second explanation follows from the belief that the phenomena of the behavioral sciences are better accounted for by Popper's (1972) "cloudlike" than his "clocklike" model. Popper's "clocklike" model assumes a precise mechanical determinism such as one finds in the workings of an old spring-wound clock with its numerous gears. Any movement of one gear immediately causes a proportionate response in others, and prediction can be precise. His "cloudlike" model assumes that behavioral science phenomena are better described by the normative behavior exhibited by a cloud of gnats. A gnat strays only so far from the center of the swarm, returning there when it becomes an outlier. If we think of our predictions as being represented by the swarm of gnats, most of the predictions will more or less hold—most gnats are in the swarm—but there are occasionally outliers. In this model, there can be no precise prediction, only an increase in likelihood of certain results. With the loose coupling of events that the cloudlike model assumes, one would expect to find unusual results of both a positive and a negative nature from time to time.

Occasional dashed hopes might be expected, because one cannot guarantee the expected effect with each treatment application. If one views the result of a study as an outlier, then one's dashed hopes might suggest that a replication is in order, since a result more central to the "swarm of gnats" is the most likely result of a replication.

In the case of surprised expectations, where negative results were expected and positive ones were found, if one is convinced the study is an outlier, then the result is a fluke of chance, and one's judgment that the study is not likely to yield positive results on replication is sound.

A third possible explanation is an error in the application or interpretation of statistics (Cook and Campbell, 1979, use the term *statistical conclusion validity*). Sometimes the wrong statistical method was used or a misinterpretation occurs. A common problem that would account for dashed hopes is that the study was designed with insufficient sensitivity to show the result that occurred. Statisticians say the study lacked sufficient power, where they are referring to a kind of analytic power. Like a microscope that is not strong enough to permit the researcher to see the event of concern, the study did not provide evidence of the effect because it was not powerful enough to sense it, so the wrong conclusion was drawn. Statisticians call this a Type II or beta error; one wrongly concludes, using inferential statistics, that there was no effect.

There are a number of ways of reducing the chances of such an error, such as increasing the size of one's sample or changing the level of significance used in the study (for example, from .05 to .10). But doing so involves trade-offs such as, in the latter case, increasing the chances of a Type I error (discussed shortly). If, from previous work, one can estimate the size of the effect one is looking for and certain other characteristics of one's sample, the study can be designed with sufficient sensitivity to ensure positive results if an effect occurs (Cohen, 1970). Similarly, by the same methods one can check an already completed study to determine whether its sensitivity was adequate. If one believes the study was designed with insufficient sensitivity, then although this study might have low internal validity (LP), it is clearly worth replicating with adequate sensitivity.

A different statistical occurrence helps to explain surprised expectations, an explanation much like the outlier, or anomaly, problem discussed in the second explanation—a chance error that falsely showed a positive result. This is the opposite of the previous statistical error and is called by statisticians a Type I or alpha error. It is the kind of situation in which ten coins shouldn't *all* come up heads at once, but it does happen—on the average, once in a little over a thousand times. It is of little comfort to believe that this is that instance, but it does happen, and there is no way of completely avoiding it. As with the previous statistical error, however, one can reduce it, in this instance by adjusting the significance level (for example, from .05 to .01, .001, or less). But again doing so also involves a trade-off; in this instance it reduces sensitivity. If one believes that an error of this kind has occurred, not only will internal validity (LP) be low, but there is little point in replicating the study.

If the study runs contrary to the explanation and to other work in the field, it is possible that one of the errors just described has occurred, or there could be a clerical or computational problem. Today's use of computers has reduced the likelihood of computational errors, but clerical errors are an ever-present danger, especially in getting the data into the computer.

Explanations That Apply to Dashed Hopes

In addition to the preceding explanations, which apply both to surprised expectations and to dashed hopes, there are explanations that apply only to dashed hopes (no effect was sensed when one was expected):

1. The proposition or theory may not be adequate to handle all situations, and some will, therefore, not turn out as we expect. Popper's famous criterion for an acceptable theory is that it should be falsifiable. Ziman (1978, p. 35) notes that this test is "strategically sound, but tactically indefensible. It turns out in practice that almost every theory is to some extent 'falsified' by the relevant observations; the question then hinges on whether, pending conceivable improvements in formulation or computation, the negative findings may be temporarily overlooked."

Falsification may result from lack of knowledge of the boundaries within which a formulation holds or of the contingencies on which it depends. The resulting dashed hopes require a judgment of whether the result reflects on the truth of the proposition or should be considered an anomalous finding, a random outlier.

2. Parallel to the concern about lack of statistical power noted earlier is a concern that the research methodology is too crude; research technique may be at fault. The observation or measures may not be precise enough, for example, or the study may be too poorly controlled.

Einstein is said to have been undisturbed when early experiments failed to confirm his theory. He believed them too crude to sense the result with sufficient accuracy and waited for technique to improve. Time validated his judgment. There are, no doubt, others whose careers never blossomed as a result of the same behavior, either because technique did not improve or because their determination was misplaced. Clearly, whether to persevere and insist the results are not credible is a matter of judgment—like so many aspects of the research process, one that some researchers are both wise and lucky enough to make correctly.

Studies That Break New Ground

Since there are no previous studies for direct comparisons, one needs to consider differently a study that is breaking new ground from those either following a traditional line of study or replicating previous work. The ground-breaking study must be judged on its own merits and in relation to the closest research one can find. Studies following a more traditional line of work can be judged against research that has plowed this ground in the past. A consensus of the latter studies makes one more certain the relationship really exists; the results are to be trusted—one has a credible but less exciting result! The ground-breaking study will be tougher to evaluate but exciting, and the stakes can be high if it is judged incorrectly, so care is called for.

Hypotheses That Oppose a Field's Beliefs

What if one's expectations are contrary to the previous results in the field? Presumably one had good reason for so deciding, and if those contrary expectations are confirmed, one's rationale for reversing the field is further supported. Because those in the field may be doubtful of such a result, one may want to use extra care in examining the evidence to ensure that it can withstand heightened scrutiny. Those in the field seeking to maintain prior beliefs are likely to seek out and attack the weaknesses of the study.

Overall Internal Validity (LP) of a Study

The internal validity (LP) of a study is a summary judgment across five separate but related judgments: (1) explanation credibility, (2) translation fidelity, (3) demonstrated relationship, (4) rival explanations eliminated, and (5) credible result. Positive answers to the questions involved in all five will indicate strong linking power. But it is not a simple summation of the number of "yeses." The heavy dependence of each of the successive judgments on the previous one invests in the fifth and last one, credible result, a special weight.

The five judgments have been presented in a logical sequence and their interdependence noted. In reading most articles this will be the order in which they will come to one's mind. But in some situations it will not. For instance, given an evaluation of a school curriculum, the first question may be whether there was an effect; if not, why go further? If there was one, was there an alternative explanation? Explanation credibility is still worth considering, since the results will be more persuasive with it. Translation fidelity will be questioned to ensure that the measure of achievement was indeed relevant to the curriculum. And there will also be concern that this might be a unique outlier, an instance in which results and expectations are at variance and one wonders whether the result is credible. So the questions are all relevant, but a reader might consider them in a different order. The interdependence of the questions, of course, remains, regardless of the order of consideration.

Internal Validity (LP) in a "Cloudlike" World

In discussing the explanations for "dashed hopes," I implied that internal validity (LP) may be difficult to demonstrate in a cloudlike world. It is reasonably clear that internal validity (LP) can be shown and easily recognized in a clocklike universe, but in a cloudlike one, phenomena are loosely coupled. In such a world, changing one variable only makes it more likely that something else may change; it does not necessarily change it. Nor can one necessarily predict the exact timing of concomitant circumstances that may be necessary for change to occur, so the timing of the change is difficult to predict. Consequently, strong prediction of individual events becomes most difficult, and one must depend on the robustness of the phenomenon showing over a number of events in which it could occur (Wimsatt, 1981). These conditions require larger and more sensitive studies and also put a premium on reducing nuisance and error variation. Even then, because of the loose coupling, the cause will more than likely appear as a weak, rather than a strong, treatment. Internal validity (LP) is possible and just as necessary if one believes in a cloudlike world, but it appears to be more difficult to achieve. To many people that sounds exactly like the situation they are facing in studying social phenomena.

An Analysis of the Internal Validity (LP) of a Study

As an example of the decisions involved in determining the internal validity (LP) of a study, let us examine a study by Coleman, Hoffer, and Kilgore (1981) that compared public and private schools with respect to achievement and several other characteristics. Coleman's study grew out of a longitudinal study by the National Opinion Research Center (1980). It involved sample survey techniques in the testing of both private and public school students. I shall confine my analysis to the cognitive achievement part of the study, which asked, "Do private schools produce better cognitive outcomes than public schools?" At the outset of the study, Coleman argued that they do. What is the internal validity (LP) of this study with respect to this finding?

Explanation Credibility. From a scientific standpoint, it is a strength of the Coleman study that the issue is not prejudged, in the sense that the arguments both pro and con regarding the role of the private schools are presented. Unfortunately, however, the arguments are cast as though the conditions that might lead to higher achievement in either sector would require moving the children from one sector to the other rather than having either sector adopt the favorable conditions. These are such conditions as more homework, better discipline, and more favorable expectations among students and teachers of the possibility of attaining academic achievement. Coleman sees tax credits and vouchers as ways of increasing the availability of private-sector schooling and therefore these conditions. Persons who object to this way of setting forth the rationale for the study find themselves antagonistic to the study from the outset. For them the study has lower explanation credibility, since it seems as though the investigators might be biased toward showing that tax credits are an answer to the public schools' problems.

Translation Fidelity. When one is comparing public and private schools, the question whether the students studied are representative of those two sectors is key to the comparison. Both the public and private samples were large random samples. Even though the schools had to agree to participate, questions about the representativeness of the public schools and the private Catholic schools seem answered. But the sample of non-Catholic private schools is small, and one does not know whether and to what extent it included (1) the prestige schools of this category, (2) schools that cater to special education and "problem" children, (3) non-Catholic religious schools (it is believed the fundamentalist Protestant schools refused to cooperate). So one question is whether non-Catholic private schooling is appropriately included in the interpretation of the results, a limitation on the study's translation fidelity and linking power (and translation generality, as discussed in Chapter Five).

The data in the study came from a longitudinal survey that used short tests, ranging from a twenty-item reading test to a thirty-two-item mathematics test. To measure growth in the high schools, however, these already small samples of student behavior had to be reduced to very, very short ones. Worse yet, the mathematics tests were "elementary, involving basic arithmetic operations, fractions, and only a few hints of algebra and geometry" (p. 159). This is hardly what one would expect of a test measuring a high school curriculum. Further, the authors admit that "explicit attention to reading comprehension and to vocabulary expansion is not part of the standard curriculum in the tenth through twelfth grades" (p. 159). Thus translation fidelity is low. Even if one were not raising questions about the way the rationale was phrased, judgment of translation fidelity might raise some questions about internal validity (LP).

Demonstrated Relationship. The data show that private education students achieved more on the tests than public school students.
Since the children were in school before the testing, precedence is
established in one sense. But the fact that the material tested was at the
elementary school level and the tests were given at the high school
level leaves in question precedence concerning where the learning took
place. Had those tested been in private schools during their elementary
school years? This question is never addressed.

The average scores on the tests were one or two items higher in
the private than in the public sector. No statistical tests are presented,
but considering the very large number of subjects in the surveys, there
is little doubt that even very small differences would show up
statistically as other than chance differences. Statistical sensitivity
(power) is very great with such large numbers of cases. Whether the
one- or two-item difference is of practical significance is a matter of
judgment. Such small differences are typical of those found to be due
to educational treatments, however.

There is no prediction as such, because no explanation or
hypothesis was stated, just pros and cons. Therefore strong prediction
does not enter as a factor.

The matter of precedence raises questions about whether the
relationship was demonstrated.

Rival Explanations Eliminated. At least two rival explanations
could explain the data. The first, a very serious one, is that there is a
strong selection effect in the kind of pupils who attend private schools.
These are pupils whose parents felt strongly enough about their
children's education that they took action to remove them from public
schools and were willing not only to pay taxes to support public
schools, which their children were not attending, but to pay private
school tuition as well. Clearly these are not "run of the mill" parents.
It seems likely that the parents' expectations for improved achievement
as a result of this special effort will be communicated to their children.

Coleman uses complicated statistical techniques to correct for
this potential bias and to remove this rival explanation. These
corrected results show that the private schools are still ahead.

There has been considerable discussion of whether the correction techniques are adequate; many believe they are not. Even if one
believes they were adequate in correcting for socioeconomic status
(SES), one datum used to determine SES was an estimate of parents'
income supplied by the student. Many seriously question whether
children, even high school seniors, know their parents' income with
any accuracy. Thus there are multiple grounds for doubting the
adequacy of the correction.

Another rival explanation is that the growth in achievement measured by the tests occurs mainly at the elementary school level. As noted, there is no evidence of whether the private high school students had attended private or public elementary schools. Hence it is difficult to attribute achievement in these skills to their private school background.

So there are questions whether rival explanations have been satisfactorily eliminated.

Credible Result. Is Coleman's result a credible one? Depending on one's prior judgments, one may come to this fifth question with so many questions about the credibility of the study that one is ready to say no as soon as the question is asked. But in the context of prior research in the field, how does it compare? This study, like Coleman's earlier study (Coleman and others, 1966), is unique in that it is the only large-scale study of its kind of private education. So placing the study in the larger context is not helpful; there is little prior basis for developing expectations.

Overall Judgment of Internal Validity (LP). Normally the rationale is a critical and determining aspect that works positively for the study. In this instance, depending on one's orientation toward private schools, it might work positively or negatively. Although ostensibly it is a study merely to determine the facts, the study unfortunately seems a little heavy in its presentation of the tuition tax-credits case.

With regard to the other aspects, in summary, translation fidelity is weak especially in the translation of the concept "achievement" into operational terms; there are questions of precedence that undermine the convincingness of the demonstration of private schools' superiority; rival explanations based on the selection factor are not entirely eliminated. The overall internal validity (LP) of this study would therefore have to be judged quite weak.

Considering the criticism that the study has been receiving since the draft copy was released (for example, Goldberger and Cain, 1982), this concluding judgment is supported by the majority of those who have read it—the workings of the fishscale network of organized skepticism that judges the work of fellow researchers and builds a consensus of what is and what is not knowledge.

Exploratory Versus Validating Studies

Although I have discussed studies as though they always advanced explanations, of course they do not. Indeed, studies such as Coleman's, which are essentially gathering data to answer a question, may not be able to anticipate even whether there will be a difference. In the prison simulation study, all that was hypothesized was that the roles affect the behavior of "guards" and "prisoners" differently.

In the absence of a rationale, there can be no strong prediction, and in the absence of both of these, the linking power is, in general, weakened. The prison study was rescued by its dramatic results; had they not occurred, this might have been "just another study."

An important point follows, discussed later—namely, that if any of the pieces of the internal validity (LP) evidence is weak or lacking, the internal validity (LP) is considerably weakened. Therefore, exploratory studies in general, except for dramatic effects or some other saving grace, will always be shorter on internal validity (LP) than those that can make strong predictions and then are able to demonstrate them.

5

Reformulating the Concept of External Validity (Generalizing Power)

External validity (GP) is the validity with which statements can be made that the generality claimed for the relationship across subjects, situations, independent variables or ways of administering treatments, measuring instruments, times, study designs, and procedures is supported by the evidence and is the only appropriate interpretation of that evidence with regard to generality. One uses the evidence to evaluate the robustness with which a relationship would appear across the above-named design facets to which one wishes to generalize the relationship (Wimsatt, 1981).

This discussion of the details of external validity (GP), the generalizing power of a study, essentially follows the format of the previous chapter. Indeed, much of what is said parallels the prior discussion of internal validity (LP) in content as well. But with external validity (GP), one is asking about the generality aspects of the questions one considered for internal validity (LP). Like internal validity (LP), external validity (GP) is a series of five sequential judgments, the fifth contributing strongly to the overall assessment of external validity (GP); see Figure 13. However, unlike internal validity (LP), external validity (GP) has no previously undisclosed subcategories, as there were in demonstrated result; external validity (GP) consists of just the five judgments. Each is parallel in name and content to the comparable category in internal validity (LP).

**Figure 13. Judgments Contributing to Internal Validity (LP)
and External Validity (GP).**

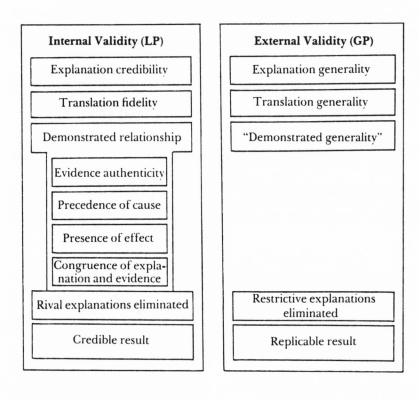

Some of the judgments of external validity (GP) depend on those made for internal validity (LP). For example, if the explanation makes no sense and has no explanation credibility, then it makes little sense to be concerned about explanation generality. If the translation of the explanation into the operations of the study is not satisfactory— the judgment made in translation fidelity—then one cares little about judging the translation generality of those operations for external validity (GP). Similarly, if the relationship to be demonstrated does not appear in demonstrated result, there can be no "demonstrated generality." There may be alternative ways of explaining the relationship so far as internal validity (LP) is concerned, some of which may restrict generality—for instance, when the study uses volunteers, a selection problem. In addition, there may be alternative explanations to be considered under external validity (GP) that restrict generality. Thus, although the judgments are made independently of whether they are alternative explanations for internal validity (LP) or for external validity (GP), restrictions on generality result from combining the judgments. Finally, if there is not a credible result, the last judgment of internal validity (LP), one can hardly expect it to replicate, which is the final judgment of external validity (GP). So all the judgments made in external validity (GP) are potentially affected by the judgments of internal validity (LP). In the detailed discussion of external validity (GP) that follows, it will be assumed without further comment, except in the case of "demonstrated generality," that the parallel internal validity (LP) judgments were positive.

External validity (GP) must be inferred from the breadth of the evidence presented. A study showing that crowding people together in living quarters leads to aggression might increase the generality of the proposition "Frustration leads to aggression" by indicating that frustration includes such stressful situations as crowding. But one could not necessarily, from that study, extend the generality to other stressful situations. By contrast, a study designed to emphasize external validity (GP) and show the generality of the basic proposition would show that it held in a wide variety of situations—crowding in an elevator, inability to get an elevator to come to one's floor, traffic jams, long checkout lines at the grocery store, inability to attract a waitress' attention—the panorama of situations, persons, and times in which it might be expected to hold. Given this contrast between a study designed to show external validity (GP) and the usual study, which is a test of a single instance of the proposition, it is clear that *most studies emphasize internal validity (LP) rather than external validity (GP).*

In this chapter, as in the previous one, we shall successively examine in detail each of the five judgments that enter into the determination of overall external validity (GP).

Explanation Generality

Explanation generality is the generality stated or implied in the explanation proposed for the relationship to be demonstrated. It is a judgment of the extent of generality that is claimed or implied by the explanation, rationale, or theory on which the study is based. The explanation may explicitly indicate the generality being claimed, but more often the generality is implied. An explanation can be stated more clearly and simply if one does not have to include all the qualifications that detail the boundaries within which it holds.

Many explanations start out as universals, expected to hold under any condition (for example, frustration results in aggression); some are more limited and apply to a specific instance (for example, being a Democrat during a Republican regime is likely to be frustrating).

The question, hypothesis, prediction, or model that stems from an explanation is usually only one of many that could be deduced and therefore is usually not representative of the breadth of generality of the explanation. For example, as noted earlier, the theory that frustration leads to aggression might lead to the idea that crowding leads to aggression. As a test of this latter idea, one examines the hypothesis that a group of individuals in a small space where they are not free to move as they please will become aggressive toward one another. The hypothesis is consistent with the theory but in no way indicates the extent of its generality. Thus the implied generality is often much broader than the particular question, prediction, or hypothesis tested or studied.

Just as with internal validity (LP), in which one judges the credibility of the explanation, so with respect to explanation generality one must judge whether the generality claimed for the proposition is reasonable. If it is, then one can comfortably proceed with the judgment of the translation of the explanation into the study. If it is not, and one rejects the extent of generality claimed for the study, then, as in the situation in which one rejects the explanation of a study, one is likely to be extremely critical of the effort to demonstrate generality and to seek ways the evidence fails.

A point that was already mentioned in Chapter Three but needs emphasis is that generality is always an inference; it is a leap of faith to generalize from any given instance to others like it and assume that the relationship will appear there as well. It is impossible to demonstrate generality in all the instances to which a relationship is to apply; there is always the next one that has not yet been tried, in which the relationship might not work in the same way. Instead we judge the demonstration in a sample of instances to which it is to generalize and, from those, make an inferential leap. But that leap is much safer if there is solid reason to believe that the instances in which the relationship was demonstrated are representative of the target instances to which the leap will be made. Therefore the next judgment, translation generality, is critical for external validity (GP).

Translation Generality

As with internal validity (LP), one is concerned about the translation of the question or hypothesis into the choices that define the study, but whereas in internal validity (LP) one is concerned with the *accuracy* of the translation, here one is concerned with the generality that can be inferred from the translation, the translation generality—whether the study as operationalized is representative of the targets to which one wishes the study to generalize. Is it representative of the kinds of individuals, situations, and times to which one wishes to generalize? Are the measures, observations, or scales representative of those spanning the breadth of operational definitions that accurately specify the constructs or concepts involved in the study? If there is a treatment, is it operationalized so as to be representative of the breadth of variations of treatment that are intended to be included in whatever treatment definition is appropriate to the study? The problem of translation is so critical to judging external validity (GP) that examining each of the design facets to see how appropriate choices can be made is worthwhile.

If, as in some studies, there is no explanation but clearly generality is claimed, then one must judge the scope of the generality claim and its targets from the way the study is carried out. A test intended to predict sales success may be a hodgepodge of empirically validated items, but clearly it is intended to predict beyond the group on which it was validated. The claimed generality and targets would be inferred from the subjects and their situations in the validation study.

Subjects and Situations

If one wishes to demonstrate generality, the subjects and situations chosen should be representative of those that are the generality targets of the study. Consider a study of how certified public accountants are able to be integrated into a business corporation and build a loyalty to that organization yet retain sufficient autonomy to exercise their own professional judgment about accounting practices

(Lengermann, 1976). Clearly the intent here is that the generalization from this study will apply to all CPAs corporately employed. If so, one must be sure the study includes a representative sample of such CPAs. This is exactly what Lengermann did, randomly sampling local and regional firms, national firms, and other organizations where CPAs worked.

In some instances, the proposition being tested is perceived as universal—for example, that watching aggressive athletic contests increases hostility and aggressiveness (Goldstein and Arms, 1971). Such a hypothesis should apply to anyone watching such contests; therefore, although individuals studied had attended a gymnastics meet followed by a football contest and are, therefore, clearly a group particularly interested in sports, they are a part of the population at large, and the proposition ought to apply to them. They were clearly appropriate subjects in that study so far as internal validity (LP) is concerned. But suppose one wants to show broad generality and build a study with strong external validity (GP). If there were reason to believe that the proposition might more readily apply to such a sports-minded group than to the population at large, then the study as originally designed is a weaker demonstration of its generality and has weaker external validity (GP) than one using a random sample of shoppers at a mall, for which any claim of the special applicability of the proposition would be unreasonable.

Kruglanski and Kroy (1976) make the point that when a particular group is the target of generalization, as in the instance of the CPAs, then a representative sample of them is the only appropriate set of subjects. The general principles and techniques of sampling—simple random, stratified, cluster, sequential, quota, and panel sampling—apply to this sampling problem just as they would to any other such problem. In discussing the same topic, Cook and Campbell (1979) note that using samples of convenience (also called "grab samples," since one grabs whatever group is handy—usually undergraduates in a required course) may save time and energy but the trade-off is that they make it very difficult to generalize to a larger universe of which they might be representative. Undergraduates are as good a place as any to start with a "universal" proposition to show internal validity (LP), however, and one can perhaps get clues from such a study where next to try it if one suspects generality is limited.

Time

We must consider the sampling of time as well as of persons and situations. We do not usually think of time as a limiter on generality.

Yet, as Cronbach (1975) points out, some generalizations decay with age, particularly as a culture changes. Childrearing patterns appropriate in one decade do not generalize to a later one. Changes in age or grade with the passage of time may obviously invalidate generalizations applicable to an earlier age.

This is a serious problem for the behavioral sciences, which progress by assembling the findings over time into larger generalities that provide greater and broader understanding. Cronbach notes: "The trouble . . . is that we cannot store up generalizations and constructs for ultimate assembly into a network. It is as if we needed a gross of dry cells to power an engine and could only make one a month. The energy would leak out of the first cells before we had half the battery completed. So it is with the potency of our generalizations" (p. 123). We are therefore left with the uncomfortable feeling that we may not realize that our generalizations are failing even as it is happening—which is probably true. For example, because the meanings and salience of words change, verbal scales may need to be revalidated before their use in another period.

Treatment

Representativeness with respect to treatment involves first determining which aspects of the treatment are its essential characteristics and defining the appropriate extent of variability in the way the treatment is administered. Then, when the treatment is administered, one must ensure both that the characteristics are present and that the appropriate range of variability in treatment administration is represented. Descriptions of treatments or instruction booklets are likely to describe the essential characteristics but rarely say anything about how far one can stray from them without lowering effectiveness. Yet, unless one trains those administering the treatment to do so in a very precise way, there will be considerable variation in the way a treatment is applied. On the one hand, one must decide how much variation can be tolerated and the integrity of the treatment still maintained. On the other hand, one must allow for some variability if one has a variety of individuals administering it; variability is inevitable, especially without special training. The problem is to estimate the in-between range of variability within which the treatment remains representative of what was intended while allowing such variability of administration as it is not practical or necessary to eliminate. That in-between range should be represented in the treatment administration sample to show generality.

The essentials of an instructional treatment might be clearly stated in the written instructions for a method involving the use of particular teaching materials; however, a teacher will typically reinterpret and adapt those instructions. Alternatively, the essential characteristics of treatment might involve a set of particular teacher behaviors that teachers might be trained to use in appropriate circumstances. Whereas individual teacher training would more precisely ensure that the instructions were correctly followed, the use of written instructions with freedom to interpret and adapt them would be more representative of the conditions to which one would expect to generalize. One would want to know whether the effect was robust enough to appear even with the variety of interpretations of written instructions that would inevitably result. Therefore, using the written description would provide a better demonstration of generality.

Measures and Observations

In judging external validity (GP), one is concerned with what Cook and Campbell (1979) call "construct validity," the validity with which the measures or observations assess the intended constructs or concepts. If one is using a measure of frustration tolerance, does it actually measure that construct accurately and well? Is it representative of such measures; might one get a different result from the study if a more representative measure were used? Is the measure affected by the way in which it is taken—paper and pencil, interview, or whatever? This last concern is what is called "method variance"; some measures give different results when taken orally than when taken by paper and pencil (or presumably by computer). The topic of construct validity is covered extensively in any measurement text, so, as in the discussion of translation fidelity, further explanation of this measurement topic would require space better used for topics not so well covered elsewhere. Nevertheless, it should be noted that, as in the parallel internal validity (LP) case, it is extremely important to the judgment of translation generality and therefore to external validity (GP).

"Demonstrated Generality"

As noted early in the chapter, "demonstrated generality" is dependent on demonstrated relationship. If the relationship is demonstrated, then "demonstrated generality" goes beyond that judgment to ask whether the relationship appeared in all the instances in which it would be expected on the basis of the generality inferred or claimed.

The term is in quotation marks to call attention to the fact that it is a logical impossibility. One cannot *demonstrate* generality to persons or conditions not included in a study; as noted previously, one can only *infer* it. If one has a representative sample, such as one of certified public accountants in a given city, then presumably a demonstration of the relationship would permit one to infer that the proposition would generalize to the other certified public accountants in that city. But unless one included all of them in the demonstration, generality is an inference, not a demonstrated fact. Inference to CPAs in other cities is a still larger inferential leap.

Restrictive Explanations Eliminated

Just as with internal validity (LP), any alternative explanations that could explain the generality or the lack of it must be eliminated in designing the study. Millman (personal communication, June 6, 1983) notes quite correctly that these alternative explanations might be better thought of as restrictions or limits on the inferred generality when they are not eliminated. When there are alternative explanations for the results, they indicate that the results showed up under these special conditions but might not have if those conditions were absent, and so one cannot infer the intended generality.

The alternative explanations that might explain the obtained results are different from those for internal validity (LP). As with internal validity (LP), several common rival explanations are to be guarded against, and again Cook and Campbell (1979) and Campbell and Stanley (1963) have been very helpful in formulating and describing them. Bracht and Glass' (1968) discussion of external validity contributed extensively to its proper formulation. Some alternative explanations suggested by the literature are described in the following sections.

Selection/Treatment Interaction. Persons may be attracted to the treatment who are especially likely to benefit from it. Therefore, the individuals who take the treatment may differ from others on a fact that enhances (or dampens) treatment. The Coleman study of public and private schools, for instance, has a problem of this sort. Only students from homes where school achievement is a serious concern are likely to be attending private schools. These are also the students most likely to tolerate and perhaps even appreciate the greater homework assignments and stricter discipline presumably found in private schools. Disentangling the selection/treatment interaction from the treatment effect, private school instruction, is a problem for this study.

Random assignment of subjects to groups, if feasible, can eliminate this problem.

Besides being an explanation for the results that private school students did better on achievement tests than public school students, selection/treatment interaction also acts as a warning that one cannot generalize from these results to infer that, in general, private school instruction results in higher achievement than public. Thus, as Millman notes, the alternative explanation acts as a limit on the intended generality as well as an alternative explanation of the results.

Selection/Maturation Interaction. This selection bias is like the preceding one except that a maturation factor is at work. Maturation includes changes in the subjects that occur during the study—short-term effects such as tiring or becoming bored or anxious as well as longer-term ones more generally associated with the term *maturation* such as growth cycle patterns. Suppose that, as often happens, volunteers in a K-8 school were assigned to the experimental group and nonvolunteers to the control group. If most of the volunteers were in the upper grades, they would be in a different part of their growth cycle than the younger nonvolunteers. In a study involving learning eye/hand motor coordination, this difference could easily account for an observed difference between the groups. Here, as before, use of a special group limits the generality of findings from what was intended.

Testing/Treatment Interaction. If a pretest is given, it may alert subjects to the important parts of the lesson to which they might not otherwise attend so carefully. The treatment will therefore appear more potent than without the experimental pretest condition. If the pretest is regularly used as part of the treatment, then one can generalize from these results. If it is not, as is usually the case, but is used only in an evaluation of the treatment, then generalizing is restricted. Using only a posttest for evaluation purposes eliminates this problem.

In some instances, the posttest may be a learning experience that helps to "solidify" or put in place aspects of the treatment. Treatment without the posttest would be less effective, so study results would not generalize to treatment use in a nonevaluative situation. If this problem is suspected, a less "instructive" form of posttest is required.

Multiple-Treatment Interference. Where multiple treatments are applied to the same subject, the residual effects of an earlier treatment may change the impact of a later one. For example, suppose one is seeking the cause of hyperactivity in children, and it is presumed to relate to diet, especially food coloring. To hold constant biological makeup, the same group of individuals is systematically deprived of a different food or coloring for each week of a ten-week period. One would have to ask whether the fact that a certain dietary item was withheld one week might affect sensitivity to another dietary restriction the next week. If so, one could not generalize to the effect of treatments taken singly.

Reactive Effects. The reactive effects described under "Rival Explanations Eliminated," in Chapter Four, not only modify the observed effect and therefore may affect the judgment of internal validity (LP); they may also restrict generality. A treatment given in more normal circumstances where there is no competition with a control group, or where the group members do not feel they are special, or where the novelty effect has worn off, may yield an entirely different result. Thus the restrictions that stem from obtrusiveness and the resulting reactive effects may restrict generality to the abnormal conditions under which the effect was observed.

Experimenter Expectancies. As Rosenthal (1976) has so effectively shown, the researcher's expectations can affect the study. They may be unintentionally and unconsciously communicated to subjects who seek to look good in the eyes of the researcher and therefore try to give responses intended to please her. Alternatively, assistants or others seeking to please the researcher may make decisions in line with expectations when situations are ambiguous ("Was the response just barely under the time limit? I guess so"). In both animal and human studies Rosenthal examined, where it was communicated that ordinary subjects were "unusually capable," they somehow turn out to be. Randomly selected rats given to researchers as "fast learners" are found to learn faster. One can eliminate this effect by using double-blind conditions, in which neither subjects nor experimenter knows who is receiving the special treatment.

As with internal validity (LP), there may be less common rival alternative explanations, some unique to a given study, that must be guarded against as well.

Replicable Result

The heart of external validity (GP) is replicability: Would the results be reproducible in those target instances to which one intends to generalize—the population, situation, time, treatment form or format, measures, study designs, and procedures? Of course one can never be sure unless one examines each of those instances, and that is an impossibility. So the judgment of replicable result comes from a comparison with previous studies whose results may have indicated generality and from mental simulations, "thought experiments," in which one imagines the target instances, mentally simulating studies that would help determine whether the relationship would be reproduced in those as well. One mentally constructs new studies to check the phenomenon. This is, incidentally, a remarkably good way to spot ambiguities in design choice and procedure that might interfere with the tightness of the chain of reasoning. For example, in reflecting on the prison simulation study and considering whether a new study would replicate the findings, one might realize that the "guards" were allowed to define their role. But aren't real prison guards trained? Does this difference limit the generality of the results? Thought experiments that redesign the study and try to replicate the results will often turn up considerations not otherwise noticed. (See also the discussion of reproducibility in Chapter Eleven.)

In weighing the similarity of this study to those target instances to which one wishes to generalize, one considers as well the certainty with which one holds the demonstration in this instance. Of course, if the latter is not very certain, one may be uncomfortable about generalizing to other instances unless one has reason to believe they would be even more hospitable to demonstrating the relationship. For example, even if the results of the study of gymnastics and football had shown only a small increase in aggressive behavior, one might expect it to generalize with considerable certainty to a boxing exhibition.

Positive results from this process produce the inferential leap to assuming generality to the intended targets. Of course this, the fifth decision of the sequence, is dependent on the previous four—the explanation must specify or imply a reasonable generality, this generality must be represented in the choices for the study design, and the relationship must appear in those choices without restrictive alternative explanations of the results.

As noted earlier for internal validity (LP), a study that reproduces the findings of previous ones in whole or in part or bears important similarities to them will be examined in light of the previous results. If the new results are consistent with previous evidence but under new circumstances, then, given the four positive previous judgments in the sequence, one has a replicable result, and external validity (GP), generality, has been extended at least to these new circumstances.

If the new results are inconsistent with previous ones, then, as in internal validity (LP), one must determine whether one has an anomalous result or a replicable one. As with internal validity (LP), a result may be anomalous because—

1. One assumes a cloudlike, plastic universe rather than a rigid clocklike universe.
2. "Statistical conclusion validity" is lacking because of a statistical error, inadequate statistical sensitivity to a weak effect, improper statistics for the situation, improper calculation or interpretation, and so forth.
3. The methodology is crude—for example, inaccurate or inadequate measures.

In addition, the result may differ from previous findings because of some subtle difference from previous studies. If one can find the reason for the inconsistency, one often better understands the phenomenon and its controlling characteristics. If one can find no apparent reason for the inconsistency, then the reason may be one of the items just listed, or the result may not be reproducible even with improved methodology and statistics. That is a matter of judgment.

External validity (GP) is not an all-or-none phenomenon. Like internal validity (LP), it is best thought of as a reduction in uncertainty, in this instance uncertainty that a phenomenon will generalize to a certain target population, situation or set of situations, and so on, and perhaps even beyond them. The overall judgment of external validity (GP) would be reflected in a lowering of that uncertainty. But how does one generalize beyond the persons, situations, and other elements of the study design? We have noted the inferential leap from a sample to the population, or universe, of which it is representative. It is an even larger and less certain inference to targets represented only in the sense that they are similar to the sampled target. How does one generalize to them? One does so by combining one's certainty of replication in the targets represented in the study with an estimate of the similarity between the new target of application and the target in the study. This is obviously a much more difficult judgment.

Take the study of certified public accountants discussed earlier. Lengermann sampled CPAs in New York State quite well, but can one generalize these results to another state? Or nationally? It is a matter of combining the probability that the results of Lengermann's study would generalize to his target, New York State, which is quite high, with one's judgment of the likelihood that the CPAs in that state are like CPAs in other target states or perhaps in states throughout the country. One would have to weigh the likelihood that the CPAs in New York State, with its many large accounting firms and large corporations, are like those in a rural state like Kansas or a sparsely populated area like Montana or North Dakota where a small-town ethic rather than a big-city or corporate ethic is likely to prevail. Some appreciation of the tentativeness of the inference to others beyond the group directly sampled can be grasped from this example.

Bandwidth, Fidelity, and External Validity (GP)

The bandwidth/fidelity trade-off is an important and frequent trade-off in research methodology. Cronbach, who first called our attention to it in the context of measurement, has most recently shown its applicability to a variety of facets of the evaluation problem (1982). Indeed, it is present wherever sampling is involved, since one may sample deeply (narrow bandwidth), gaining greater information (greater fidelity) about the narrow target sample, or one may use the same resources to sample a broad target (wide bandwidth) shallowly, gaining less information (lower fidelity) about the nature of that target. This trade-off is present in the replicability problem. With an intensive sample of a target population, situation, or behavior—narrow bandwidth—one might have greater certainty of generality to that limited target but less certainty about other, similar targets, since one has no direct information about the applicability of the result to them, only inferred information. By contrast, a sketchy sampling over a broad and varied target—broad bandwidth—yields an inference of less certain generality in any one instance but greater certainty that generality is not limited to the small target of the narrow-bandwidth study.

Variability of Experimental Findings

If one is to have generality, one must have findings that replicate in the sense discussed under "Replicable Result." This has been a problem in the behavioral sciences. Recently, with the advent of meta-analysis (Glass, McGaw, and Smith, 1981), we have learned much more about the variability of experimental results, particularly in the fields of education and psychology. The data are not encouraging: "The outcomes of educational experiments are enormously variable across the conditions of the world in which experiments are performed. . . . A huge experimental field evaluation of a dozen or so models of primary school compensatory education revealed that the average differences among the models in basic skills achievement were insignificantly small compared to the differences among different experimental sites evaluating the same model" (Glass, 1982, p. 634). For reading achievement, the variability across sites *within a model* was ten times the variability among the experimental effects for the thirteen models. In a study of the efficacy of psychotherapy, the standard deviation of the effects was larger than their positive mean effect, indicating a tremendous variability in effectiveness (Smith, Glass, and Miller, 1980).

Interestingly, the problems in the fields of education and psychology may extend to other fields dealing with humans. Glass cites a study by Gilbert, McPeek, and Mosteller (1977) showing that 100 experiments comparing an innovative surgical technique with a traditional one showed half in favor of each and no pattern of findings.

If one is concerned about the slow progress of the behavioral sciences, and many researchers are, perhaps here is a central problem. It suggests that Popper's cloudlike analogy may not be far from the mark. Yet, despite these difficulties, there does seem to be progress, sufficient reason to continue our quest for improved understanding of how research works.

External Validity (GP) Applied to an Example

The example of the Coleman study of public and private schools illustrated how the various criteria in internal validity (LP) apply. Let us look at the same study with respect to external validity (GP).

Explanation Generality. We saw earlier that the study had no explicit rationale that justified the superiority of either the public or the private system. But the language in which the study is discussed leaves the implication that the study is intended to generalize to the public and private school systems as aggregates. So the targets to which the authors expect to generalize are all clearly implied in the initial discussion:

> Subjects—public and private school students.
> Situations—public and private schools.
> Treatment—instruction in the public and private schools.
> Time—immediate past and immediate future.
> Measures of effect—relevant measures of achievement.

Translation Generality. Each of these targets is translated into the study, some with greater generality, some with less. The careful sampling of public and private school students is consistent with the kind of work that a large government agency such as the National Center for Education Statistics is able to mount. There was even an extra large sampling of certain groups and schools where special studies were to be done. The sample of Catholic schools was substantial, and special sampling and analyses were done of the schools in the public and private sectors with high-performing seniors. However, although 894 public schools and 84 Catholic private schools were sampled, only 27 private non-Catholic schools were. It is not clear what the composition of the latter might be because there is too little comment in the report that is currently available. They could be elite schools, military academies, special education schools, and so on. With this exception, however, the translation of the study into samples of subjects, and therefore into situation and treatment (which are linked to the population sample chosen), seems admirable. Given this sampling, generalization to public and private Catholic schools seems possible. Generalization to private non-Catholic schools may need caution. Twenty-seven is not necessarily too small a sample, but non-Catholic private schools are a very diverse group. It is not clear how well that diversity is represented or whether, for instance, special education schools are so different that they should not be lumped with the others in any case.

As noted in the discussion of internal validity (LP), the translation into instruments to measure achievement is considerably less than satisfactory.

"Demonstrated Generality." The data demonstrate superiority of the private school sample over the public school sample. The inferential leap from sample to population can be made with greater certainty when, as in this sample for the public and Catholic private schools, the sampling is done well. The inferential leap for the non-Catholic private schools is tenuous, however, because it is unclear how well the sample represented this group.

Whether one believes that the superiority demonstrated is real in the well-represented groups, however, depends especially on the next judgment, whether there is a restricting alternative explanation. But note that "demonstrated generality" depends, among other things, on having translation fidelity. If one judges the measures of achievement to be inadequate, as I do, the whole question of generality becomes moot.

Restrictive Explanations Eliminated. The matter of who attends the private school was covered extensively in the discussion of internal validity (LP). It need not be further discussed here, except to note that this is another example of persons selecting themselves for treatment. In this case the treatment was selected for the students by their parents, but the effect is the same. This selection-by-treatment interaction causes problems in inferring generality, because if one wants to argue that the private school treatment would have the same effect on public school children, the lack of comparability of the two groups makes the inference risky. As noted before, Coleman attempts, at great length, to justify generality with statistical adjustments intended to compensate for the selection effect. I believe, with others (Goldberger and Cain, 1982), that the methods used could make only inadequate corrections for selection.

Replicable Result. It seems likely, considering only the samples used, that the results would be reproducible with the same instruments for other samples of the public and Catholic private school sectors. It is quite possible that the results for the non-Catholic sector might be reproducible as well, since twenty-seven schools is by no means an insubstantial sample if that population is relatively homogeneous. As noted, one can't tell that it is from the data given.

But would one be able to replicate the result if one took into account the problem of translation fidelity? There is a real question whether a more appropriate measure of achievement, one based on subject matter and skills taught at the secondary rather than at the elementary level, would yield the same result. One really can't judge from the results of this study. So generality to more appropriate measures of achievement is highly uncertain, and replicable result and therefore external validity (GP) are very low on this basis.

Would the study replicate if the alternative explanation, selection/treatment interaction, were eliminated? Here is an interesting thought experiment of the kind suggested earlier as a way of assessing whether the results are reproducible as one would like to generalize. If public school children were all somehow put in private schools and vice versa, would the private schools still be superior? Imagine private schools trying to cope with the problems of inner-city public schools, carrying over the current methods that have presumably made them more successful than public schools. Imagine private school teachers trying to cope with the discipline problems that, while daily events for public school teachers, can be avoided in private schools by refusing to accept the unruly pupil. Again the likelihood of a replicated result seems small, and therefore the external validity (GP) of the study is low. Therefore the support for tuition vouchers and tax credits that the researchers appear to wish to draw from the study seems highly dubious.

Weighting Internal Validity (LP) and External Validity (GP)

Ideally studies are designed to show enough internal validity (LP) that they can create a consensus that the relationship truly exists and to show simultaneously as much external validity (GP), generality, as resources allow. Thus, to the extent that we can, we try to optimize both; one usually wishes to have both internal validity (LP) and external validity (GP) in a study. But for each study the researcher must decide how to weight internal validity (LP) in relation to external validity (GP).

To strengthen internal validity (LP), one tends to narrow the scope of the question studied so that the phenomenon can be easily observed under as controlled conditions as necessary for sufficient internal validity (LP) to be developed. Strengthening internal validity (LP) this way shrinks external validity (GP); a study done in controlled, limited, perhaps artificial conditions, over a narrow problem, has limited generality. Bronfenbrenner (1977, p. 513) described this problem very neatly when he characterized the field of developmental psychology as "the science of strange behavior of children in strange situations with strange adults for the briefest possible time."

The existence of resource limits typically makes one choose one direction or the other so that a satisfactory level of at least the chosen direction is achieved. Thus one trades off the advantages of gaining a certain amount of internal validity (LP) for some external validity (GP) and vice versa. The problem is to find the point that maximizes the information needed by the audience for whom the study is intended.

The balancing point between these two will typically vary over the course of knowledge development. Internal validity (LP) is usually stressed in the early stages of the study of a phenomenon, external validity (GP) in the later ones. Initially, one wishes to be assured that the relationship exists at all. Until the relationship is well enough demonstrated that we are sure it exists, we are typically not as interested in building studies to show how broadly it can be applied. If a study fails to show generality before the relationship link has been established, one can't tell whether it failed because the relationship does not exist or merely because the relationship does not generalize to the circumstances in which the study tried to demonstrate it. Prior establishment of the relationship link eliminates this problem. Once the link has been established, one wants to know how generally it applies to other kinds of persons, situations, and so on.

If, as in the prison simulation study, one can demonstrate a striking phenomenon with high internal validity (LP), one is much more comfortable about leaving external validity (GP) to a later study.

6

Other Criteria
of Research Studies

Constructing a Framework

Internal validity (LP) and *external validity (GP)* and their proper
relative *weighting* have now been presented as the main criteria of a
good study. But it is already apparent that if one is to build a chain
of reasoning that is strong enough to create a consensus, there is more
to consider. For one thing, how one *formulates a problem* makes a
great difference to what the study contributes and how successfully it
can be carried out. For another, to build a consensus, one must be
aware of how one gains *credibility with one's audience*—what are the
audience's expectations? How one maximizes *information yield* in a
study is a factor both in the success of that study and in what it leads
to in future studies. Finally, how one *allocates one's resources* to the
various parts of the chain of reasoning determines how well the design
can be carried out and how well internal validity (LP) and external
validity (GP) can be achieved. So each of these factors must be
considered in designing a study or judging one; the criteria are more
complex than simply appropriately weighting internal validity (LP)
and external validity (GP). Further, beyond optimizing the balance of
internal validity (LP) and external validity (GP), one seeks to optimize
the fit of the study to other criteria as well.

    As before, good judgment is essential, but here it involves an
even larger cluster of decisions. One must simultaneously optimize
question formulation, balance internal validity (LP) and external
validity (GP), achieve audience credibility, and get the best informa-

tion yield and appropriate resource allocation—all within the limits of available resources, ethical standards, and institutional constraints. And, as previously, there are trade-offs. For example, the optimal choice may balance the commitment of resources to rework the question into a better formulation against those needed to build audience credibility or to gather information on side effects.

Because one person's judgment of the optimum may differ from another's, the design of a study is more the art of making many carefully considered and balanced judgments than a science that can be completely expressed in rules and principles. In addition, each optimization is very much a unique function of either a given problem or its combination with particular expectations of an audience, often created by previous work. It is difficult, therefore, to provide guidelines to optimization. It is possible, however, to suggest considerations that may be useful in meeting particular criteria and note possible trade-offs.

The particular problem situation determines the priority to be given to each decision. In a program evaluation, audience credibility may be the highest priority; if the results of an evaluation are not used, there is usually little point in doing it. In a continuing series of studies, information that points to the most appropriate direction for future studies might be a prime concern. Then that would be maximized in determining the best information yield. In basic research, finding the best question formulation combined with building strong internal validity (LP) may be the criteria with priority.

So, rather than indicating primacy, this discussion will arrange the characteristics to be optimized in roughly the order in which they come under consideration in designing a study: (1) question choice and formulation, (2) audience credibility, and (3) and (4) information yield and resource allocation (discussed together). The constraints within which these criteria are optimized will also be discussed: (1) the resource limits the researcher must observe, (2) the boundaries set by ethical standards, especially as these are formulated and enforced by institutional human-subject protection committees, and (3) institutional constraints, which are reflected in the extent to which an institution (or person) will permit research activities that may disrupt its routine, challenge its values, reflect on its reputation, or change the way it goes about its business.

Figure 14 shows schematically the way these criteria and the constraints on their optimization relate to the criteria for internal and external validity previously discussed. With these final pieces in place, Figure 14 portrays the entire framework.

Figure 14. The Complete Framework, Including Criteria to Optimize and Their Constraints.

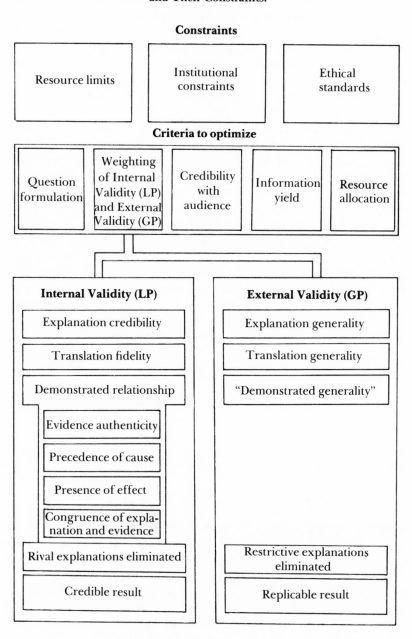

Optimization of these decisions within the constraints and limits is critical to designing a study and to the process of implementing it. The outcome of these decisions determines the success or failure of the study. The process of optimization is a covert one, rarely reported in the write-up. In fact, it is often not a conscious series of choices on the part of the investigator. But it is precisely because many of these decisions just happen as a result of other choices that this chapter is so important. These optimizing decisions *should be consciously made*.

Once made, they are reflected in the product, the research report. The reader, with almost no direct reporting of what was considered in the optimizing process, is in the position of second-guessing the researcher after the fact—judging whether the problem formulation was the best one, whether the researcher appropriately weighted internal validity (LP) and external validity (GP), whether she built audience credibility, whether the information yield and resource allocation resulted in the appropriate mix of data and adequate attention to those things about which data should have been gathered, and whether the constraints observed were necessary ones or, if the reader had been doing the study, they might have been breached to yield a better study. It is always easier to see flaws in retrospect; facing that prospect is all the more reason for the researcher to give careful and conscious attention to the optimizing process.

Question Formulation

> When faced with a dilemma, seek the right question.
>
> —Getzels, 1982, p. 37

Question Choice and Formulation: An Intertwined Process

The decision in question choice is usually whether it is better to work with a question that poses problems for its investigation but which is in hand or to work toward a reformulation that lets things "fall into place" for an easier and stronger study. Clearly some formulations lend themselves to particular methods and to investigation of the question better than others. "What happens to persons who seek jobs as prison guards?"—lots of uncontrolled variables. "What happens to normal, stable individuals who become prison guards?"—better, at least input is better controlled; but may there be few such persons? "What happens to normal, stable individuals in a simulated prison situation?"—the Haney study, and better still. In reformulation, occasionally one has to change the question slightly to make it fit the method—a simulation rather than the real thing, young college students rather than relatively uneducated individuals who take prison guard jobs because they can't get others, and so forth. How much time and resources does one put into reworking the question in contrast to strengthening other aspects of the study? Which of the potential formulations of the study lend themselves best to building a chain of reasoning likely to gain a consensus? These are the kinds of questions involved in optimizing question formulation.

Although this chapter offers advice on question choice and question formulation as if they were separate topics, for the researcher they are often parts of the same problem. Getzels (1982), in a superb chapter "The Problem of the Problem," quotes Henry Moore (1955) on problem finding in art, a process analogous to the often chaotic problem-finding activities of the new researcher: "I sometimes begin drawing with no preconceived problem to solve, with only a desire to use pencil on paper and only make lines, tones, and styles with no conscious aim. But as my mind takes in what is so produced, a point arrives where some idea becomes conscious and crystallizes, and then control and ordering begin to take place" (p. 77). As we saw in the first chapter, the mind is a pattern-seeking instrument. As it finds pattern and order, the question is formulated.

The dilemma, of course, is how to get from the chaotic state to the right question. There is considerable testimony to the fact that the unconscious mind is a better pattern finder than concentrated conscious effort. Many are the insights that occurred when the researcher was off target—driving, staring into a fire, watching a movie, or dreaming (grab that pencil and get it down, it won't be there in the morning; some executives regularly keep tape recorders near their beds to capture their ideas). Periods of concentrated reading, thinking, trying to find patterns, and filling the mind with material it can digest are alternated with off-target activities that allow the mind to ruminate at will. It is a process well worth trying.

The same problem can be formulated in different ways: There is considerable testimonial evidence on the importance of problem formulation to problem solution. Getzels quotes Albert Einstein: "The formulation of a problem is often more essential than its solution, which may be merely a matter of mathematical or experimental skill. To raise new questions, new possibilities, to regard old questions from a new angle, requires creative imagination and marks real advance in science" (Einstein and Infeld, 1938, p. 92). He notes that this is extended by Wertheimer (1945, p. 123): "Often in great discoveries the most important thing is that a certain question is found. Envisaging, putting the productive question, is often a more important, often a greater achievement than the solution of a set question."

Getzels gives an excellent example of the importance of formulating the question in the work of Leo Sachs on leukemia. "Somehow in leukemia the body becomes infected by cells that refuse to age and die naturally the way normal healthy cells do. These harmful cells thus remain trapped in a perpetual state of youth. Current treatment tries to kill these hostile cells by poisoning them. Unfortunately, the drugs are so toxic, they usually also kill the perfectly healthy cells, often causing death by the potent side effects. *So Professor Sachs posed a new question. Would it be possible to find a drug that would make the leukemic cells mature and simply die?* Professor Sachs' fresh approach was soon to pay dividends in opening a wide range of previously unforeseen possibilities" (Griver, 1979, p. 7).

Getzels and Csikszentmihalyi (1976) present evidence that the quality of problem finding and formulation determines the quality of the solution. In studying artists, they found that ratings of the students' problem-finding and formulation capability correlated with rankings of the quality of the art they produced (r = .54). The correlation continued beyond student life; this capability positively correlated with success as a professional seven years later (r = .41).

Researchers choose problems for many reasons, often personal ones—they want to show up someone who said it couldn't be done, someone close to them was affected by it, or perhaps they are simply attracted to it, they don't know why. Some prefer to find their own problem, one that represents them, one that is *theirs;* they reject suggestions of others. Others, particularly graduate students, are happy to have a problem legitimated for them by the suggestion of their major professor. There are clearly many influences affecting problem choice and formulation. This section has made some suggestions and given an indication of the importance of problem formulation. It is hard to be more definite about how to perform a creative art. In order to narrow the field to the point where we can say something definitive, such advice as follows is directed largely at designing a good study within the general area that an investigator has chosen.

Guidelines for Question Formulation

1. *Connect the study to previous work in the field and, if possible, build on it.* Such connections permit the work to be placed in context and thus more easily understood. Its implications and importance become more readily apparent. This means "standing on

the shoulders" of previous researchers not only by building on their ideas conceptually but also by avoiding their mistakes and capitalizing on their methodological strengths. The best researchers seem to have read further back to the seminal minds in their field and are better able to place their contributions in the historical context of prior solutions.

2. *Consider feasibility.* Feasibility may be limited by the skills and resources that can be commanded by the researcher, by what present instruments or methods permit, and/or by what science can do. Although it is only reasonable to be prudent, it is easy to be overly constrained by feasibility boundaries when in fact some can be extended.

Skills available to the individual researcher continue to grow rapidly. Complex statistical procedures once beyond everyone's computational capacity are routinely available through computers, and aids to their interpretation widen their accessibility.

Computers can help, too, with the problem of reducing large quantities of notes gathered in the field if one goes to the trouble of putting them into a computer memory. But even though computer programs will find the similarities, still required is the kind of mind that is able to see the larger generalities above the mass of detail, that sees pattern where most of us see chaos. Consider that Blau (1963) gathered *three file drawers* of notes in his study of two bureaucracies. One's limits in these instances are best probed by experience.

The lack of suitable measures is often a problem. Because availability of measures determines what can be precisely researched, that which can be finely and accurately measured is often considered an indication of the maturity of a field of study. Certainly, compared with the natural sciences, the behavioral sciences are at a disadvantage in this respect. Yet, for many difficult-to-measure concepts, observation or relatively crude devices will provide enough information to yield useful data. Backer (1977) is an excellent bibliography of sources of information on tests that may save the researcher from constructing a new measure when one already exists or help find a better measure than one already located.

A criticism by politicians, administrators, teachers, and others concerned with research applications is that behavioral science problems are too often chosen mainly because of their feasibility rather than their importance. From the researcher's viewpoint this choice is only sensible, since efforts that yield to one's methods are more rewarding than beating one's head against apparently insoluble problems. Yet, to wait for methodology to overtake problems so they are ripe for solution results in a high social cost. This is a matter of risk management, a decision area where people differ greatly; the payoff in a breakthrough is high, but the odds of success may be low. Fortunately, there are always some people willing to bet on the long shot.

Cost feasibility is a problem for nearly all studies. Resources used for one study are not available for others, and a study with high cost may not be worth it. A large, high-cost study may require so much management overhead to get clearances, handle public relations, and gather data that a smaller study might be a better use of resources. There is probably some optimum point after which costs rise dramatically in relation to reduction of uncertainty.

3. *If impact is a goal, consider leverage.* Cronbach (1982) uses the term *leverage* for the impact that knowledge gained in a study will have on the reduction of uncertainty about the effectiveness of an evaluated treatment. Will the evidence change the minds of opinion leaders? This is a matter of special concern to applied researchers doing evaluation studies intended to have an impact. In some instances evidence has little initial effect on individuals, so strongly are they committed to a position. Are these concerns irrelevant to knowledge development? Not entirely.

As I have noted, science is consensual, and knowledge claims must be judged valid by audiences for the claims to be accepted. It is to be hoped that these judgments are less political than those that often follow an evaluation study. Nevertheless, to have impact, one's evidence must be accepted as reasonable and of value by those audiences important to building a consensus around one's knowledge claim. I shall discuss this further under "The Researcher's Credibility with the Audience." But Cronbach's point is that some applied studies may not be worth doing if the individuals they are intended to affect have opinions so deeply entrenched that they will pay no heed to fresh evidence.

Concern with long-term impact, however, means seeking new knowledge regardless of whether one's efforts are accepted or viewed as trivial. One U.S. senator has gained publicity by giving "Golden Fleece" awards to researchers who he believes are "wasting" taxpayers' money on trivial problems. But to most researchers, such studies are central to the advancement of knowledge and must be encouraged, nourished, and protected. Both short- and long-term-impact studies are important.

4. *Be aware of the effect of the perceptual set induced by the context of the problem.* One thing we know is that the situation can have considerable influence on how a problem is perceived. We have all had enough experience with rephrasing questions to realize intuitively that the perception of a problem usually determines our efforts

to solve it. The initial formulation focuses our efforts in a particular direction and so forecasts the answer we will find—or, if no answer lies in that direction, our failure to find one.

That the setting is a major determinant of problem perception has been illustrated many times, beginning with Maier (1931). In a typical experiment, two strings are suspended from the ceiling too far apart for one person to be able to reach both at once and tie them together. When only a pliers was available in the room, subjects tended to frame their solutions in terms of how they could use the pliers as a tongs to reach the other string and wished that it were longer. But no solution lies in that direction. However, if a hammer or a plumb bob was present, the solution of using a tool as a pendulum eventually presented itself. The subject tied the tool to one string, set it swinging, and, holding onto the other string, caught the pendulum on the upswing and tied the strings together. The person who is able to break the set induced by the setting is better able to solve the problem.

How does one break the set? There are a number of ways, the simplest of which is just to leave the problem for a while and then come back to it. But one of the best is to talk with someone else about it. The neutral observer has a considerable advantage. Researchers following Maier noted that observers were much more likely to solve the string problem than subjects actively involved in pursuing the solution.

In addition to the problem of set, the way a problem is phrased may affect one's reaction to it. Some of the research on this topic has been pulled together by Hogarth's (1982) monograph, which includes the chapter by Getzels referred to earlier. In it Tversky and Kahneman (1982) and Slovic, Fischhoff, and Lichtenstein (1982) describe how formulating a problem changes reactions to the solution. Noting, for instance, that resistance to wearing a seat belt is not unreasonable when one realizes that a fatal injury occurs only once in 3.5 million person-trips and a disabling injury once in every 100,000 trips, they reformulated this information: During a fifty-year lifetime of driving, the average motorist takes thousands of trips, so that the probability of a fatality rises to 1 percent and of a disabling injury to 33 percent. Whereas 54 percent of persons favored mandatory seat belt protection when exposed to single-trip information, 78 percent did when the same information was presented in terms of lifetime probabilities. This and other studies investigating ways of framing choices suggest that such choices are not irrational. Although we wish our decision to be free of the effects of framing, we are typically not aware of them. Simon (1955, 1956) has discussed this phenomenon as "bounded rationality." Undoubtedly it affects problem choice and the quality of solutions. Being aware of it is at least a start on attacking the problem of the problem.

5. *The bandwidth/fidelity problem requires finding an optimal breadth of problem focus.* Bandwidth/fidelity (a concept introduced in Chapter Five in a different perspective) borrows from electronics the idea that a communication channel can carry only so much information. One alternative is to try to cram the channel with a wide spectrum of messages having little redundancy and take a chance that some will get lost in the noise of the circuits. Another is to use the channel capacity to concentrate on getting a few messages through accurately by building in sufficient redundancy that even if part of the message gets lost or scrambled, we can figure it out from the rest. With a fixed-capacity communication channel, we can't maximize both bandwidth and fidelity at the same time. We trade one for the other and seek an optimum balance.

We can think of our research resources and efforts as being the fixed capacity of the communication channel. We can spread them over many questions (sometimes pulled together as a single, very broad question) but with a less dependable answer to any one of them. Alternatively, we can concentrate on obtaining more dependable answers to one or a few narrowly focused questions. The optimum for a study will be found, typically, in the balance between internal validity (LP) and external validity (GP). This balance has already been discussed but is also noted here because the optimum balance may well be determined by how the problem is formulated. A related aspect of this question is considered in the next point.

6. *Maintain sufficient holistic perspective to keep the study in proper context.* Maintaining a holistic view helps one to keep perspective on the problem in relation to its context. Qualitative research methodologists are often critical of quantitative workers because they perceive that the latter deal only with those aspects of problems that can be measured, thus cutting the problem to fit the method and thereby omitting important aspects of it. Cutting the problem to increase control is another reflection of the need to balance internal validity (LP) and external validity (GP).

Sometimes one loses holistic perspective by oversimplifying. Consider, for example, teacher enthusiasm. An analyst might consider the relation of enthusiasm to achievement a simple cause-and-effect phenomenon. A more holistic view might include student perception of the situation. For example, balance theories suggest that the teacher's enthusiasm about a subject for which a student has no previous positive feeling might be perceived as creating a potential conflict in the student. To balance the liking for the teacher that the enthusiasm created, the student adopts the stance of at least tentatively liking the subject. From this view, we have a feedback process rather than the overly simple cause-and-effect relation originally suggested.

The Researcher's Credibility with the Audience

Building a consensus around the interpretation of the evidence that supports one's knowledge claim requires gaining credibility with the audience. Cronbach's ingenious phrasing of the problem, quoted in part earlier, bears repeating: "Validity depends not only on the data collection and analysis but also on the way a conclusion is stated and communicated. Validity is subjective rather than objective: the plausibility of the conclusion is what counts. And plausibility, to twist a cliche, lies in the ear of the beholder" (1982, p. 108).

To build that consensus, one must anticipate the expectations of the audience in designing and implementing the study. Remember that the audience includes such gatekeepers as journal editors, committees that review proposals for funding, and those who select presentations for professional association programs. Persons in the latter groups can prevent a study's being funded or, when completed, from being adequately disseminated.

Ignoring concerns about audience credibility may only slow consensus development in the case of published basic research. Such concerns, however, are critical to applied research. Audiences that do not understand or accept the research are not about to apply it, thus negating the purpose of the study.

Relation to Integrity

Let us first be clear about the fact that, for the researcher, the most important audience with whom audience credibility must be built is oneself! Maintaining one's integrity as a scientist and a scholar is a first priority. Merton (1968) notes that among the norms that facilitate the functioning of science is disinterestedness. Disinterested researchers are not lacking in interest or motivation. Rather, in spite of their motivation, they not only do an honest job of gathering data but also analyze and interpret it as independently as possible from their expectations, hopes, and aspirations.

The quality of integrity conveyed when a study is presented depends on one's own. Given that one's personal integrity is genuine, then it is important to convey to the audience a sense of that commitment. This involves building a chain of reasoning with the strength that the data permit, not using hucksterism or propaganda to build an apparently stronger one. On occasion scientists are chided for their showmanship; when that occurs, their research tends to be suspect. *The line between propaganda and a solid presentation may be a fine one, but it is a boundary that must be found and observed.* Erring on the conservative side may delay appropriate recognition of a knowledge claim but is more generally viewed as acceptable.

Is there a role that the researcher can adopt? The researcher's task is more akin to that of a judge writing a decision than to that of a lawyer trying to make a case. Having come to a decision, the judge prepares a document that, while recognizing the cons, presents the strongest possible argument for the pros, explaining how and why the conclusion was reached. In preparing that decision, the judge, as the researcher must, considers the expectations of the audience and what objections its members are likely to raise from their orientations.

The foregoing should make clear that building credibility with the audience has nothing to do with hiding a study's weaknesses, misconstruing the data, or overgeneralizing. Protection of the progress of science alone is enough reason for such a stance. But purely from the standpoint of self-interest, such errors reflect on one's professional competence as well.

Ways of Building Audience Credibility

What can one legitimately do to gain audience credibility? One can predict which audiences are key and anticipate the expectations they either will bring to the study or will develop as they review the report. Although each audience is unique, some common considerations are important:

1. *Start where the audience is.* Build the study on knowledge that is accepted by the audience; otherwise your case rests on a foundation that will be questioned from the start. The balancing of internal validity (LP) and external validity (GP) in a study depends on whether internal validity (LP) has previously been demonstrated. A study intended to show generality usually takes for granted that the relationship between the variables has already been accepted in the audience's minds in at least a limited circumstance; be sure it has.

2. *Avoid the weaknesses of previous similar studies.* One will undoubtedly make some original mistakes, but to repeat the mistakes of others indicates an inability to learn from experience that is damaging to audience credibility. Few if any studies are able to eliminate all possible criticisms; the trade-offs involved in covering certain problems inevitably leave others exposed. Where you repeat problems previously encountered, however, explain how you decided that this was still the best design for the study.

Audience credibility is enhanced if the researcher is knowledgeable about current literature on method. For example, the person who is reporting an analysis of covariance should comment on recent articles that raise questions about its use, explaining why he continued to use it. Doing so builds reader confidence.

3. *Other things being equal, use accepted methods, measures, definitions, and terminology.* Unless the contribution of the study lies in new methodology, new measures, or new definitions or terminology, use of accepted forms will increase credibility. The audience's greater familiarity with the conventional facilitates communication. The reader is more comfortable, feels capable of judging the study, and has confidence in that judgment.

Using standard methods permits the audience to readily find the hallmarks of excellence that have come to be associated with particular approaches. The questionnaire study that takes steps to ensure that the nonrespondent responses match those of respondents, the participant observer who records personal biases before starting the study so that they can be recognized if they influence data collection and interpretation, the study that reports reliability and validity data for a new instrument—these are all signs of careful workers, and they build audience credibility.

In the same way, using standard methods helps the audience know what to watch out for: A remedial group, for example? Unless there is a control group, the audience will look for a possible regression effect. Multiple correlation? It will look for cross-validation.

Similarly, use of accepted instruments means that the results are more readily interpreted and that the audience that knows something about how the instrument behaves will be in a position to judge the results with more confidence.

If one hopes to reach a lay audience, use of only common terminology with few technical terms is a minimum requirement. Within reason, technical terms are appropriate, understandable, and impressive to professional audiences. But nothing is so devastating to credibility as inept use of technical language or inaccurate simplification of technical concepts. Face validity of measures is especially important for lay audiences. For example, although a measure of writing ability based on multiple-choice test items may seem acceptable to a researcher, only an actual writing sample is likely to have validity in the eyes of a lay audience.

4. *Justify use of the nonstandard.* Where one departs from the accepted, the burden of proof is on the researcher. Pioneering a new method, coining new terms, developing a new instrument all require

making it "self-evident" to the audience that this was an appropriate thing to do. Usually this demonstration requires pointing out the relation to the standard choice, giving the reasons for not using it, and showing how the new one advances the field. This book demonstrates this practice, it is hoped successfully. In Chapter Three the terms *internal validity (LP)* and *external validity (GP)* were introduced in relation to their predecessor formulations. In Chapter Eleven this demonstration is further pursued with a fuller discussion of the other formulations in relation to these two.

In some instances one must teach the audience the hallmarks of excellence for a technique and then show their existence in the study in question. Sometimes there is an accepted instrument that is not quite "on target" for the study; a less well-known one measures more precisely what one wishes. One trades ready acceptance of the standard measure for a more precise study but also has the extra effort of "educating" the audience in the merits of the new measure. Education may also be necessary when writing for an untutored or, especially, a lay audience; otherwise niceties of method may seem unnecessary complexities.

5. *Indicate the basis for trade-offs that leave apparent weaknesses.* Trade-offs by definition permit a gain in one respect at a loss in another. The resulting weakness may be viewed as a sign of incompetence if the reader does not understand why it was allowed to exist. Stating one's rationale for accepting such weaknesses shows that at least they did not result from oversight or stupidity. It provides the reader a basis for empathizing with your problem and possibly accepting your solution. Give yourself a break and your reader that chance.

Resource Allocation and Information Yield

Resource allocation determines whether a study can be successfully carried out. It involves the allocation of both tangible resources, such as time, energy, money, equipment, and office and laboratory space, and intangible resources, such as interpersonal skills, social capital and favors owed, friendships, and use of persons appropriately placed in the bureaucratic or social hierarchy. Since resources (tangible or intangible), once used one way, cannot be used again, the allocation act is crucial.

Resource allocation involves such decisions as balancing time spent developing and reformulating the question against time spent actually investigating it; balancing field observations with reading and reflecting on the observation notes; carefully developing the study design against implementing it; spending more time in the field gathering data against time analyzing the data already collected. Regardless of research method, optimizing resource allocation is a key factor in success.

It is obviously easier to optimize resource allocation when the study can be planned in advance, as with experimentation. By contrast, field studies, in which one knows less well what will be encountered or how long the study might take, require optimizing decisions made as one goes along, a much more difficult process but equally important to the success of the project. Probably the degree to which resource allocation can be optimized depends on the feasibility of advance planning.

Resource allocation often sends the researcher back to the drawing board. One finds that the resources are not adequate to do the study as planned or that more economical ways of designing the study exist. An often-repeated cycle frequently results, successive iterations of the design proving to be better as well as more economical and efficient.

Some researchers believe that, being unfunded, they have no resource allocation problem. (See "A Note on Dissertations" at the end of this chapter.) Quite to the contrary, the most expensive item in any budget is professional time. Even without money to manage, there should be a time and energy budget; these resources are not inexhaustible. It is true that without funding there is no deadline on the project, and time and energy limits are quite elastic. Economists, however, call our attention to "opportunity costs," the likely returns for alternative uses of one's time and energy. Too rarely do we raise this question, which should be a part of the planning for every study. The planning of a research program is therefore advisable (Lakatos, 1970, 1978), with resource allocation planning that extends beyond the immediate study. Opportunity costs are more easily assessed when research programs are planned than in single studies. Further, more fruitful results are likely to come from a research program; only rarely is a single study highly significant.

Viewed in its broadest perspective, resource allocation involves optimizing two aspects: (1) information yield and (2) efficiency and effectiveness. These are discussed in more detail in the following sections. Because of its importance, even though it is a resource allocation function, information yield is broken out as a separate set of decisions both in the discussion to follow and in Figure 14.

Information Yield

Optimizing information yield means allocating resources in such a way as to simultaneously gather evidence to:

1. Maximally reduce uncertainty with respect to one's main knowledge claim(s).
2. Ensure accurate interpretation of evidence bearing on those claims.
3. Alert one to important side effects, especially unexpected ones.
4. Facilitate formulating future studies.

Since resources put to one purpose do not serve others, one must set priorities. Doing so involves answering such questions as: How likely is it that unexpected or unusual data-gathering conditions will weaken the knowledge claim? That the treatment will not be administered as planned? That side effects will occur that need to be noted? How important is it to start thinking now about the next study?

Reducing uncertainty about one's main knowledge claim is nearly always first priority. For example, the prison simulation study showed first of all that the hardening attitudes of the "guards" occurred even in the simulated situation. But what happened to the self-concepts of the "prisoners"? Is this an important side effect that should have had resources allocated to its observation?

What aspects of the design are particularly crucial to accurate interpretation of the data? For example, the treatment plan may be excellent, but if not implemented well, it goes for naught. Did the police carry off their arrest of the "prisoners" as though it were the real thing? Personally collecting evidence helps researchers be assured that they did. One cannot plan for the observation of *unexpected* side effects, but one can have enough resources in a contingency reserve that when one suspects them or when something goes wrong, resources are available. Murphy's law, "Whatever can go wrong, will!," was born of experience.

Planning for the next study of a research program involves such questions as: What assumptions must be tested? Which propositions? How will the data gathered during this study advance the general scheme of the research program? If one is planning to apply for funding, it is always impressive to funders if one has preliminary data that indicate the potential success of the proposed study. Many successful investigators collect enough data for their next study in their current one that they are always working one step up on the study ahead.

Efficiency and Effectiveness

Allocating resources so as to use most efficiently the available time, energy, and skills is clearly important. A good research design makes for very efficient planning if events can be correctly anticipated.

Concern with efficient resource management can be overdone, of course, especially if it becomes so critical that research efforts are restricted and creativity is stifled. But many research projects err on the side of too little, rather than too much, advance planning.

Efficiency is linked to effectiveness in that efficiently allocating resources in accordance with priorities will also usually produce the most effective use of resources. The entire design of a study must be kept in balance; there is no point in putting resources into an elaborate sampling plan, for example, when some of those resources should be used to strengthen a weak measuring device. The maxim that a chain is only as strong as its weakest link suggests one should allocate resources so as to make all links equal in strength. Researchers' file drawers contain numerous unpublished instances of elaborate statistical analyses that cannot be interpreted because inadequate resources were put into finding and eliminating various design flaws.

Clearly in the category of project resources, but not usually so considered, are the space likely to be available for publication and the time allocated for a seminar, workshop, conference, or convention presentation. If the goal of one's research is to bring about the consensus required for acceptance of one's contribution to knowledge, these are more important resources to use wisely than any of the rest, for unless one reports the study so it gains the acceptance due it, the other resources have not been well employed; their use was intended to ensure that the best appropriate report was possible. The researcher must decide what issues are critical to address in order to resolve important questions in the minds of the audience and yet, at the same time, make a full enough presentation to satisfy the usual expectations of a research report. In some instances, the researcher may find it is better to omit a minor or secondary topic rather than try to address it in the space likely to be available. To address a concern that cannot be adequately allayed in the presentation may be a waste of a precious resource better allocated elsewhere. An instance is found in one of the studies analyzed in Chapter Ten. A major feature of the treatment was to hypnotize the subjects. The journal in which the report appeared has many readers likely to be skeptical of hypnosis. One alternative was to use precious journal space to allay readers' mistrust and to justify use of hypnosis—a task that would have been extremely difficult if not impossible in the space allotted. The alternative chosen was to provide no justification of the technique at all and to use the allotted space to discuss the important features of the study for those willing to accept the technique.

Limits and Constraints

Three sources of constraints restrict what can be accomplished in a research study: (1) limitations on the total available resources, (2) ethical standards, and (3) institutional constraints. The first constraint, resource limits, is a factor in nearly all research; the extent to which the second and third are serious problems varies from study to study.

Limitations on Total Resources

Resources are rarely sufficient to do all one might hope. But as one quickly finds when one writes proposals for funding, a study can be built in a variety of sizes and designs and still attain one's goal. The same question can be answered within a wide range of budgets—very large to impress a congressional committee on a policy issue, very small to help one better understand what is going on in a situation. As noted under "Question Formulation," there is probably an optimum size for many studies, which is determined by the needed sensitivity to show the relationship, the needed size for representativeness, and the needed impressiveness for uncertainty reduction. This last is no doubt related to audience familiarity with research methods; lay audiences, such as Congress, may require large and impressive demonstrations. Professional audiences may be well satisfied with smaller studies done to very high standards.

There is another sense, however, in which resource limits need to be considered. The preceding remarks relate to the maximum resource figure and the problem of staying within it and yet doing what needs to be done. The minimum may also be important. This is particularly true in a policy study to satisfy Congress; unless the study is done with a sample of substantial size and considerable representativeness, it is unlikely to be sufficiently impressive to have the desired impact. A minimum resource limit may also be important when one is seeking a particular effect. I have referred to the sensitivity or power of a study. There may be a minimum number of subjects or an expensive but sensitive test without which there is hardly any point in doing the study, since the effect, even if present, will not be sensed. So knowing the minimum limit on resources is sometimes as important as knowing the maximum.

Questions that help determine the level of resources needed are these: How clear are the goals of the study? How likely is it that one can accurately predict how the study will go? If one isn't sure what is being sought from the start, that isn't necessarily bad, but is finding it likely to take longer? How real is the threat of important rival explanations for study results? What will it take to eliminate them? What are the audience's expectations in this regard? Sometimes ways of answering these questions can be found that reduce the cost of the study to within one's limits. Finally, there is the question "What are the minimum characteristics of a study, below which the study is not worth doing?"

Ethical Standards

Ethical standards have tightened considerably over recent years. Originally the main concerns were with physical harm or severe psychological trauma. But some widely publicized experiments in which individuals found themselves doing things they would not normally do, such as the cruelty shown to prisoners in the prison simulation study, caused considerable criticism because of the potential psychological cost to subjects. Exposure to self-knowledge that subjects had not sought could be most disturbing and difficult to handle. Such studies could leave a psychological scar on individuals who now realized they were capable of behavior they would not have dreamed possible.

Human-subject protection committees have therefore been established to ensure that the potential for such harm is minimized in every possible way. An institution that receives federal funds for any purpose must establish a committee to approve all research involving human subjects, whether the research is funded by the federal government or not (animal protection committees are similarly required). Such safeguards are desirable, however, even if not federally required. Such committees ensure that if the potential for such harm exists, the study is deemed important enough to warrant it. But just when, if ever, such risks are justified is a topic of increasing debate and consideration both by these committees and by the public generally.

Federal and state privacy laws may make it difficult to match data on the same person in longitudinal studies, because certain personal data must be gathered under anonymous conditions. There are ways around this constraint, however, such as asking subjects to make up a personal code number involving information not available to the researcher but using a standard set of questions for everyone: "Make up a number the first digit of which is the number of children born to your father's family; the second, the number born to your mother's family; the third and fourth, how long you lived at the address before your present one," and so on.

Some federally funded projects must receive clearance before they can administer a questionnaire or measuring instrument. Originally this requirement was to reduce the paperload and to eliminate overlapping requests for the same information. The clearance can now involve concerns about the adequacy of the instruments and invasion of privacy. Where highly sensitive information is being requested that can be given on a yes-or-no basis, there is a way to conceal a given respondent's answer. Ask the respondent to flip a coin and, if it lands heads, to answer yes, if it lands tails, to answer the question honestly. The true frequency can be estimated from probability theory without knowing whether any given individual answered yes in response to the question or because the coin landed heads. Of course, be sure to phrase the question so that "yes" is the response that is sensitive to give, since the "no" responses are presumably truthful and self-revealing. If the latter is a problem, a somewhat more complex procedure can be used: flip the coin twice, and if it comes up heads both times, answer yes; tails both times, answer no; one head and one tail, answer honestly (see also Bradburn, Sudman, and Associates, 1979).

Many professional associations have developed codes of ethical standards. Examples are the statements of ethical practice published by the American Psychological Association (1981), standards for evaluation projects (Joint Committee on Standards for Educational Evaluation, 1981), standards for tests (American Psychological Association, 1974), and ethical standards for research with children (Society for Research in Child Development; for the text of the statement, see Vasta, 1981). Although compliance is voluntary, such standards often find their way into federal regulations and are the basis for legal decisions. The test standards, for instance, have been frequently cited in legal briefs where testing is involved. Conformance with such standards also contributes to audience credibility.

Not all constraints are externally imposed. Ethical decisions abound in field studies and must be made in the absence of such standards and on the spot; in some instances serious value conflicts arise. A classic case is whether researchers should report criminal activities to authorities when observation of them resulted from the trust gained through participation in the group. Humphreys (1975) not only did not report them, he acted as a lookout for policemen in order to observe homosexual culture in public washrooms. Further, noting the participants' license numbers, he traced them to their homes and interviewed them about their lives. It was later pointed out to him that his notes could have been subpoenaed and he would have had no way to protect his subjects, even though he had promised them anonymity. He went through some anguishing moments and destroyed his records. (See the appendix to the second edition of Humphreys, 1975.)

When do the ends justify the means? Humphreys obviously thought they did. As a former clergyman who had worked with homosexuals, he thought his study and methods proper; others were extremely critical (see references in his appendix). Like Humphreys, Milgram, the designer of the electrical shock study cited earlier, would probably argue that his ends justified the means. His study helped people see that the Nazi acquiescent mentality was unique neither to Germans nor to wartime situations. It could happen here any time as well! Is that knowledge worth the guilt and anxiety borne by the individuals who participated and who came to realize they might commit such acts? In Milgram's defense, it should be noted that he maintained that the subjects' guilt and anxiety were only temporary and that he did everything possible in the debriefing session to help subjects see the study in perspective. He felt that subjects left the study with positive feelings toward it (Milgram, 1973).

To guide behavioral scientists and, as well, medical professionals who are involved in even more difficult situations, institutions like the Hastings Center have been developed to study ethical questions. The *Hastings Center Report* is that institution's periodical for reporting its deliberations. It also publishes a newsletter, *HRB*, for human subject research committees.*

Institutional Constraints

Constraints are imposed by institutions trying to keep things operating normally. Requirements that disrupt schedules or other normal operating procedures usually reduce access to desired research sites, since most institutions insist on maintaining business as usual. This fact raises questions about the representativeness of those that will let a researcher in and weakens the implied generality of findings.

Gaining access can be especially difficult when controversial topics are to be probed or when the study results may reflect unfavorably on the institution. An administration may grant access to observe what it perceives as a favorable development and nevertheless find that the development is reported unfavorably. Rist (1977), for example, observed the integration of black children bused to previously all-white schools in Portland, Oregon—a program of which the admin-

*HRB: A Review of Human Subjects Research, published by Hastings Center Institute of Society, Ethics and the Life Sciences, Inc., 360 Broadway, Hastings-on-Hudson, New York 10706.

istration was quite proud. Rist, however, found that integration meant assimilation to the point that the black children's culture was devalued in their own eyes. The school administration was offended. This and similar incidents cause administrators to be reluctant to admit researchers whom they perceive as more interested in revealing unfortunate conditions than in protecting the institution. Every researcher who reports in a highly critical way probably raises barriers to similar studies as the controversy over the last such study spreads. Levin (1981, p. 52) notes that it may be impossible for the researcher to please all parties, and the decision becomes one of "which people to harm rather than avoiding harm altogether."

Clearly this is also an ethical dilemma for the researcher, who unquestionably feels that society should know about such conditions. Yet such revelations may be detrimental to the institution's reputation and may affect its support. Indeed, in some instances its existence may be threatened, as well as the professional careers of the administrators who permitted the study. Although some researchers might argue that such consequences are deserved, that in no way endears the researchers to the administrators. The result? Any social problem needing correction and worth studying may often be inaccessible.

A Concluding Note

Although this chapter points to very important aspects that are often overlooked, researchers almost intuitively sense and attend to many of these aspects. Audience credibility is an example. The researcher certainly considers the audience when writing the report—but not necessarily when the study is being planned. It is later, when one is writing the report and some unanticipated demand of the audience comes to mind, that the demands of the audience become real. Thus these aspects may not always be considered at the most appropriate time, and even when some are, frequently some are omitted. So there is merit in making these points more apparent and salient. They are then much more subject to conscious control.

Still, it would be nice to be able to say more about how to choose and formulate a problem or how to adjust information yield, for example. Many of these decisions are problem-specific, so that experience in a given research area is very helpful. Consulting an experienced researcher when one begins work in a new area can often save much trial-and-error learning. Such individuals often seem intuitively to know what to expect. But the framework provided in this book can also help by making explicit some of the problems to attend to. Good decisions require one to know what is to come—will there be side effects, unexpected deviations from plan, and so on? It is partly the fact that we are bumping into the barrier of the unknown that makes the chapter less than might be hoped. Partly, too, it is a matter of maturity. As the behavioral sciences develop, more can be said.

Now that the entire model of design choices has been described, perhaps it is more easily understood why the design of a study is an art, why individuals differ in judging whether a study is a good one, and why people disagree on whether a given design is the best possible one for the goal intended. And such disagreements often exist regardless of the skill and competence of the individuals involved, the time given to developing the design, or the research method used. One reason is the complexity of the model with which we are all dealing; another is the differences among conceptions of how the behavioral sciences are best built and what they ought to be.

By now you realize the complexities of decision making in designing, conducting, and reporting a study. And I have not touched on the niceties of measurement reliability and validity, sampling, statistics, and the many other topics that have their criteria of proper use and are extensively covered in the more typical research text. There are so many decisions, many of which could be made differently by someone else on a completely rational basis. One operates within limits that may be perceived differently by different persons, and people differ in the extent to which they will try to change whatever limits they perceive to exist. One must simultaneously optimize five judgments—how best to formulate the question, weight internal validity (LP) and external validity (GP), build credibility with the audience, get information yield, and allocate resources. Those decisions must be made within the perceived limits of institutional and ethical constraints and available resources. And all this must be done in such a way as to build the strongest chain of reasoning that the evidence allows. Clearly a complex task—but one that researchers are accomplishing quite satisfactorily every day, so not an impossible one. These complexities produce more possibilities for disagreement than we generally consider. Nevertheless, some of that disagreement comes from another source.

I have been proceeding on the assumption that all behavioral scientists believe we can develop generalizations, at least approximations of the kinds of rules, laws, and theories that the natural sciences have. Some behavioral scientists do not believe that is ever possible. They would, therefore, reject this whole approach. Others believe that each of us must develop for himself an understanding of the way the behavioral world works; we construct our own cognitive map, if you will, that guides our behavior. Some behavioral scientists distrust verbal explanations for things they cannot physically sense; they prefer not to deal with constructs like happiness and anxiety that they cannot directly measure. They prefer to build a behavioral science that deals only with the behavioral manifestations they can directly observe and measure, and they would be unhappy with the emphasis given to explanations in the previous material. You ·can begin to sense that there are different orientations to behavioral science that, in addition to everything else we have considered, must also be taken into account. The next chapter will describe a typology of behavioral scientists that divides them in accordance with the way they work and the kind of behavioral science they are seeking to build. The chapter following will examine that typology in relation to the model that has been the subject of the preceding chapters.

A Note on Dissertations

The doctoral student's main resource to allocate for her dissertation is her own time; how she allots it to the various phases of her study usually determines whether she is able to complete it in the time she has allowed. Too many fail at this task; they leave the university planning to finish on their first job and find the new responsibilities combined with the unfinished ones too much. These failures are also mute testimony to the difficulty of time management, since many faculty members fail at this task as well. The usual solution, to plan the study in its entirety, removes much of the exploration and excitement and can turn it into a mechanical task. We want our students to experience the fun of research as well. It is another problem of finding the middle ground, and although students must be free to make some mistakes, we probably need to give them more help.

There is another aspect of resource allocation in which we could train students quite successfully but in which we now give them negative training because of the dissertation format. We continue to act as though the research report form were the most important form of research communication. Such reports are much less widely read than journal articles; indeed, probably the main readers of dissertations are other doctoral students doing dissertations. Research reports and dissertations are the only forms in which the length is uncontrolled. Convention time and publication space are scarce resources to be allocated carefully and used well. Some doctoral committees insist that the manuscript include every "jot and tittle." This requirement does the student the triple disservice of (1) not using the dissertation as an opportunity to learn how best to use journal space, (2) having to learn this skill on her own without faculty guidance, and (3) learning it at the same time that the crush of the first job's unfamiliar responsibilities makes adequate time allocation for such learning impossible.

How much better a learning experience if the dissertation format were that of a manuscript of appropriate form and length for publication (possibly more than one article if the work warrants it)! A review of the literature, the raw data, or such other documentation as a doctoral committee might desire for training or complete report purposes could be put in an appendix.

The advantages are obvious: (1) learning journal format and how to reduce a complicated study to abbreviated length with the appropriate inclusion and exclusion of aspects of the argument and of detail, (2) doing so when not burdened with a new position and its unfamiliar demands, (3) having the guidance of experienced faculty members to facilitate learning, (4) having the dissertation "wrapped up" on getting the degree and the freedom to devote full energies to one's new tasks without feeling "I really ought to get back to it and do something with it!," (5) possibly a publication on entering the first position, and (6) the reinforcement of successfully accomplishing these gains, which would make it more likely that future research will be seen as rewarding. Universities willing to modernize their training modes will clearly give their students a head start over others.

7

How Orientations
to Knowledge Affect
Research Methods

> If we understand that science is not simply about
> the acquisition of knowledge but is a means of express-
> ing ourselves—and of forming, transforming, and gener-
> ally coping with our world—we can approach this
> endeavor in a new way. In so doing, we will be able to
> steer clear of the delusion that it is possible to know in
> an absolute sense of "being right" and devote our
> energies to the more constructive process of dealing with
> the implications of our different ways of knowing.
> —Gareth Morgan, 1983a, p. 18

Sarah is a doctoral student working on an interesting dissertation. She is trying to be as objective and unbiased as possible in determining the factors contributing to the outcome of the presidential election. Sarah has worked long, hard hours with her major professor to develop a comprehensive questionnaire to be used in predicting the outcome of the election. She is presenting it and the plans for its use to the committee she has chosen to guide her through this phase of her studies. The committee members seem to tolerate, more than be enthusiastic about, the questionnaire; indeed, one of them reacts by suggesting that she extend her plans to include mingling with the voters as they leave the polls to learn how they made their decisions. That leads another committee member to suggest that she add some case studies of how these voters made up their minds over the ninety days prior to the election.

Sarah thinks, "She must be crazy! Not only is that a lot of extra work, but it doesn't belong in an empirical study like mine where I'm just trying to see what predicts the results. Mingling with the voters gets one into a lot of soft stuff that can't be measured! And for that matter, how could such a small sample of case studies predict anything? It takes such a large number of representative cases to really mean anything!"

Before she can voice her reaction, however, another committee member adds his suggestion: "How about reading the various analyses of the election and then doing a retrospective that merges the best of the questionnaire results, the case studies, and the analyses into a single discussion of the event?" Sarah despairs, "It gets even worse! How can one call that science when one picks and chooses among the data and their analyses to select whatever one wishes? It's so confusing! Here are all these competent behavioral scientists clearly sincere in their efforts to help me; each seems bent on making my study the best ever, but their suggestions are so diverse! And worse yet, they seem to ask me to do things that run counter to what I've been trained a science is. Why can't they live with the questionnaire study as first designed, a predictive study of what determines the outcome of the election?"

It is hoped that, with the perspective provided by this and the following chapter, Sarah and students like her will better understand that, yes, each is bent on improving her study but *from his or her own point of view—and those views differ.* For the quantitative methodologist like her major professor, objectivity is critical. By contrast, the historian member of her committee recognizes that selecting what to include in a study is a subjective decision—indeed, the quality of a historian's work is judged by how well those decisions are made (Barzun and Graff, 1977)! Yet, both are researchers contributing to the behavioral sciences. Working from their orientations, her committee members sought different evidence to provide the best demonstration of the determining factors of the election as they would approach the problem. Each was interpreting the criteria of a good behavioral science study in terms of what seems to contribute to building that science as he or she understood it.

The quotation from Morgan with which the chapter opens both describes the problem and suggests the solution. We need to understand the personal factors influencing research. It seems unlikely that we can understand them at a level at which we can predict why Sarah picked the particular problem she did. But we can understand the commonalities and differences that result from the differing streams of socialization processes to which all of us are subject in the process of learning how to become behavioral scientists. If we could do that in this instance, it would suggest why Sarah was using the method she chose and why she had difficulty with the suggestions made by her committee members. Once we are aware of the common factors in these streams, we can better understand them and their influence. Then we can begin to compare and contrast them by their consequences. No longer hidden and covert, the differences will be apparent and articulated so that we will be in a better position to deal with them and their effects.

This chapter describes a typology intended to cover the major ways in which different types of behavioral scientists approach problems and propose solutions contributing to the behavioral sciences as that type envisages them. It is intended to make these approaches visible, increasing their salience in behavioral science discussions so that we can, as Morgan suggests, "devote our energies to the more constructive process of dealing with the implications of our different ways of knowing." The following chapter displays some of these consequences as it relates each of the types to the model developed in the preceding chapters.

The typology was stimulated by a set of four types based on Jungian thought described by Mitroff and Kilmann (1978). Two of the types, the particularist and analyst, are close to their types. Their work considerably facilitated this derivation from it and is gratefully acknowledged.

The typology describes a continuum of orientations and methods from those closest to the natural science traditions to those closest to the humanistic ones. Each point on the continuum characterizing a type describes one of the patterns of work that occur with some frequency, patterns in which graduate students are trained. As in any field of study, behavioral scientists are socialized by those who have gone before; they *learn* their points of view and methods of research. Fields tend to be characterized not just by their content but also by the dominant research methods that have proved effective with that content. These, in turn, tend to characterize the way their users think about the behavioral sciences and what they ought to be. It is an interactive process. Like the blind men each of whom characterized this strange beast, the elephant, by the part he was holding, so researchers come to views of behavioral science that are molded by their ways of working and the content they work on, and the knowledge claims they present reflect their orientation.

Although researchers are typically socialized as graduate students to the orientation and methods of their major professor or mentor, some find that they desire a broader approach and learn additional methods and points of view. Some come to routinely straddle two or three as they encounter a variety of problems demanding different approaches. Usually their "home type" reflects the orientation of initial socialization, but most adjust even that to fit their growing experience and over time use research methods that fit their own unique patterns of capabilities. For many individuals this adjustment continues throughout their careers as their capabilities grow, as they experience how their research contributes to the knowledge of their field, and as their research skills broaden. For many such persons, the types are much better thought of as roles, roles they may assume as the characteristics of particular problems demand them. Many, trying to characterize themselves or others in terms of the types, will find that they fall between types on the continuum. Equally often, individuals will find that their roles span a segment of the continuum. Probably mature researchers bridge across types more often than novices.

The types seem most meaningful when you can personalize them, matching them to persons you know, thus giving a greater sense of reality to these abstract conceptions. The fit typically will not be exact (everyone wants to adjust the scheme to fit his predilections). But the scheme has proved useful in stimulating thought about the linkage of method to conceptions of what the behavioral sciences are and ought to be. This is its use here.

Fellows at the Center for Advanced Study in the Behavioral Sciences, where I was when this typology was originally developed, very constructively commented on the set of orientations. They searched for one that fit themselves: "That really describes me," "Oh, there's Joe," "Tom is most like. . . ." Their enthusiasm and that of others since have provided the main validation for the scheme. Some readers may object to this lack of empirical evidence; clearly it would have been desirable to have some. But the types serve a heuristic and illustrative purpose. The variety of orientations encourages people to introspect into the characteristics of their own approaches, their own understanding of methodology, what the behavioral sciences ought to be, and the extent to which their view is determined by their socialization or whether they have moved beyond that and are consciously determining what methods and views are most appropriate on the basis of their experience. Such thought will help considerably to advance both methods and the sciences themselves. Since it serves this purpose, I decided to use it despite potential objections to the lack of data.

Some may see the typology as incomplete. For example, where does one put modelers of phenomena? They seem to fit with one of the types, the analyzers. They start with a holistic conception—for instance, a theory—and then bit by bit match it to reality just as analyzers test propositions that stem from theory. One could no doubt think of others that appear to have been omitted. Perhaps empirical work will suggest these. But in my role as a theorist (also one of the types), I decided to leave empirical verification aside for the moment until that is a more central goal. In doing so, I applied the practical principle of research that underlies all the decisions on trade-offs mentioned so often in this book: "Apply standards appropriate to your central goals; trying to perfect everything is impossible and may leave important priorities poorly done."

A Typology of Behavioral Science Orientations

Researchers' orientations to knowledge are highly varied. Although we don't need a special part of the brain to keep track of the distinctions, as we do with facial recognition, we need nonetheless to reduce their variety to patterns we can readily understand and use. Consistent with this need, I have imposed order on the variety of orientations by organizing them into seven types: pragmatist, analyzer, synthesizer, theorizer, multiperspectivist, humanist, and particularist. A description of each type follows, accompanied by examples of research conducted by that type.

The Pragmatist

Pragmatists seek instruments, rules, principles, equations, and models that predict with better-than-chance accuracy and therefore permit some measure of control. They seek operations that permit them to control without the necessity of using constructs and concepts that cannot be physically sensed and therefore are never directly measured. They are concerned with finding *what works*—regardless of whether it can be explained or seems reasonable. The Strong-Campbell Vocational Interest Inventory (Strong and Campbell, 1981) is a product of pragmatist work. It compares the interests of persons seeking to make a vocational decision with those of persons who have already chosen a particular field of work. It predicts that individuals like those already in a field will be most successful. This inventory has been one of the most successful predictive instruments in some difficult areas for many years. From the standpoint of explanation credibility, however, there is no particular reason that an interest in music should predict success as a mathematician, but it turns out that it does!

Another example is "wait time" (Rowe, 1974). If one can increase the amount of time the teacher waits for a response to a question before supplying the answer or calling on another student, the nature of classroom discourse changes markedly toward longer and more thoughtful comment and a higher level of student thinking. Typical wait time is only about one second or less, and a small increase to three seconds creates the effect. Rowe's early work does not explain why the effect occurs or what creates it; it is enough that this technique is effective.

Still another example is the work of Skinner (1957) and those who follow his example. They define the terms they use in their work strictly operationally, trying to build a psychology without having to use constructs, without having to infer what is in the mind, the "black box" they can't sense directly. For example, a reinforcer is something that has the effect of increasing the probability of a behavior the next time the same circumstances occur—not something that gives pleasure, although that is the meaning the term has come to have with many persons, especially as it is associated with M&M candies. Nonpragmatists may infer that it is the pleasure (a construct that can't be directly sensed) that results in learning (another construct), which results in the increased frequency of the correct response. Pragmatists skip all that in-between speculation about what goes on in the mind.

Pragmatists often use statistical prediction techniques such as multiple correlation, discriminant function analysis, canonical correlation, and factor analysis. They are most often found in psychology and economics.

Pragmatists assume Popper's "clocklike" world. They endorse the classical norms of the natural sciences as the most valid ways of knowing. Subscribing to Merton's norms (see Chapter One), they see science as impersonal, value-free, precise, reliable, valid, causal, and exact, with clear standards for judgment.

They are less concerned with explaining, with understanding, or with theory than with that "it works." One may not entirely understand why an economic model works; it involves so many variables, and their relations are so complex. The important point is that it predicts. To pragmatists science is more finding operations that work than finding explanations.

Lee J. Cronbach, an eminent educational psychologist, is sympathetic to this view. In a personal communication (April 9, 1981), he says, "I will always take theory lightly, thinking the play's the thing and you can stage a play in many ways." I interpret "the play's the thing" to mean that the researcher must attend closely to the relationship he is observing, learning as much about it as possible, looking for unexpected effects, fine-tuning apparatus, checking treatment—in short, being sure of what is occurring, the "play." There may be a number of possible explanations of what occurred, "the way the play is staged," and the one advanced may or may not be correct. But so long as the researcher is sure that the relationship exists, both practice and science advance, because such "knowledge" leads to prediction and control and eventually the correct explanation will be found (see also Cronbach, 1975). For the pragmatists, what is crucial is not the way the play is staged: "The play is the thing! Period!"

Lincoln Moses, graduate dean at Stanford University, on reading this section in an earlier manuscript, also commented negatively on the importance of explanation credibility out of his extensive experience as a medical statistical consultant. He noted many instances in which the explanation for a treatment was incorrect but the treatment worked. He admitted that explanations helped to get a finding used, and he saw good in using them to that purpose. What is important, however, is the operational success. Each orientation differs in what is of most value and is most important.

Although pragmatist research was very much in style during the days of "Minnesota dust-bowl empiricism," before and after World War II, recent published examples are harder to come by, probably in part because of the recent emphasis on the importance of theory. Perhaps although individuals may subscribe to the pragmatist point of view, journal editors are less inclined to publish articles in that vein. Mitchell and Klimoski (1982), for example, compare empirical with rational keying, using a personal history blank for predicting the licensing of real estate salespersons as a vehicle for the comparison. It is not a rabid pragmatist piece, since it includes a review of psychological and sociological theories, the kind of rational explanation an analyst would seek, but the empirical keying is strictly pragmatic.

Indeed, such empirical keying is a prime example of the pragmatist orientation. Items are weighted according to data regardless of whether the weights appear to make sense. In this instance, responses to biographical items in multiple-choice format were weighted in accordance with their relation to whether a subject in the researchers' first sample became licensed. These weights were then used to predict licensing in other samples. It is pragmatic but not obviously rational that owning one's home (+5), renting a home (-1), renting an apartment (-4), or living with relatives (-2) should be weighted as shown by the figures in parentheses. Thus it counts strongly for you to own your home, and it is a negative factor if you live with relatives but still worse if you live in an apartment. These weights are proportional to the correlation of those particular responses with getting licensed.

This article shows the basis for the success of the pragmatist position; the empirically keyed blank proved a better predictor (a correlation of .46) than a blank that was keyed on the basis of a job analysis, a "perusal of the literature," and a "review of psychological and sociological theories regarding the influence of background factors on career success" (a correlation of .36). There is an "8.2 percent improvement . . . in favor of the empirical . . . over the rational . . . approach" (pp. 413-414).

As already noted, other examples are Skinner (1957) and Rowe (1974).

The Analyzer

Analyzers seek to confirm rules, principles, or propositions that relate variables or events; such confirmation may also constitute a test of theory. Validating hypotheses is typically their main business. Analyzers prefer carefully designed studies with experimentation as the main technique, but they may also use natural or field experiments. Ideally, they integrate findings to build an explanation or theory, although many are often satisfied to confirm a single hypothesis. Other researchers are critical of the latter practice, believing that it leads to a fragmented literature of bits and pieces of research that do not add to anything important.

Analyzers are more likely to assume (or hope for) Popper's "clocklike" than his "cloudlike" nature of phenomena; the latter makes patterns so much harder to confirm. Although they look for prediction at some level of accuracy and generality, they are not always as sanguine about mechanistic linkages as those who characterized this type a decade or more ago. They are now more aware of the possibility of "loose couplings" between presumed cause and effect. They are also more aware of system relationships in which variables so interact that disturbing one variable may cause change somewhere else in the system to adjust and possibly resist change.

Like pragmatists, analyzers subscribe to science as the prime method of knowing and support its norms. They place considerable emphasis on science as a method of reducing or eliminating the biasing effects of personal values on observation, and they try to be value-free. Often they give the appearance and sometimes the reality of cutting down a problem to fit the method rather than adjusting the method to fit the problem.

Behavioral science literature, particularly in psychology but also in sociology, political science, and economics, heavily represents the work of analyzers. Indeed, whole issues of the *Journal of Experimental Psychology*, the *Journal of Educational Psychology*, and even the *Journal of Counseling Psychology* are filled with such writing. The Milgram electrical shock and the prison simulation studies are further examples; in addition, a third analyzer study is presented and critiqued in Chapter Ten.

The Synthesizer

Synthesizers study phenomena in their natural surroundings; they are oriented to fieldwork. Out of these observations they produce an explanation of the essential characteristics of the phenomenon. They may produce theory grounded in these observations (grounded theory) and do fieldwork involving careful observation, possibly as unobtrusive participants in the groups being studied (participant observation). They are more oriented to inductive reasoning than to the deductive reasoning heavily used by the analyzer. They more likely attribute a "cloudlike" than a "clocklike" nature to phenomena.

Some synthesizers view the world as a system with homeostable states being maintained by constant adjustment of variables and conditions to one another. For example, when the students are tired, the teacher must exert herself to attract their attention and maintain order. By contrast, when students are fresh, eager, and seeking stimuli, maintaining order is more a matter of providing a focus for their efforts. In this view, there is no simple correlational relationship between the frequency or strength of a particular teacher's behavior and classroom control, such as some analyzers might seek, nor from the synthesizer's point of view would one expect there to be; relationships are more complex than that. Both teacher and pupil behaviors are continually adjusting to each other, in this instance involving at least four variables: student tiredness, teacher attention-attracting activity, teacher providing foci for attention, and student attending.

Synthesizers are more concerned with description and explanation than prediction. In providing generalized explanations, as in grounded theory, they delineate the most common causative factors from relatively rare ones. Much sociological and anthropological literature is of this nature. For example, one participant observer developed a description of the stages a used car salesperson goes through in selling a car—first establishing personal trust, then trying to match customer needs with possibilities, and so on (Browne, 1976). Some historians are synthesizers as well, using the records of the past in the way sociologists use contemporary observations.

Synthesizers subscribe to the norms of science and to science as a way of knowing. But they are much more aware of the role of values in science because of the potential of values for biasing the observations that are the mainstay of their work.

Synthesizers prefer a holistic approach to phenomena rather than piecemeal studies that are likely to cut the phenomenon to fit the requirements of method.

Most sociological and anthropological case studies that seek to derive generalizations or develop theory are examples of synthesizer writing (for example, Blau, 1955, 1963). Many make understandable the behavior of groups and individuals we would not typically encounter by showing how these subjects perceive the system in which they are immersed and showing that their behavior is consistent with what we know about how individuals and groups behave under such circumstances (Humphreys, 1975; Liebow, 1967; Rubin, 1976; Whyte, 1955). The example from Becker (1963) in Chapter Ten is of such a nature. Often such studies are intended to drive home a social lesson, as in Rist (1977). Some such case studies are mainly descriptive, however, leaving the integration of their potential usefulness to the reader's cognitive map construction, as the humanists do.

The Theorizer

The theorizer, like the synthesizer, works back and forth between abstractions designed to capture essential characteristics that explain a phenomenon and the study of the phenomenon itself. But whereas the synthesizer puts considerable emphasis on the observation aspect and may even defer development of the description and explanation until after leaving the field, the theorizer puts the main emphasis on developing out of the observations an explanation that makes a conceptual contribution to knowledge. In theorizers' typical method of work a few cases are carefully observed or some past research is integrated and an explanation derived. Perhaps a few small studies or more observations are done to check the explanation. The conceptual explanation is adjusted to fit, further checks made, and so on. Construction of the typology of this chapter was a typical theorizer effort.

Theorizers are found in nearly every field. They typically produce very attractive explanations that keep analyzers busy trying to confirm the explanations. Consider all the studies that have been inspired by Durkheim, Erikson, Freud, Kohlberg, Maslow, Piaget, Redfield, Riesman, and others like them who did substantial theorizer work.

Theorizers, like synthesizers, are sufficiently close to observations that the "cloudlike" character of phenomena can be a problem, but they have an uncanny ability to find common patterns across groups, aggregating at an appropriate level so that the random noise cancels and pattern is apparent. Some historians fit this pattern, like Toynbee and Spengler, although whether these two tended to go beyond their data in building their theories, as many theorizers do, is a matter for critics to debate.

As just implied, theorizers' ideas are not always on target, often being generalizations beyond their data, and their ideas are often modified by subsequent research. But their captivating conceptualizations contain enough of the germ of reality that their proposed patterns usually persist.

Compared with the previous three types, successful theorizers are rare, but those who succeed are tremendously powerful figures who can set the course for a field and strongly influence its research agenda. Although they subscribe to the norms of science, rather than presenting typical scientific evidence with a sizable formal data base, they depend more on the method of intuition (that is, the self-evidently true nature of their theory or explanation) to build a consensus of belief. Rather than extensive evidence, they depend on carefully chosen and very powerful examples to make their case. Confirmation, as already noted, becomes the work of others.

An interesting example of a theorizer's writing with considerable impact is that of Piaget (1929, 1930). In it the alternation between theoretical explanation and example is obvious and very compelling. It is indicative of the fact that these orientations are often better thought of as roles rather than indelibly categorizing types that a person like Skinner can be considered a pragmatist in *Verbal Behavior* (1957)—building a psychological theory without constructs, using only behavior that can be directly sensed and manipulated—and at a later stage be an example of a theorist in "The Science of Learning and the Art of Teaching" (1968). The latter article is said to have been inspired by visiting his daughter's schoolroom. It starts by citing very convincing incidents of animal training, showing how such training has progressed to very complex behaviors, and then contrasting it to education:

> Some promising advances have recently been made in the field of learning. Special techniques have been designed to arrange what are called contingencies of reinforcement—the relations which prevail between behavior on the one hand and the consequences of that

behavior on the other—with the result that a much more effective control of behavior has been achieved [p. 9].

In all this work, the species of the organism has made surprisingly little difference. It is true that the organisms studied have all been vertebrates, but they still cover a wide range. Comparable results have been obtained with pigeons, rats, dogs, monkeys, human children, and psychotic subjects [pp. 13-14].

From this exciting prospect of an advancing science of learning, it is a great shock to turn to that branch of technology which is most directly concerned with the learning process—education [p. 14].

Skinner then proceeds to give a very convincing explanation of how current education fails:

First . . . what reinforcements are used? . . . The child at his desk, filling in his workbook, is behaving primarily to escape a series of minor aversive events—the teacher's displeasure, . . . low marks, . . . criticism or ridicule. . . . In this welter of aversive consequences, getting the right answer is in itself an insignificant event, any effect of which is lost amid the anxieties, the boredom, . . . the by-products of aversive control [pp. 15-16].

Secondly, . . . how [are] the contingencies of reinforcement arranged? . . . The contingencies . . . [the teacher] provides are far from optimal. It can easily be demonstrated that . . . the lapse of only a few seconds between response and reinforcement destroys most of the effect. In a typical classroom, nevertheless, long periods . . . elapse. A third shortcoming is the lack of a skillful program which moves forward through a series of progressive approximations to the final complex behavior desired [p. 16].

Perhaps the most serious criticism . . . is the relative infrequency of reinforcement. Since . . . many pupils are usually dependent upon the same teacher, the total number of contingencies which may be arranged during, say, the first four years is of the order of only a few thousand. But a very rough estimate suggests that efficient mathematical behavior at this level requires something of the order of 25,000 contingencies [p. 17].

The result of all this [:] . . . Even our best schools
are under criticism [p. 17].

There would be no point in urging these objections if improvement were impossible. But the advances
which have recently been made in our control of the
learning process . . . tell us how the revision can be
brought about [p. 19].

In what follows, the theoretical position is translated into
classroom activity and technology in the form of a teaching machine.
Then the advantages of the machine are summarized: "The important
features of the device are these: reinforcement for the right answer is
immediate. The mere manipulation of the device will . . . probably
keep the average pupil at work for a suitable period each day. . . . A
teacher can supervise an entire class . . . yet each child may progress
at his own rate. . . . The gifted child will advance rapidly. . . . The
device makes it possible to present carefully designed material . . .
therefore the most efficient progress to an eventually complex reper-
toire can be made" (p. 24).

Finally, even objections are anticipated and undercut: Will it
handle complexity of thinking? "If the advances . . . can give the child
a genuine competence in reading, writing, spelling, and arithmetic,
then the teacher may begin to function, not in lieu of a cheap machine,
but through intellectual, cultural, and emotional contacts of that
distinctive sort which testify to her status as a human being" (p. 27).
Will it cause technological unemployment? "Mechanical devices will
eliminate the more tiresome labors of the teacher, but they will not
necessarily shorten the time during which she remains in contact with
the pupil" (p. 27). Can we afford it, economically? "The answer is
clearly Yes. The device I have just described could be produced as
cheaply as a small radio or phonograph" (p. 27).

Skinner's enthusiasm and his cogent argument sparked a substantial literature of experimentation on programmed learning and
teaching machines. It gradually became apparent that it takes more
than small steps and giving the right answer to put together a program
that students and teachers will use, and the fires of enthusiasm were
banked. The wide availability of microcomputers in education may
rekindle the flames, but as of now, most of that literature stands as a
tribute to the tremendous efforts of analyzers to validate a position set
forth by a skilled theorizer.

Sigmund Freud, of course, is a prime early example of theorist
writing. With generalizations and explanations derived from his

clinical cases, his work had a tremendous impact on psychology (Brill, 1938).

The Multiperspectivist

Multiperspectivists, depending on their work, may be more like theorizers or like humanists. They are therefore placed between these types. Like theorizers, they usually operate from observation and examples rather than a formal data base. Many of them, like humanists, deal with the explanation of a single phenomenon rather than setting forth propositions with sweeping generality.

Platt (1964) attributes to T. C. Chamberlin (1897/1965), a geologist at the University of Chicago, the statement of the "method of multiple hypotheses":

> The moment one has offered an original explanation for a phenomenon which seems satisfactory, that moment affection for his intellectual child springs into existence, and as the explanation grows into a definite theory his parental affections cluster about his offspring and it grows more and more dear to him. . . . There springs up also unwittingly a pressing of the theory to fit the facts and a pressing of the facts to make them fit the theory. . . .
>
> To avoid this grave danger, the method of multiple working hypotheses is urged. It differs from the simple working hypothesis in that it distributes the effort and the affections. . . . Each hypothesis suggests its own criteria, its own means of proof, its own method of developing the truth, and *if a group of hypotheses encompass the subject on all sides, the total outcome of means and of methods is full and rich* [as quoted in Platt, p. 350; emphasis added].

Chamberlin very neatly states both the multiperspectivist position and some of its advantages in contrast to other modes of work.

Multiperspectivists are still fewer than successful theorizers, although they seem to be increasing and their work is widely admired. Potentially their impact is great, but so far the potential has not, in general, been realized. Perhaps one reason is that we are not accustomed to handling more than one explanation of a phenomenon. Whereas most of us are delighted to find one reasonable explanation, multiple explanations are the goal of the multiperspectivists. But we are often uncomfortable with multiple "correct" ones, having been taught to look for "the" explanation all our lives. The often uninte-grated, sometimes almost contradictory nature of the proposed expla-nations stimulates considerable thought and interest but decreases the ease with which explanations translate into action. The explanations might, for example, be competing ones, as in Marxist and capitalist explanations of our economy, or they may be complementary, as in an examination of an institution such as a school or hospital from political, social, psychological, historical, and economic viewpoints.

Whereas theorizers aim to find explanations with generality over persons, places, and times, like Piaget's stages of growth or Skinner's learning principles, by contrast multiperspectivists usually take on more limited tasks. Their explanations are more like those of the historian, explaining, as Allison did, an event like the Cuban missile crisis or the rise of a phenomenon, as Tyack did for compul-sory school attendance (discussed shortly).

Like theorizers, multiperspectivists assume "clocklike," "cloud-like," or system orientations but are looking for a level of aggregation at which patterns are discernible. The other comments about theoriz-ers are also applicable.

One very good example of multiperspectivist work and perhaps a piece that dramatically called attention to this approach is Allison's (1971) study of the Cuban missile crisis. This book examines the puzzles of the crisis from three perspectives: that of the rational-man model, that of an organizational bureaucracy with standard operating procedures, and that of governmental politics and bargaining. Each viewpoint raises different questions, provides different answers, and reaches different conclusions. The rational-man model views nuclear war as unthinkable and suggests that low-level military actions can be engaged in without fear of escalation. But both the organizational and political models suggest that "irrational" stumbling into a nuclear war is quite possible and nuclear crises "are inherently chancy" (p. 260).

Another good example is Tyack's (1976) examination of the rise of compulsory schooling in the United States, using five explanatory models:

1. Compulsory education was a form of political construction: "How can one construe the political construction of education? New nations are commonly composed of . . . individuals who identify with regions, religions, ethnic groups, tribes, or interest groups. . . . The central purpose of universal education is . . . to create citizens and legitimize the state" (p. 365).

2. It was an outgrowth of ethnocultural conflict: "During the nineteenth century Americans differed significantly in their views of

citizenship and the legitimate domain of state action, including compulsory attendance legislation. A number of interpreters . . . have argued that these cleavages followed ethnic and religious lines. . . . Were . . . compulsory school attendance laws . . . largely passed by Republican pietists? . . . The interpretation seems plausible. . . . Evangelical ministers were at the forefront of the common-school crusade as the frontier moved westward" (pp. 369–370).

3. It resulted from organizational integration: "At the turn of the century a powerful and largely successful movement centralized control of city schools. . . . Advocates of these new forms of governance argued that education should be taken out of politics and that most decisions were best made by experts. As decision-making power shifted to superintendents . . . the number of specialists . . . ballooned. . . . By 1911 attendance officers were numerous and self-conscious enough to start their own national professional organization" (pp. 373–374).

4. It was an investment in human capital: After World War II it became apparent that physical capital was well utilized only where "qualified men knew how to use it" (p. 377). Economists found education to have considerable power in explaining development. They assumed that individuals would maximize their investment in schooling until the marginal rate of return equaled the marginal cost and showed that states with compulsory attendance laws had higher investments in education than those that did not. But they found that such levels had been achieved before the laws were passed and thus merely formalized what was already fact.

5. It can be explained from a Marxian approach: "Schooling has served to perpetuate the hierarchical social relations of capitalist production. . . . Workers won schooling for their children, but by controlling decision making in education, . . . the ruling class maintained the social relations of production while ameliorating conditions and dampening conflict" (pp. 383–384).

Tyack examines the fit of each of these explanations to the facts, noting discrepancies. He ends with this: "One of my purposes in this essay has been to extend the boundaries of discussion about the history of American education . . . much of the recent work in the field—my own included—has used causal models too implicitly. . . . Entertaining explicit alternative models and probing their value assumptions may help historians to gain a more complex and accurate perception of the past and a greater awareness of the ambiguous relationships between outcome and intent—both of the actors in history and of the historians who attempt to re-create their lives" (p. 389)—clearly a statement of a multiperspectivist point of view.

The Humanist

The humanist believes that causation is so complex, each event being the result of a nearly unique pattern of causative factors, that rules and principles will not provide adequate explanations. One must personally find the parallels between patterns of events, the coming together of certain factors and forces that help to explain past occurrences, that inform one's view of the world. Through the study of enough such accounts—some of which may be personal, some group or institutional, and some even fictional—one learns to recognize patterns that help one adjust behavior successfully to meet future events. The humanist is seeking the nature of such accounts as have the power to usefully instruct and the models of literary, personal, and historical accounts that most completely embody that nature.

Presumably, timeless literature has successfully found these models; certainly much literature consciously attempts this goal. Prescott (1982, p. 77) noted a current attempt in his eulogy to John Cheever: "He observed and gave voice to the inarticulate agonies that lie just beneath the surface of ordinary lives. . . . In 'The Bus to St. James' a man watches his daughter in dancing school: '. . . It struck him that he and the company that crowded around him . . . were bewildered and confused in principle, too selfish or too unlucky to abide by the forms that guarantee the permanence of a society, as their fathers and mothers had done. Instead, they put the burden of order onto their children and fill their days with specious rites and ceremonies.' "

The humanist still further disassociates explanation from prediction, being content to explain a given event or historical movement as completely as possible. Humanist studies may be historical or may be descriptions and explanations of current phenomena, such as White's *Making of the President* (1961, 1965, 1973).

Rather than laws, rules, and principles of a physicslike behavioral science, the humanist helps us build "cognitive maps" so we can recognize parallel situations when we encounter them. For example, President John F. Kennedy is said to have read Barbara Tuchman's *Guns of August* just before the Cuban missile crisis. In it Tuchman describes how Germany's generals in World War I persisted in their preconceptions of situations even in the face of contrary evidence. Kennedy saw a parallel to Khrushchev's handling of the missile crisis and modified his behavior accordingly.

Many historical accounts are examples of humanist writing; as just noted, Tuchman (1962) and White (1961, 1965, 1973) are examples. The line between the synthesizer and the humanist traditions is a fine one but is basically determined by whether the author has adopted the physical science model, seeing the behavioral sciences as consisting of generalizations that he is trying to explicate and illustrate, or whether he resists this model and prefers to explain a situation and let the readers make the inferences for their own cognitive and affective maps and lives.

In classifying writing as an example of one orientation or another, one is, of course, making inferences about the author's view of the world and his intent, items that only the author himself could confirm. Judging from only the writing itself, many historical pieces—Spengler (1926) and Toynbee (1948), for instance—may be difficult to classify. One could imagine that cases could be made for their being synthesizer, theorist, or humanist writing. That, of course, isn't the point, however; the point is that some authors have a humanist orientation to the world and being aware of that helps us to recognize them and to appreciate what such individuals are seeking to accomplish.

The Particularist

For the particularist, the useful organization of the events of the world is a personal phenomenon, unique to each individual. The world is certainly not clocklike; possibly it even has different cloud patterns at different times and places for different people. The particularist assumes that each person must discover those patterns that work for her. Much of the grist for that discovery comes from personal experience and intuition but some from vicarious experiences described by others. Because it is a personal pattern, esthetic criteria are applicable in some cases as well as more cognitively oriented criteria.

The researcher working from a particularist orientation learns from the subject, and in turn the subject learns from the researcher, but this information instructs the individuals involved rather than builds a science.

A position very close to the particularist is that of action research as described by Zwier and Vaughan (1984); they note that it is also called "participatory," "endogenous," or "dialectical" research with slight changes in emphasis. Action research assumes that researchers are active participants in the situations researched rather than passive observers. The relationship of the observer to the situation deserves study, and the situation is seen as changing during the research; indeed, the researcher often introduces social knowledge into the situation to test its effect. The knowledge acquired is seen as specific to the particular constellation in which it was generated rather than generalizable. The social scientist is seen not as objective but as learning from those in the situation and as making them part of it by helping them to learn along with him. Examples of this research in Reason and Rowan (1981) involve voluntary desegregation programs, prison environments, and banking systems, the main benefits accruing to the subjects participating in the research—very similar to the particularist position.

The particularist contributes little to science except to suggest possible leads, stimulating those of other orientations to consider an idea.

One might expect that there would be no published examples of particularists' writing, since they do not contribute substantively to behavioral science. But a section of a recent publication, Reason and Rowan (1981), gave examples of the particularist in action. One chapter, Torbert (1981), described the evaluation of the process of voluntary desegregation in Boston. The evaluators are clearly products of mainstream orientations, but as a particularist would, they strongly emphasize the involvement and participation of their clients as well as the mutual learning that comes from such participation. These values caused them to reflect on their process as well as that of the behavioral sciences. The flavor of their efforts to combine a more traditional with a particularist outlook can be sensed in this final paragraph:

> Thus, from the point of view of an action research design, in which data collected on any given round of research are tested for empirical validity, political useful-ness, and existential illuminatingness by feeding them back to the participants themselves, analytical validity is not the only, nor the final, criterion of truth. A political criterion of validity—does this information help me to act more effectively in given situations? and an ontolog-ical criterion of validity—does this information help me to experience more directly my-real-situation-in-the-world?—complement the analytical criterion of valid-ity—is this information internally consistent and exter-nally replicable? Western science has until the present time concentrated its attention solely on developing increasingly elegant analytical tests of validity. As a result, analytical criteria and explicit validity testing of all three types remain relatively primitive and rare in most people's lives and in most social settings (including the conduct of social science itself) [p. 346].

Rather than moving all the way into the particularist's corner, these authors think it important to add the particularist point of view to conventional ones—an interesting possibility. To do so would increase self-perception of one's place in the methodological scheme of things, also a goal of this book. It would cause one to evaluate the worth of one's work on a quite different scale of values from those conventionally emphasized.

Summary Chart and Examples of the Types

Table 2 summarizes the characteristics of the seven types, one to a column. Descriptions of the characteristics of each type are organized in rows to highlight similarities and differences in (1) their guiding principles, (2) what they believe is the nature of behavioral science knowledge, (3) the criteria of good work, (4) their preferred research method, (5) some suggestive stereotypes, (6) the role of values, (7) strengths, and (8) weaknesses. The suggestive stereotypes in the fifth row may help or hinder; they are intended to bring images to mind. Because stereotyping is always controversial, I am taking the chance that they help more than hinder.

Table 2 goes considerably beyond the text in detailing the characteristics of each type and presenting them in a form that facilitates between-type comparisons. Read down the columns to get a renewed sense of each type and then across the rows to note differences.

Comparisons of the Types on Important Research Decisions

Choice of Research Problem

Researchers typically view problems through two screens: (1) their subject matter orientation and (2) their typology orientation. The first suggests what in the problem to focus on, the second the approach to studying it. Consider how an analyzer psychologist and a synthesizer sociologist might study professional/parent interaction in an intensive care facility for newborn infants. The analyzer psychologist might focus on the personality characteristics and typical social response tendencies of staff and parents and hypothesize how and where these mesh or clash. She might then set up experimental situations that should minimize clashes and maximize meshings and see whether they do.

The synthesizer sociologist might act as a participant observer of the social communication of staff and parents and, from these data,

Table 2. A Typology of Orientations to Behavioral Science Knowledge and Methods.

	Pragmatist	Analyzer	Synthesizer	Theorizer	Multiperspectivist	Humanist	Particularist
Row 1 Guiding principle	Produce an instrument, rule, principle, and so on that will usefully predict.	Test propositions and, through testing, confirm them.	Produce an explanation embodying the essential characteristics of a phenomenon.	Produce theory to explain phenomena.	Produce explanations of phenomena from different perspectives—for example, political, economic aspects.	Find the most powerful images and models that foster human understanding.	Emphasize importance and uniqueness of person or organization; help them know selves and achieve self-determination.
Row 2 Nature of behavioral science knowledge	Impersonal, that which empirically predicts.	Impersonal; the consensus of a scientific community where individuals with relevant competencies monitor work of peers and pass their approval or disapproval to those less qualified to judge.				Largely personal, provides understanding to self and culture in terms of conceptual patterns and schemes that have value in guiding future behavior.	Personal, provides self-understanding as unique person or group; science often less useful than older ways of knowing (art, poetry, mysticism, and so on).

Row 3 Criteria of excellence	Predictions replicate on new samples.	Solid theory or rationale produces strongest possible prediction confirmed by data. Alternative explanations eliminated. Narrowing problems for control.	Production of an accurate description of phenomenon and, if possible, an explanation of its essential characteristics. Production of theory grounded on data. Holistic view.	Production of a theory or framework that explains a phenomenon. Logically internally consistent, convincing examples.	Choice of approaches that significantly contribute to understanding.	Explanation that mediates well between the world and persons. Provides useful models and examples of analysis.	Personal growth of person or organization; may also be esthetically pleasing.
Row 4 Preferred research method	Quantitative data involving statistical prediction techniques; usual forms of correlation.	Quantitative data and as close to good experimental design as one can get.	Qualitative data, verbal descriptions, case studies, enthnography, participant observation.	Very careful observation of few cases. Often cases chosen for special characteristics and sometimes placed in special circumstances.		Gathering of personal accounts that will stir minds, hearts, and souls and bring new insights.	Sharing of personal experiences and knowledge by subject and researcher. Action research.
Row 5 Stereotypes helpful in visualizing types but likely to be controversial	Developers of instruments like the MMPI and Strong-Campbell; some personnel psychologists, some economists.	Most quantitatively oriented psychologists and sociologists, many economists.	Most sociologists and anthropologists and many historians.	Famous theorists of behavioral science like Freud, Parsons, Piaget, Skinner.	Allison (see examples in text), possibly Marshall McLuhan. Well-known persons in behavioral science are rare but Bronowski, Sagan, Asimov in natural sciences.	Many historians, some ethnographers, many clinicians, literary critics.	Some clinicians, people reacting against the dehumanizing of persons by science.

Table 2. A Typology of Orientations to Behavioral Science Knowledge and Methods, Cont'd.

	Pragmatist	Analyzer	Synthesizer	Theorizer	Multiperspectivist	Humanist	Particularist
Row 6 Role of values	Research is nonpartisan, sees self as value-free.		Researcher tries to control possible value positions but describes personal bias to reader to allow judgment of its possible effect.	Can be either like analyzer or like synthesizer.	Value differences may highlight different aspects of a phenomenon and so may be sought, but their presence is made explicit.	Values are an integral part of knowledge; they help give it meaning and serve as motivators.	
Row 7 Strengths	Starts new fields where little understanding exists; trial-and-error approach serendipitously produces leads, which can then be studied to gain explanations; empirical keying of measuring instruments often yields most accurate predictions.	Tests and confirms propositions; experimentation is the strongest and most convincing method for demonstrating relationships.	Locates "heart" of phenomena; theory has close correspondence to data; provides theory and propositions for analyst to confirm.	Explains important phenomena in ways that, in hindsight, fit conventional wisdom; usually very convincing, especially in use of examples.	Reflects the complexity of reality; contrasting viewpoints provide breadth and depth of view.	Emphasizes the personal, human, and historical as a repertoire from which to draw; source of ideas for scientific validation; an answer where laws and theories fail.	Knowledge is highly useful to person or organization; source of ideas for scientific validation.

Row 8

Weaknesses						
Requires ability to handle statistics; does not supply understanding and explanations; some items counterintuitive, others may be without any apparent logical basis for predicting.	Requires ability to handle statistics; narrowing of problems may reduce significance; hard to do "tight" validation and show wide generality at same time; not all important phenomena are measurable.	Requires ability to integrate masses of data and find patterns; biases of observer a potential problem; requires separate validation step for theories and propositions.	Typically not grounded in demonstrations of any size or representativeness; leaves validation to others; boundary conditions within which theory holds are rarely set forth, must be found.	Requires breadth of skill and training; heavy conceptual load; relative importance of contrasting points of view requires synthesis.	Contributes little to consensual knowledge; requires conceptual grasp of large amounts of material to select relevant portions to weave into integrated story.	Little generality, each person and institution must make the "trek" anew.

establish types or roles each has created in its perception of the other. He might use these with examples to explain how parents and professionals interact and why. In each instance the researchers have focused on the part of the problem to which prior training has sensitized them and then applied the research procedure that their training suggested would typically be applicable.

Some researchers' work is narrowed by these two screens to a single research method and a strictly held orientation. Some even have a single-minded missionary zeal about the "rightness" and power of their approach. Other researchers work at avoiding being constrained by the screens. Each has its advantages. Those with a single orientation have the advantage of focusing their attention so they develop methodological excellence, but they may not have the broad perspective on problems that those not constrained to one orientation have. The latter may deem unimportant aspects important to those of one persuasion. Further, with less practice in any one method, they may have less methodological expertise. Many persons, probably most of them, try to work between these extremes.

Along the same lines, some problems have greater appeal than others for a given orientation because of the special suitability of a preferred method. Problems with few clues to their solution have greater appeal to the synthesizer than to the analyzer, who prefers to work from a hypothesis. Similarly, field-oriented problems appeal more to synthesizers than to analyzers.

In professional fields where methodological socialization is less strong, some individuals are eclectic in both orientation and method and flexibly adopt the role that the problem seems to require. Many persons in each field are mixtures rather than examples of pure types; to them, this flexibility comes easily and naturally. Where acculturation to method is strong, however, or method requirements are difficult, as in statistics, such eclecticism is reduced.

Criteria of Excellence

The variation in characteristics of excellence (see Table 2, row 3) is one of the most striking contrasts among the types. Note the differences, reading across from pragmatist to particularist: being able to predict and control; well-controlled, though possibly narrow, experimental studies that are very satisfying demonstrations that a relationship exists; production of theory that is grounded in observations and captures the holistic characteristics of a phenomenon; developing a theoretical approach to a problem supported by very persuasive and compelling examples; application of a variety of perspectives to a single problem; stories that mediate well between reality and the person; personal growth and meaning. That is quite a spectrum.

More detailed analyses of the types and the criteria of good research discussed in previous chapters are undertaken in Chapter Eight, but with such a range of "hallmarks of excellence," one can already see that the seeds for communication problems and even conflict among persons of differing orientations are sown. Increasing the chance of conflict is the smoldering resentment of some persons in orientations further from the natural science model; the often greater acceptance of work close to that model results in an implied lesser status for theirs.

Choice of Research Method

As noted, for each type there is a preferred method or technique of research that fits that orientation's view of what is important and what kind of knowledge one seeks. These are described in the fourth row of Table 2, and the matches of orientation to method appear to make good intuitive sense. What has not been made clear, however, is that types are not limited to preferred methods. Indeed, each type often uses a variety of methods, but it uses them differently.

Consider, for example, questionnaire technique. A pragmatist would likely convert questionnaire responses into a single score, weighting the questions according to their predictive value. The analyzer might either convert them to a single score or examine them item by item to determine their relation to a proposition or theory. The synthesizer might use the questions as a basis for observations or possibly an interview. For the humanist and particularist, the questions might provide a basis for mutual exploration in a discussion between researcher and subject.

We have come to think of method as a prime descriptor of behavioral scientists, but the research type or orientation, by describing how a given method is used, may provide a more comprehensive descriptive label for use in differentiating among behavioral scientists.

Strengths and Weaknesses of the Types

Strengths and weaknesses are described in rows 7 and 8 of Table 2. I shall comment on each of the types in turn.

Pragmatist. Pragmatists' research is important because whatever predicts also has potential for control. Control can be used to remedy a situation, avoid a problem, or select an option with greater payoff. These benefits can all be important to our daily lives. The weakness of the viewpoint is that, without an explanation, showing that something works in a situation may not be strong enough evidence to build the consensus needed to be accepted as knowledge. For example, we don't know why achievement is greater when the teacher calls in turn on each child in a small group of children arranged in a reading circle than when he calls on them randomly, but research evidence indicates that it is (Anderson, Evertson, and Brophy, 1979). That finding is counterintuitive. It seems as though children would learn more if they tried to be ready just in case they were called on rather than getting ready only for their own predictable turn. Yet, the finding can be used to increase reading achievement. The weakness of pragmatic research is illustrated by the questions that pass through people's minds about this finding. Is it really true? Without an adequate explanation it leaves one questioning.

Consider another example that demonstrates this weakness. The Adjutant General's Office developed a Biographical Inventory Blank after World War II that weakly predicted which officers would be ranked high by fellow officers. But there was no way of logically justifying the scoring of many individual items, such as that the best officers came from small towns and from large families. Why should they? If such an instrument were being used to select officers, as an only child from Chicago, I might strongly object to the employment of an instrument that so arbitrarily penalized me.

Since one is always more certain if one knows why and how something works, the pragmatist's results are often not an adequate demonstration to build the needed consensus. There is always the concern that although it has worked in the past or in the instance when the research was done, it might not in another instance. If one knew how it worked, one could better predict instances in which it might succeed or fail.

Analyzer. In our culture that reveres science, analyzers, who typically do experimental research, are generally considered to be in the strongest position to command the consensus needed for acceptance as knowledge. This is one reason that analyzers find confirming ideas generated by others rewarding; as they confirm them, the ideas gain the most complete general acceptance. With satisfying explanations, unbiased and representative samples, confirmed predictions, and the elimination of alternative, otherwise reasonable explanations, the studies provide strong confirmatory evidence. Or—when negative evidence appears—they raise strong doubts.

When analyzers "narrow" and "clean up" a problem to adequately control for other explanations, however, it can be argued that they change the problem, a definite weakness. They are more likely to dissect and work on parts of a problem than on a problem with all its holistic interrelationships, for they prefer controlled situations rather than naturalistic but uncontrolled fieldwork.

To be an analyzer or pragmatist, one must have some measure of mathematical skill to master the increasingly complex and sophisticated statistical techniques their methods use. These are not everyone's "cup of tea."

Synthesizer. Synthesizers are oriented to holistic approaches and to discovery of the key variables in the larger picture. Whereas analyzers are interested in finding the strongest variables too, they are more likely to leave determination of that role to statistics. Where analyzers typically look for a consistent role across situations, synthesizers typically use careful observation to determine the role of a variable in actual situations (remember the example of the teacher interacting with students to hold their attention when they are fresh as opposed to when they are tired). The methods lend themselves well to exploring phenomena and discovering new approaches. Data analysis and reduction of data to generalizations are serious problems for the synthesizer. Not everyone is able to integrate a mass of detail into holistic pictures and discern the patterns that identify the determiners of significant actions. Some gather mountains of data and then are unable to complete the task, a heartbreaking experience for all concerned.

Potential observer bias is a persistent problem. The synthesizer's confirmatory evidence is like that of the theorizer, the selection of compelling examples rather than data based on random and representative samples. On occasion this may be enough for acceptance of a knowledge claim, especially when it is backed by a strong explanation or rationale. More often, however, it must undergo a separate confirmation test before it gains general acceptance.

Theorizer. Theorizers have the considerable advantage of being able to propose very believable explanations. These are often sweeping generalizations with important implications, so theorizers potentially have considerable impact. In fact, of all the orientations, they are the most likely to have persuasive effect. They find the simple, powerful explanations that seem to basically underlie phenomena.

But their empirical evidence is usually limited to their examples. They rarely delineate the boundary conditions within which a generalization holds and beyond which it must be modified or abandoned. To do so complicates their explanations, reducing their impact. One of the real concerns about theorizers is that they often oversimplify reality. Indeed, their sweeping statements often considerably annoy analyzers, who, as a result, challenge the claims, try to validate them, and, in the process, limit and modify them.

Multiperspectivist. Multiperspectivists have both the strengths and weaknesses of the theorizers but have the additional strength of illuminating multiple facets of a complex situation or phenomenon. Like the synthesizer and analyzer, the multiperspectivist requires special skills. First, one must be able to master several subject matters well enough to be able to apply them. Second, one must have the breadth of vision to be able to keep the different perspectives separate and yet integrate them in relation to the facts of a phenomenon. This requires a considerable intellectual and conceptual grasp.

Humanist. Humanists must have considerable conceptual capability as well, since to see patterns and parallels is often difficult and requires the ability to abstract generalizations and ignore the mass of detail in extensive descriptive data. They formulate the accounts and stories that are most likely to lead to good internal cognitive maps of how the world works, a most difficult task. Where they are successful, this kind of map considerably exceeds the explanatory and the predictive power of simple propositions and sometimes of theories.

Humanist accounts draw attention to the situational aspects of behavior that so often are determining factors but are very difficult to describe in sufficiently general terms that they can be added as boundary conditions to generalizations. To do so would make the theories as complex as the humanists' stories, so the simplifying advantage of theory would be lost.

Particularist. Particularists reject claims of generality of knowledge about people. Each person is unique, and laws about behavior threaten that uniqueness. One cannot build a behavioral science with such beliefs.

As the particularist knows, nothing is so useful as knowledge that one has ferreted out for oneself, that has been intuitively built out of one's own experience. It usually comes more readily to mind than that which has been learned vicariously. For others, however, such knowledge has value mainly in what it suggests for further investigation or in what can be built into an explanation or theory.

Particularists believe researchers of other orientations often must play the role of satisfying others rather than themselves. Particularists feel that they are "truer to themselves." To some extent this is true. Cast over all orientations is the shadow of the natural sciences. Insofar as research does not meet the criteria and norms of the natural sciences, regardless of whether these are applicable, some will perceive the work as less than satisfactory. Particularists, some humanists, and others perceive their peers to have been inappropriately swayed to use statistics and experimental methods by this pressure.

An Overall Comment. Clearly greater understanding of the orientations should lead to greater tolerance of positions other than one's own as well as to greater appreciation of each orientation's strengths as well as weaknesses. The latter are more often emphasized. It is worth repeating that, except for the particularist, all these orientations are valid contributors to research. For an example of a similar effort to show different approaches to the social sciences and their potential, see Morgan (1983b).

What is more, the behavioral sciences have benefited from this variety; no one of them has so far demonstrated that it is the sole source of significant knowledge. We need all the orientations; each has its advantages. We should educate audiences about the strengths and contributions of all the behavioral science orientations and about the problems created by insistence on applying natural science criteria to the behavioral sciences.

Dimensions Underlying the Types

Although the types may be considered on a continuum, they are best portrayed arrayed around a broken circle as in Figure 15. Underlying the continuum and helping to define it are the dimensions noted: (1) emphasis on prediction, an orientation toward data vers emphasis on explanation, and an orientation toward higher-level abstractions and (2) action orientation versus theory building and knowledge orientation. The particularist and pragmatist ends of the continuum are related to concrete applied knowledge—applications that guide behavior. The middle positions, by contrast, are more closely related to abstract descriptions and explanations of phenomena.

Note that as one moves from pragmatist around to humanist, phenomena are perceived as more complex. The pragmatist deals with a straightforward equation, a score that predicts a criterion or a procedure that works. The analyzer typically includes an explanation or theory as a part of the study or perhaps a prediction embodied in a hypothesis or question. The analyzer may deal with either simplified problems or sections of problems that are amenable to carefully controlled research. The synthesizer is more likely to deal with problems holistically, looking for the significant variables in the larger context. The theorizer's view is an aberration in the pattern, since her theory may be no more complex than the positions advanced by the analyzer or synthesizer. But the multiperspectivist, bringing to bear multiple viewpoints each with something to contribute, is clearly

Figure 15. Dimensions Underlying the Types.

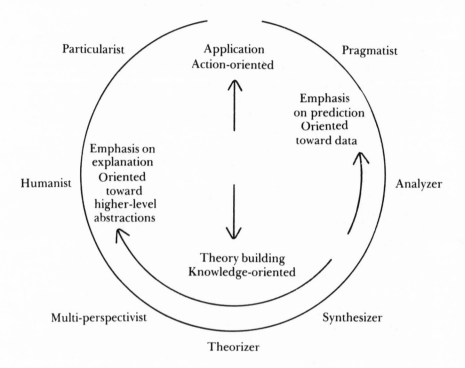

seeing a more complex view. And the humanist, who sees so much unique in each set of events that it cannot be understood by general rules and principles, views the world as still more complex. The particularist, for whom knowledge is unique for each person, has the most complex view of all, so complex it is difficult even to reduce it to the common patterns of the humanist. So the types from the right around the circle to the left seem to view the world as more complex and differentiated.

As positions closer to the humanist end of the continuum are adopted or become dominant, a science composed of simple generalizations and principles, the natural sciences model, becomes increasingly difficult to attain but also less attractive.

Emphasis on prediction yields to explanation as one goes clockwise around the types in Figure 15. The pragmatist totally emphasizes prediction. Explanation is closely associated with prediction for the analyzer, and the predictions of a hypothesis or theory are demonstrated as confirmed or disconfirmed by the theorizer's studies. Synthesizers and those to their left are content to explain; if prediction seems possible, that is an added plus. Explanation and prediction are disassociated for the humanist. Historians, for example, clearly realize this; they may be able to explain what happened in a particular battle, a series of battles, or even a war. But that does not mean they can predict the next battle or a new war.

As Scriven (1980) notes, an explanatory pattern is open-ended— it can be implemented in many ways that are impossible to predict. Scriven uses the example of coroners not being able to predict that a person fifty pounds overweight would die of a heart attack if he ran up fifty stairs. "But they can nevertheless be sure of that exertion as the cause of death after an autopsy . . . the fit can be made *exact* when the events fall into place. Explanations are possible where predictions are not" (p. 18).

For an example closer to the behavioral sciences, consider human development. We have many examples of stages of development—infant, child, adolescent, youth—and several psychological accounts of stages (for example, Erikson, 1950). Gergen (1980, pp. 34-35) makes the same point as Scriven in his description of the aleatoric account of development, one that calls attention to the flexibility of the developmental pattern: "From this perspective, existing patterns appear potentially evanescent, the unstable result of the peculiar juxtaposition of contemporary historical events. For any individual the life course seems fundamentally open-ended. Even with full knowledge of the individual's past experience, one can render little more than a probabilistic account of the broad contours of future development."

How Types Are Perpetuated

The characteristics that determine one's orientation or type are partly brought to the acculturation process and are partly the result of it. The part brought to it results from the match of one's skills and values to those of the professionals already in the field, a match that attracted one to the field in the first place. As Roe's studies show (1953a), there are differences in capabilities and interests among scientists in different fields—indeed, even between the theoretically and the experimentally oriented in a single field. Preferred methods are, in part, a function of subject matter. Thus the psychologist's experimental skill would be of little use to an anthropologist trying to capture the essential characteristics of a primitive culture. Where experimental methods require precise measurements and statistical manipulation, anthropological ethnomethodology uses verbal narration. It is no surprise, therefore, to find eminent anthropologists with lower mathematical scores but higher verbal scores than psychologists (Roe, 1953b, p. 28).

One may speculate that many factors probably contribute to choice of orientation, only a few of which have been studied. Consider that synthesizers working in the field must, on the one hand, be socially oriented persons who can mix with and appreciate people and their differences. But on the other hand, as Gans (1968) puts it, to be good observers, they must be "psychologically on the margins of social situations and relations" (p. 304). "My hunch is that fieldwork attracts a person who, in Everett Hughes' words, 'is alienated from his own background, who is not entirely comfortable in his new roles, or is otherwise detached from his own society'" (p. 317).

An aura of detachment also exists among analyzers, who typically interpose instruments such as questionnaires or tests between themselves and their subjects. Are such researchers' needs for direct human contact less; are some perhaps even threatened by close human contact?

All professionals, to some extent, must accustom themselves to deferred reward, but there is immediate satisfaction for synthesizers as they are directly guided by the data and personally immersed in them. Analyzers must wait for their affective reward until the end of data analysis, when they learn whether the study was successful.

Since some orientations tend to be associated with certain fields of study, one's capabilities, predilections, interests, and values are all likely to influence the selection of a field and the socialization process that results. Students without appropriate skills either select themselves out to avoid failure, are counseled out by faculty members, or find themselves unable to find someone to serve as their adviser. Those remaining find that those with whom they work respond positively to their interests and values; a mutual attraction binds them cognitively and affectively.

These bonds are strengthened by the extensive socialization processes that accompany graduate training. Socialization takes place not only in course work but also in apprentice work on a research project. The many informal discussions among students and between faculty members and students are especially important in forming the affective undergirding of attitudes, values, and interests that develop and maintain the socialized role.

The socialization continues as the graduate student becomes "a member of the club" through joining a university faculty or some other work unit of like professionals. "In-service socialization" occurs through contacts with fellow workers both at the local level and in professional association affairs—at conventions, in various committees, in the promotions given for "good" work, in the models set by those successful, in professional association prizes and awards for outstanding research, and in the prestige of association officer positions.

Indeed, one might wonder why variation exists in a discipline at all were it not that competition also does. Everyone wants to succeed, and where success is defined as new knowledge, other orientations may be perceived as more successful routes, especially for certain problems. Competing graduate students and faculty members see advantages to differing from a discipline's modal training, and some break the pattern to exploit the potential of another orientation. Thus, although traditional modes dominate, one finds a variety of methodological orientations in any field.

Socialization is not always successful, however; individuals may appear to accept an orientation during graduate school and then change when they are on their own. Like adolescents who behave while under parental control, they may go to the opposite extreme when the controls are no longer enforceable. One professor, for example, was recruited into a university because he had graduated with superb recommendations from one of the best analyzer-oriented psychology learning research programs in the country. When given teaching responsibilities, he adopted a particularist stance that caused him to reject much of the work he had been engaged in. He eventually left his original field entirely for a clinical psychology position compatible with the particularist orientation. It was as though, in working through his independence from his graduate mentor, he had to go to an opposite orientation.

No doubt some failures of socialization occur because many graduate students experience reduced control of their fate at the time of entrance to graduate school. They typically go where the financial inducements are the highest and only later realize the nature of the commitment they have made. Many are able to live with their choice, but some are not and become resentful. Probably faculty members are more consciously aware of the prerequisites for a successful match than graduate students are. But their ability to predict who will be good partners in the match is far from perfect, and their breadth of choice of sufficiently capable potential students is often not sufficient for them to apply what they do know.

Team research is increasingly prevalent because of the different skill requirements, the problems of mastering more than one orientation, and the advantages of having different perspectives brought to bear on a problem (from the standpoint of subject matter as well as methodology). To facilitate team formation, research corporations have developed a "matrix type" organization. Individuals are employed in disciplinary departments that are responsible for recruiting the best personnel in a given field, and such personnel, in turn, have a disciplinary "home" with support from others with their point of view. The work, however, is done in interdisciplinary task forces chosen from appropriate departments as the problem dictates. This pattern combines the advantages of depth of specialization with the breadth of viewpoint that provides for exploration of the widest range of approaches. It is interesting, however, that this interdisciplinary structure provides for assignment of each member to a disciplinary "home" department through which in-service socialization persists.

An eminent sociologist in tribute to Everett C. Hughes noted that Hughes called attention to the difference between a learned society that welcomes contributions to knowledge regardless of the source and one that restricts its membership to those for whom it can vouch (Becker and others, 1968, p. ix). The latter is an example of the socialization process at work, and it contrasts with that ideal of science, the free marketplace of ideas, methods, and viewpoints. The pressures that make socialization important are apparent, but it is equally significant to keep some perspective on the trade-offs that result.

_____

Now that the whole framework has been discussed, readers may wish to again review the Introduction.

8

Ways Researchers
of Various Orientations
Emphasize Different Criteria

At the outset of the last chapter, Sarah, a doctoral student, was getting varied advice from different members of her committee, each representing a different typology orientation. Similarly, behavioral scientists brought together to advise the federal government or other clients about a problem or a research direction often markedly disagree. In fact, there is a saying, "The only point on which two behavioral scientists can agree is how deplorable is the work of a third." This may be too disparaging. But given the variety of research orientations and their implicit criteria of excellence, it seems likely that these underlying differences in orientation may often cause disagreements and disparagement of work done to fit the criteria of another orientation. Such discussions can be more productive if the basic differences among orientations are understood and the reasons for disagreements recognized. A much greater appreciation of alternative orientations can result as well.

Both the typology of research orientations described in the previous chapter and the criteria of a good study described in Chapters Three through Six take on new significance when they are examined in relation to each other. Audiences with dissimilar orientations differ on what they deem the most important criteria. In being socialized into an orientation, behavioral scientists incorporate value positions about what is good science and hence what is a good study. They bring these criteria to research both as the enacters and as the audience for it. As a result, a researcher must know the criteria his intended audience thinks is important. Accurately anticipating an audience's expectations regarding the criteria is critical in building a study that will have credibility with that audience.

Usually researchers are writing for their immediate peers, a group that typically has considerable influence on them. Since peers are usually of the same research orientation, there is little doubt about what they will consider the important criteria of excellent research, and that makes clear the hallmarks of excellence the study ought to achieve. The more homogeneous the audience's research orientations, the clearer the expectations of criteria. But even though the majority in a discipline may give allegiance to a particular orientation, one can find nearly every orientation represented in every discipline, sometimes in significant proportion. For that matter, many individuals within a discipline may be mixtures rather than pure types. So depending on the homogeneity of a discipline, one may be confronted with a heterogeneous audience even within a particular field of study.

When the audience is heterogeneous, the whole set of criteria comes into play. That, of course, makes for a more difficult set to satisfy, particularly when using certain research methods. For example, it is difficult to satisfy the conditions for generality with the small samples typical of field methods.

Knowing the relative importance of the criteria to each orientation also helps one to understand how orientations view one another and what each would consider the weakness in a research method that might be another's preferred one. Orientations with similar emphases are likely to view each other favorably. Orientations with different patterns are likely to view lack of emphasis on a criterion they deem important as a weakness of the other. Anyone with extensive contact with behavioral scientists knows they create stereotypes of one another. One basis for them can be recognized in the descriptions following this section.

Finally, the perception of the behavioral sciences by those in the physical and natural sciences is, in part at least, determined by which of these types is seen to form the foundation of behavioral science knowledge. To the extent that physical and natural scientists examine method, they are likely to have most confidence in the work of the analyzer and pragmatist, whose values are closest to theirs. To the extent that they see behavioral science knowledge as based on methods they value less, they are likely to be concerned about the quality of behavioral science research.

For all these reasons, we need to understand the importance that each orientation attaches to the different criteria. These patterns are portrayed visually, one orientation at a time, in Figures 16 through 21. Criteria in heavy lines are most important to the orientation portrayed; those in thin, solid lines, of intermediate importance; those in broken lines, of least importance. Readers should be aware, however, that although the figures are good shorthand ways of conveying the emphases of a given orientation, *there are a number of qualifications of the way boxes are coded, so that it is important to attend to the text as well as the figure to avoid getting the wrong impression.* This is particularly true of boxes shown in intermediate emphasis (solid thin lines). In many instances this coding is used to indicate that the emphasis depends on the study; it could be very heavily emphasized and a real strength or the opposite.

Probably no orientation has a corner on ethical problems. The electrical shocks of an experimenter, the jeopardy in which homosexuals were placed when they were studied by a field observer, the overgeneralization of data that led to theories or historical propositions that did not stand up under examination—all would be considered under some circumstances to be ethical misconduct. Ethical problems cut across types. So do resource and institutional constraint problems. Therefore resource limits and ethical and institutional constraints are not included in the following discussions or coded in the figures.

Comment on each figure may help to explain the judgments made about the perceived importance of a given criterion to an orientation.

The Pragmatist

Pragmatists are concerned with building instruments and models that permit one to predict and, therefore, to control. Their emphasis is on finding operations that work rather than on explaining why they work. For all other orientations, such explanations are very important, because understanding how the world works is what science is noted for.

It is easy to understand, therefore, that for the pragmatist, prime criteria in Figure 16 are "demonstrated relationship" and "internal validity (LP)." Within demonstrated relationship, the box "congruence of explanation and evidence," or what one might call "prediction congruence" is critical. When one can predict and show that the predictions are indeed congruent with the data, then one can predict and control the aim of the pragmatist.

Pragmatists, like most scientists, want their predictions to apply to groups other than those on which they are demonstrated.

Figure 16. The Pragmatist.

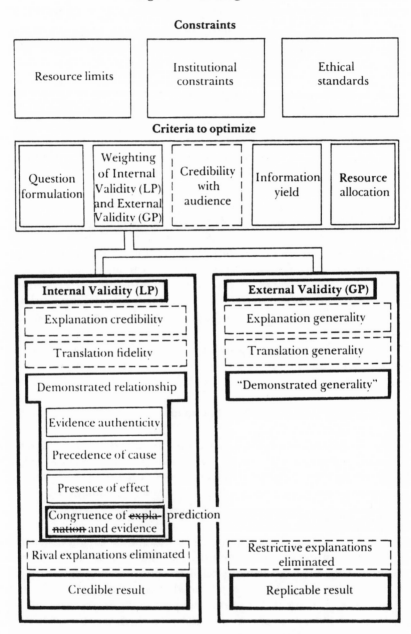

Therefore, knowing that the result is not a one-time thing, knowing that the study has external validity (GP), is also important. Consequently, the boxes for "external validity (GP)" as a whole and especially for "demonstrated generality" and for "replicable result" are heavily outlined in Figure 16.

Because the emphasis is on demonstrations rather than explanations, "explanation credibility" and "explanation generality" are deemphasized, and so, consequently, are "translation fidelity" and "translation generality." Similarly, the word *explanation* in "congruence of explanation and evidence" is changed to *prediction*. This does not mean that the pragmatist spurns explanations entirely; indeed, good ones are welcomed where they make the task of selling the procedure to others easier. But without a good explanation, audience credibility is likely to be low. Realizing this, pragmatists may use an explanation in order to get acceptance for what they consider a good procedure.

But they do not trust the explanation and do not consider it essential. Their emphasis on what works comes from a concern that explanations are too often incomplete, overly simplistic, or actually incorrect. They see numerous examples about them. For example, we know that drill and practice helps individuals to learn. But the old explanation that it strengthens a particular neural bond in the brain is no longer accepted, although for many years that was used as its justification. Pragmatists are quick to point out that drill and practice was the proper procedure—indeed, for some kinds of learning it is essential—but the explanation was wrong. Cognitive learning appears not to be localized in a single neural bond that can be strengthened. To the pragmatist, however, whether this explanation or some other version is correct makes little difference. The point is that drill and practice works.

Pragmatists will often promote a procedure without any explanation. For example, as noted in the last chapter, since the evidence indicates that the best army officers tend to come from small towns, a selection instrument would be so keyed. Such evidence may not be adequately plausible to others, who want to have some rationale before they would accept such a thing. So it seems reasonable to place "credibility with audience" in broken lines. Similarly, rival and restrictive explanations are of little interest.

The Analyzer

Analyzers, though concerned with demonstrations, as are pragmatists, give much greater importance to the fact that science is

Figure 17. The Analyzer.

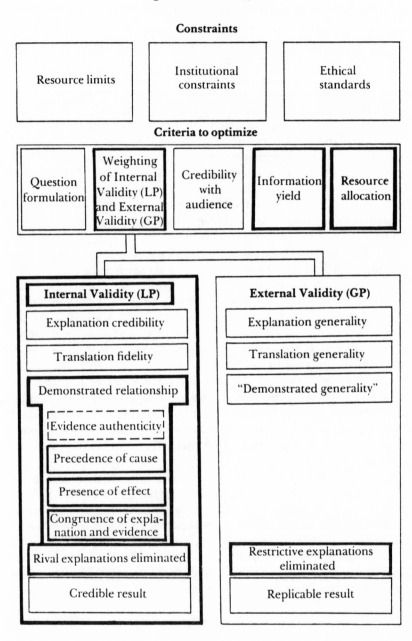

Constraints

| Resource limits | Institutional constraints | Ethical standards |

Criteria to optimize

| Question formulation | Weighting of Internal Validity (LP) and External Validity (GP) | Credibility with audience | Information yield | Resource allocation |

Internal Validity (LP)

Explanation credibility

Translation fidelity

Demonstrated relationship

Evidence authenticity

Precedence of cause

Presence of effect

Congruence of explanation and evidence

Rival explanations eliminated

Credible result

External Validity (GP)

Explanation generality

Translation generality

"Demonstrated generality"

Restrictive explanations eliminated

Replicable result

advanced by explanations and understanding. Prediction and control are still goals, but the understanding that leads to prediction is a major concern. Analyzers are noted for carefully planned, well-designed studies with tight controls that eliminate rival explanations. Because they are frequently involved in validating the hypotheses or guesses that flow from theory proposed by others, they emphasize the "internal validity (LP)" subset of criteria.

Many behavioral scientists perceive the experimental methods of the analyzer as the strongest of any for ensuring that an explanation is valid and that a proposed relationship exists. Therefore, in Figure 17, "internal validity (LP)" and within it "demonstrated relationship," "precedence of cause," "presence of effect," "congruence of explanation and evidence," and "rival explanations eliminated" are all heavily outlined. Analyzers are sensitive to the relative "weighting of internal validity (LP) and external validity (GP)" in designing a study, so this is also heavily outlined. Typically they believe that internal validity (LP) should be shown before one considers external validity (GP).

Analyzers are concerned with external validity (GP), but to the extent that the tight controls necessary for a clean study are not possible in a natural setting, they prefer the clean study. Therefore an intermediate emphasis is given to external validity (GP) and its parts. When external validity (GP) is an important goal of a study, however, the careful design intended to "eliminate restrictive explanations" is an important criterion and a strength of such studies, so that box is heavily outlined.

To the extent that controls do not detract from the believability and naturalness of a demonstration, analyzers can build high credibility with an audience. Because controls do sometimes detract, especially when the study is moved into a laboratory to achieve tight control, audience credibility depends on the study and consequently, like external validity (GP), is shown with halfway emphasis even though for many this is the most satisfying method of demonstrating a relationship.

The possibility of carefully planning a study makes for efficient "resource allocation" and hence also high "information yield" in most instances. So these are heavily outlined.

The desire for careful design and tight controls often results in a change in the question to be studied. So for many who see analyzers as cutting the question to fit the method, "question formulation" is a weakness. Countering this, however, is the iterative reformulation that leads to better understanding of the question that results from developing the design. This increases the emphasis on question formulation. Question formulation is therefore given middle emphasis.

The Synthesizer

As we move through the orientations, they more and more emphasize explanations and are less concerned with prediction. This is true of synthesizers, who seek especially accurate descriptions of situations and explanations of what is going on in them. They are thus very interested in ensuring that the problem is properly formulated. They like to build a base for their theory building in the data and to construct what they call grounded theory from it. More often than not, they try to take the same perception of the situation being studied as its participants take. Through immersing themselves in the situation, through interview, or through observation, they try to find out how the participants perceive it.

Relating the participants' view of the situation to their actions emphasizes the internal validity (LP) aspects of the study and provides a basis for understanding the behavior. In Figure 18 "internal validity (LP)" and "explanation credibility" are therefore shown as important criteria. Since the explanation is grounded in the data, there is little problem with "translation fidelity"; data and explanation use the same terms. These are therefore heavily outlined.

Judging the weight to give "demonstrated relationship" is difficult because it varies so much from study to study. Ideally relationships are verified several ways in a study, and indeed, sometimes they are. Where relationships are identified before the investigator leaves the field, additional data can be gathered to verify them. But when, as often happens, the data are not analyzed until after the investigator leaves the field, then in the limited data already gathered the situations required for validation may not have been recorded. So one cannot say that "demonstrated relationships" are either emphasized or deemphasized; it depends on the study—hence the intermediate-width line.

As a result of the lack of controls that naturally accompanies work in the field, rival explanations can often be raised to account for the phenomenon. Hence this weakness of the method is surrounded by broken lines. There is usually little basis for comparing the study with previous ones, so "credible result" is also shown in broken lines. But where the situation or group under study has been the subject of several studies, as is true of some primitive cultures and some organizational situations, credible result can be quite strong.

Figure 18. The Synthesizer.

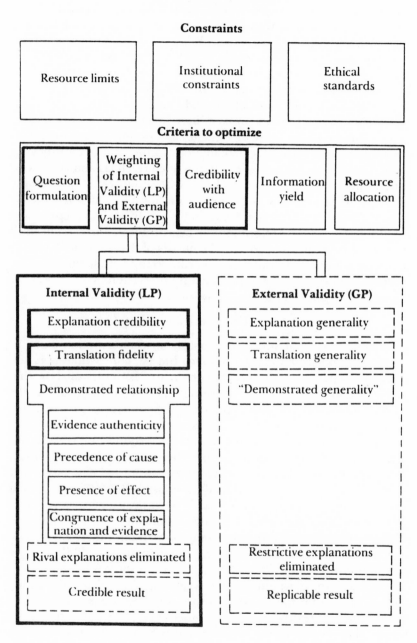

Because it is difficult to generalize from the limited data that can be gathered in a single-site field study, "external validity (GP)" as a set of criteria is placed in broken lines. One is never sure whether the group one is studying is unique. What generality there is, is carried by explanation. Often explanations do have this kind of generality— we see them as applying to our own experiences. But this situation can be uncomfortably similar to the plight of the youngster who reads the symptoms section of a medical text and imagines himself possessed of all kinds of serious diseases. Broken lines, therefore, seem appropriate.

The synthesizer's use of vignettes and examples is a strength of the method. They bring the explanations to life, and credibility with the audience is high. Synthesizer studies often reach lay audiences with little if any modification. "Credibility with audience" is accordingly heavily outlined. So also is problem formulation, which is typically solidly elicited from the data. Field studies are difficult to preplan, and it follows that resource allocation can be a problem. Further, one must save enough resources to analyze the masses of data collected, so some planning is important. But planning can occur in studies using interviews or passive rather than participant observation. Thus, "resource allocation" is placed in intermediate lines.

The Theorizer

Theorizers put still less emphasis on demonstration and still more on explanation than synthesizers. Indeed, both synthesizers and theorizers depend heavily on very convincing examples to show that the explanation is tied to reality. But there is a difference in the foundations underlying the explanations. Synthesizers base their explanations on extensive data and typically have a number of instances to draw on. Some synthesizers use frequency counts and correlations to present their data, techniques more often associated with analyzers.

By contrast, theorizers usually have no formal data base. Very acute observers, they have compiled the relationship from current and past experiences and, in that process, have collected persuasive examples. Often the same examples are used repeatedly. Thus, in Figure 19, "demonstrated relationship" is deemphasized, but otherwise the emphasis on "internal validity (LP)," "explanation credibility," and "credibility with audience" is heavy, as it is for the synthesizer.

The two viewpoints differ with respect to external validity (GP), however, for the theorizer advances explanations that typically claim broad generality. But as with internal validity (LP), there is no formal data base to provide a firm demonstration. The claim is typically carried by the apparent generality of a very credible explanation and credible examples. Thus a heavy line has been put around

Figure 19. The Theorizer.

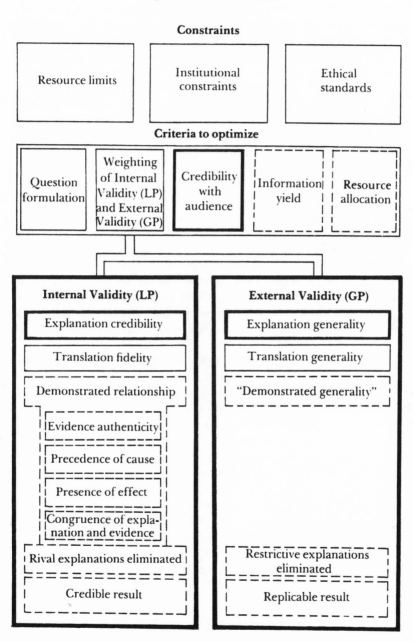

"external validity (GP)" and "explanation generality" for the theorizer because they are emphasized. Except for "translation generality,"
the other boxes are in broken lines because of the lack of a formal data
base.

"Translation fidelity" and "translation generality" are shown
with intermediate emphasis because they depend on the correspondence of explanation to reality. Translation fidelity and generality are
usually high, but in some instances, such as Piaget's notions of conser-
vation, there are questions about the way the explanation can be translated into situations, such as school curricula. Some see the translation
as very apparent, others as obscure and uncertain. It is not uncommon
for theorizers to use stipulative definitions; in this instance *conserva-
tion* is so defined. Such definitions reduce the user's ability to translate
the idea immediately into practice and slow the impact of theorizers'
work. This has probably been true in Piaget's case.

Question formulation is often quite important to theorizers.
Indeed, sometimes it is their new view of the problem that is the major
contribution. Further, proper formulation facilitates the presentation
of ideas. However, it seems not to have a special emphasis in all work
of theorizers. Therefore, it is shown with intermediate importance, but
it probably should be higher, somewhere between very important and
of intermediate value if the diagram judgments were more finely
coded.

Since there is typically little formal empirical study, "information yield" is deemphasized. Resource limits are rarely a problem. Few
theorizers are funded; except for universities, few funding agencies will
pay researchers to sit around and think. Primarily their own time is
involved, and that can be scheduled as appropriate. Therefore, "resource allocation" is also deemphasized.

As might be expected, analyzers and pragmatists in particular
see the lack of a formal data base as a weakness of this orientation;
perhaps as a consequence, many analyzers find their life's work
validating pronouncements of theorizers. For more than a decade after
Piaget proposed that cognitive development follows stages dependent
on the physical maturation process, analyzers were still doing studies
to determine the extent to which the stages were valid and how
susceptible they were to training and the environment. Thus, in the
diagram, all aspects of the criteria that have to do with demonstrations
are in broken lines.

The Multiperspectivist

As noted earlier, the multiperspectivists in many respects are
most like the theorizers. But most examples of multiperspectivist

Figure 20. The Multiperspectivist.

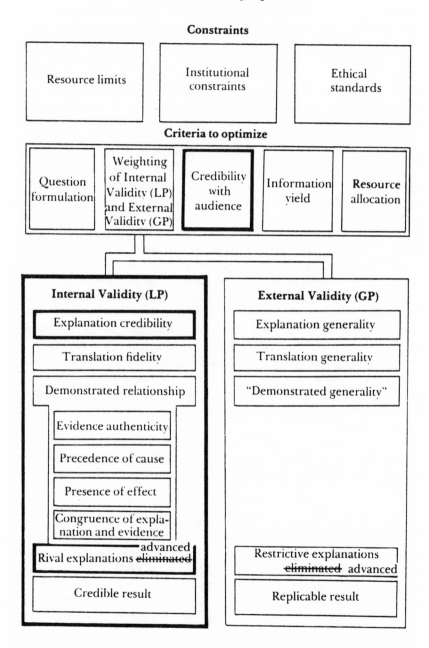

work, like Graham Allison's explanation of the Cuban missile crisis, explain a single event or set of circumstances and therefore are like the humanist's work. So multiperspectivists bear some resemblance to both theorizers and humanists. The emphasis on "internal validity (LP)" and "explanation credibility" is common to all three, as is that on "credibility with audience" (Figure 20). Multiperspectivists dealing with single events usually develop a data base to support the relationships described. But more ambitious efforts, as in David Tyack's "Ways of Seeing" (1976), examine evidence more cursorily and globally and, in their lack of a formal data base, are more like the theorizer's work. Alex Rosenberg recently pointed out to me that studies of the progress of developing nations are both data and generality oriented. Thus, the generality, or external validity (GP), claimed may be like that of the theorizer or that of the humanist. As a compromise, intermediate lines are used for "demonstrated relationship" and "demonstrated generality," indeed for all external validity (GP), in the diagram for the multiperspectivist.

A unique feature of the multiperspectivist is that rival explanations are sought rather than eliminated. The effort to explain the phenomenon from many viewpoints in order to further understand it calls for a heavy line around "rival explanations" in Figure 20. But note that it is modified to read "rival explanations advanced" rather than "eliminated." Indeed, in many instances, there is no effort to choose among the explanations or to completely integrate them. That, of course, is probably more a comment on the state of the behavioral sciences than a desirable state and is not necessarily characteristic of the orientation. Eventually multiperspectivists will seek integrated explanations.

"Question formulation," "information yield," and "resource allocation" are coded in intermediate status because their importance depends on the particular study and whether it is more like that of the humanist or the theorizer.

The Humanist

With the humanist's orientation, we come to the complete disassociation of explanation from prediction. The humanist sees the world as too complex for rules and principles. The humanist tries to explain an event as completely as possible, expecting thereby to enrich the vicarious experience of the audience. Through this experience the audience will come to have a more complete understanding of reality and of the interrelations of variables and events in it. Gradually the audience develops a cognitive map of what the world is like, a map

Figure 21. The Humanist.

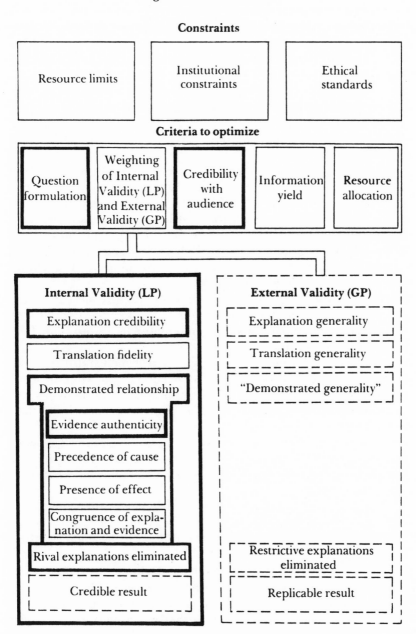

Constraints

Resource limits	Institutional constraints	Ethical standards

Criteria to optimize

Question formulation	Weighting of Internal Validity (LP) and External Validity (GP)	Credibility with audience	Information yield	Resource allocation

Internal Validity (LP)

Explanation credibility

Translation fidelity

Demonstrated relationship

Evidence authenticity

Precedence of cause

Presence of effect

Congruence of explanation and evidence

Rival explanations eliminated

Credible result

External Validity (GP)

Explanation generality

Translation generality

"Demonstrated generality"

Restrictive explanations eliminated

Replicable result

that helps guide one's behavior by helping one see (or merely intuit) relations between present and past experiences (real or vicarious). But, in contrast to the theorizer, we return to a more formal, data-oriented approach.

Since the humanist emphasizes the advancement of an explanation to account for a single event or set of events, "internal validity (LP)" is important, and "external validity (GP)" and its various parts are of little concern. This is shown in their treatment in Figure 21.

Within "internal validity (LP)," "explanation credibility" is very important, since this is the meat and potatoes of humanists' work, and so is heavily outlined.

"Translation fidelity" may or may not be a problem, depending on the availability of evidence. In the study of past events, the humanist is limited to the evidence left behind. That may be less than satisfactory, and often surrogate evidence must be used. For example, there may be some question whether the records of shipments on the Erie Canal are really a good measure of the harvest; accidents that drained part of the canal could affect a whole season of shipping. Translation fidelity is therefore in intermediate status.

Humanists more often deal with past than current events, so the matter of "evidence authenticity" becomes, for the first time, a factor of importance. Because of its special importance in historical method, it is ringed in heavy lines.

Although the various other aspects of demonstrated relationship—"precedence of cause," "presence of effect," and "congruence of explanation and evidence"—are not emphasized as for analyzers and synthesizers, they are all part of making the case and so have more than bottom-level importance.

Most humanists pride themselves on anticipating their audience's most likely alternative explanations of events and showing why they are not adequate. Therefore, "rival explanations eliminated" is given special emphasis.

Like the preceding three types, which gain high "explanation credibility" through apt use of illustrative events, the humanist also uses this advice and gains high credibility with the audience. It is heavily outlined.

Even more often than the theorizer, the humanist specializes in trying to look at events from a fresh perspective. Thus "question formulation" is especially important to this orientation.

The humanist is involved with data collection, in which although one can by no means know where all evidence is or how much will be found, usually some semblance of planning is possible. One of the special geniuses of the humanist is the ability to track down new and previously untapped data sources. Humanists have some of the same data reduction problems as synthesizers, so resource allocation takes on some importance. Thus "resource allocation" and "information yield," a form of resource allocation, are given intermediate importance.

The Particularist

These criteria are irrelevant to the particularist orientation. Particularists are not concerned with persuading others of the value of a knowledge claim but with finding knowledge claims that they themselves will accept. Each person develops her own criteria for knowledge and determines the consistency of their application. Since the process of criterion determination and application is covert, and there is no attempt to build commonality, it may be of considerable interest to the behavioral scientist as a field of study but does not contribute to this particular discussion.

Speculation: Is There a Progression Toward Orientational Maturity? An Ecological Succession of Types

Before we leave discussion of the types, it is worthwhile to consider whether there is a progression toward "orientational maturity" in the behavioral sciences comparable to "ecological maturity." Those who have studied forests describe the ecological succession of plants and trees that eventually results in a relatively stable condition, a "mature" forest. Thus lichens on rocks are followed by mosses that can hold onto the little soil that has begun to form. These yield to grasses and sedges. Coniferous trees are able to live where the grasses take hold, but they, in turn, give way to deciduous trees that crowd out and shade the conifers. Each stage produces the proper growing conditions for the next stage. In a sense, each stage is mature at the time it appears in that it pushes to the limits the possibilities permitted by the soil, shade, protection from the elements, and so on. But in time each yields to another stage of more complex, more efficient energy use as a given stage changes the ecology it started with.

Does science have an ecological progression as well? If so, what is a "mature science?" The closest models we have to such a state are the physical sciences, in which successive comparison of mathematical models, using data developed to test such models, seems to represent the epitome of method. Does mathematical modeling represent a mature state for the behavioral sciences, with its less-than-ideal measures, its complex phenomena, narrowly bounded and situation-specific generalizations, questionably stable variables, and possibly a large element of chance determinism? There is even an interaction between behavioral science knowledge and the areas studied. For example, principles of perception that contribute to sales by deceptive packaging are counteracted by unit pricing that defeats its effect.

From this chapter's analysis of different types of researchers, it is clear that natural science mathematical modeling approaches would be rejected by substantial numbers among any of the types except the analyzers and pragmatists. Yet, the modeling approach is being used to some extent in nearly every discipline. There are even historians who are statistically oriented, called cliometricians, after Clio, the muse of history. (But also resisted there—see Kousser, 1980, and Winkler, 1984.) What is going on?

Just as each species of plant, having the capacity to further exploit the situation it confronts, crowds out its predecessors in the fight for soil, sun, and water, so methods and orientations that promise to explain phenomena more fully and more precisely replace methods already in use. There seems to be an "ecological succession" of methods.

Further, the stages in a forest merge into one another and are not distinct; even in a forest of deciduous oaks and maples one may find some pine and spruce conifers. So, too, one finds a melange of methods as the succession progresses. The change comes in alternating emphases as new methods seem to succeed, then a shift back to old ones as progress slows and new breakthroughs are slow in coming. Consequently, in a given field one may find the entire continuum of methods used at one time or another, with work shifting from too sophisticated methods back to simpler ones as one finds the field not yet ready for that advance. Occasionally some investigators may shift all the way back to basic methods to find new roots from which to grow.

The desires of researchers to succeed, the drive of funders to get the greatest return for their investments, and the monitoring of both these parties by administrators, trustees, and the public, who wish to see resources allocated most effectively, mean that as the succession can take place, it will. In a "survival of the fittest" sense, a methodological Darwinism seems to be at work.

But it is much harder to predict the nature and the direction of methodological succession. It seems safe to say that there are certain types one could rule out as representing maturity of the behavioral sciences. The pragmatist orientation is fine for getting a field started, but even pragmatists agree that explanations are important to the acceptance of "operations that work." It seems unlikely that the synthesizer's position is a mature one, since ultimately the findings of the synthesizer must be validated and their generality tested. The analyzer orientation is much more effective in building a consensus around evidence for a proposition than the others. The particularist orientation does not lead to a behavioral science of common understanding, so one could eliminate it. The theorizer position seems subordinate in the long run to the multiperspectivist position, since increased understandings undoubtedly result from different perspectives. But the theories of the multiperspectivist need to be validated, and again the methods of the analyzer seem of value. The combination of analyzer and multiperspectivist is very close to the role of the modeler in the natural sciences. But the humanist position is left, as well.

Whether the modeling approach or the humanist position is more feasible in the long run depends, as noted earlier, on the nature of phenomena and on how one understands it. Scriven, a philosopher, argues, "Maturity, here, is the ability to stare a stochastic [chance] process in the eyes, to recognize randomness not as noise getting in the way of the signal but as a part of reality that will never be reduced to insignificance" (1980, p. 16). Scriven is probably right. Given the earlier-indicated interaction between gaining knowledge that permits control and its neutralization by those who do not wish to be controlled, there will always be an element of unpredictability. For example, if one could predict certain aspects of the economy with accuracy (the price of silver is going to rise), those predictions themselves would initiate actions that would falsify the predictions (silver producers hoping to make a killing increase production).

But even if one takes Scriven's inevitably cloudlike world as a given, that does not answer the question whether the randomness is so great as to drive us to patterns in cognitive maps, the humanist position. Nor does it tell us whether to abandon the search for general propositions and theories, the analyzer position. The inevitability of unpredictability suggests that we will continue to need humanist as well as analyst approaches. So perhaps even a mature behavioral science will have multiple orientations and methods.

If that sounds like where we came in, perhaps that is because it is. But it is hoped that the journey has not been in vain, that the reader has a sharpened appreciation for the complexities of the problem and for the different points of view on it, as well as a perspective that will contribute to more constructive and fruitful exchanges when behavioral science types disagree. Until it is much clearer that the ecological succession suggests one particular direction over another, we will need to maintain a multiplicity of orientations if we are to progress. It will probably be many years before we are in a position to posit a definite orientation preference, if ever. And even when we do, some will object because they feel that what they value is not given a proper place. In a sense the particularists play that role now. Their contribution to consensual behavioral science may not be great, but their position is a continual reminder that human subjects are not instrumental means to a *scientific end*—their fuller development and growth *is* the end.

9

Causal Explanation

Possible Complexities

I have emphasized the role of explanations in science and noted the important role of explanation credibility in building linking power. Many explanations depend on the concept of causation. When your car suddenly stops and the gas gauge needle points to empty, you quickly jump to a cause-and-effect conclusion: There was a lack of gasoline (cause), so your engine quit (effect). Such analyses are useful and familiar. Yet, the analysis of causation involves such complexities that some philosophers and some scientists, especially those who view the world as an interactive system, have suggested we would be better off without cause-and-effect analyses. The research community is not convinced and offers great resistance; cause and effect is too useful a conceptual model to abandon. As Nagel (1965) notes, even where the term has been abandoned, the idea has wide currency. It is pervasive in everyday speech as well as in the studies of academicians. Nagel concludes that "the idea of cause is not as outmoded in modern science as is sometimes alleged" (p. 12). Köbben (1973, p. 89) puts it even more strongly: "The notion of 'cause' is indispensable" and banning it "impoverishes our intellectual tool kit." Yet, philosophers are right about there being problems and complexities. If we are to continue using such analyses, the least we can do is understand their concerns.

This chapter examines some of these concerns and describes alternatives that ought to be considered when the simple "A causes B" model of causation seems inadequate. Philosophers have argued at length over the matter of causation; some of that discussion will be evident here. I can in no way do justice to that voluminous body of literature in the space provided for this treatment. I shall suggest some ideas that might be useful, exposing you to what appear to be some of the more common possibilities. This will be enough to open your mind to the topic, and you can search for more as needed.

Complexities of the Concept of Cause

Causal Histories

Let us return to our stalled-car example and ask whether the car's running out of gas was really the cause of the effect. Are there alternative views of the cause? One might consider that the real cause was my carelessness in not watching the gas gauge. Or it might be argued that the cause was my "muddle along" attitude toward life in general that addresses emergencies as they happen; a planned and careful approach would avoid them. Perhaps the real cause was parents who too little emphasized the preventive maintenance tasks of life and the necessity of planning time for them. Each is a step back toward a more basic cause. Clearly, we are engaged here in the development of a causal chain, any aspect of which could be considered the "real" cause, depending on how we define the term *cause*. Use of the term always means selecting some part that is salient for a particular inquiry. One must infer from its use which is being selected: the most immediate part of the causal chain, the most blameworthy part, the most remediable part, the least obvious part, the most deeply buried part, and so on. Often we make that inference quickly and think little about the other possibilities until someone says, "Wait, what about . . .?"

We commonly think of "the cause" as being "the most important immediate cause." But even in that context, stop and think. What does it mean to be "the most important immediate cause"? As we shall see in the next section, there are a variety of patterns of causation, and comparing one with another on "importance" is like comparing apples and oranges. Is "the cause" a condition without which the effect cannot occur? Is it the set of all the causative elements when they happen to be present? There is considerable room for disagreement here. As Lewis (in press) notes, one cause may be salient in a particular context, another in a different context. Some links may be part of the causal chain but never be salient, such as "the lack of divine protection" or "the birth of the driver's paternal grandmother" (Lewis, p. 3).

The cause is often defined as the last link that completes the causal chain. In such an analysis, we would distinguish conditions that are constant over the time of the event from the cause, which changed and which was the last link in the chain. Oxygen is present before a match is lit to start a fire. Oxygen is a condition; the lighting of the match is the last link in the chain, the cause.

When we speak of "the" cause, as we often do, will our analysis be understood? be persuasive? Only if our audiences interpret "cause" in the same way we do! If they are looking for "deeper" or more "basic" causes, they may find our analysis shallow and unconvincing. A very complex causal history can be found behind each action, and by selectively choosing from that history, we say we "explain" an action. As Lewis notes, *"To explain an occurrence is to provide some information about its causal history."* And when the explanation is a theory or a hypothesis about some class of phenomena, then the treatment or experimental variable introduces a common element in the causal histories of all members of that class. If it is not intentionally placed there, as in the manipulation of an experimental treatment, it may be a common part of the naturally occurring phenomenon.

The analyzer, synthesizer, and theorizer seek to describe these common elements in the causal chain. The humanist describes the causal history of a given event and leaves to others the finding of parallel events with common elements.

The problem of the researcher of any orientation is to convey to the audience the point in the extended causal chain that he has chosen for the term *cause* in that study. Further, the audience must be helped to understand that this use, combined with the data from the study, will result in a knowledge contribution.

For example, in considering the causes of decline in Scholastic Aptitude Test scores of high school juniors across the United States, a researcher might address immediate causes, such as a lack of practice in certain subject-matter-related skills, or less specifically involved causes, such as reduced motivation due to too much television watching. Whichever the author chooses, the audience must be helped to see it as an appropriate and effective conceptualization of the causation for the phenomenon in question.

Cloudlike and Clocklike Worlds

One's view of the nature of the world affects one's conception of causation. The notion of cause and effect is most compatible with Popper's clocklike world. In such a world it is easier to isolate a single condition as the cause. Such a cause would be sufficient to produce the effect and, being the only cause, also necessary. "Necessary and sufficient" are often taken as the conditions of causation.

But in a cloudlike world it is hard to find conditions that inevitably and necessarily produce an effect. Certain conditions may increase the probability that an effect will occur, but they won't inevitably produce it. Therefore it is difficult to say, in such a world, that any cause is both "necessary and sufficient"; relationships are probabilistic. But to say something is probabilistic doesn't mean one gives up the idea of trying to find its determinants. Skinner, in fact, defined a reinforcer in probabilistic terms: It increased the probability of recurrence of the behavior in the same circumstances; the reinforcer is a behavior determiner in that instance. But just as the auto mechanic has great difficulty locating an "on again, off again" problem— another of Murphy's laws: It always stops acting up when you take it to the garage—so probabilistic determinants are more difficult to locate.

Parenthetically, it may be noted that although one's conception of the world determines what causation pattern to expect, it is very hard to determine the nature of the world from the causation pattern found. There are so many alternative explanations for our inconsistent results besides the explanation that the world is probabilistic. The long list of alternative explanations proposed earlier to explain results that do appear—selection, maturation, history, and so on—could in alternative instances often be used to explain why they didn't. But if inconsistent results may be part of either clock- or cloudlike worlds or even worlds where generalizations are impossible to establish, then it is difficult to determine the kind of world we live in—a fact that makes the different orientations of the previous chapter viable.

Patterns of Causation

There are a variety of patterns of causation besides the simple "A causes B" that first springs to mind. Knowing a range of such patterns makes it more likely that you can find a good match to your data. Further, hypothesizing the precise pattern of causation permits more accurate, stronger predictions; strong predictions result in more convincing studies. Ultimately, as we shall see, the complexities become such that one is modeling the interrelationships of the variables within a system. Systems are combinations of simpler relationships, and it is examples of the latter we shall examine. The term *cause* is used very loosely in this discussion—it refers to an event of type A that results in an event of type B.

Illustrative Simple Patterns

Where A and B occur together, it may well be that A causes B. This is the pattern we typically expect to find.

$$A \rightarrow B$$

For example, we may think that spastic children's slurred speech and awkward movements (A) cause them to be dependent on those around for help (B). But it is possible that B causes A.

$$A \leftarrow B$$

That is, their dependency (B) causes such expectations of helplessness in adults that the children conform to those expectations with awkward behavior. One can imagine two independent studies of the same phenomenon taking these different causative approaches.

Including parts of the causal chain is often helpful in the analysis. For example, it is likely that A and B interact.

$$A1 \rightarrow B1$$
$$A2 \rightarrow B2$$

The child's awkwardness creates expectations and actions among adults, so that a learned helplessness is created in the child that causes even greater efforts by the adults, which reinforces the expressions of helplessness in the child, and so on.

It is difficult to define terms like *the child's learned helplessness* and *the adults' helping behavior* in "cause" and "effect" terms when one is describing a causal chain or a causal process in which there are interactive relationships, as in this instance, or in which feedback loops produce homeostatic relationships. Examples of the latter are the thermostat on the wall that controls temperature and the automatic pilot of an airplane that directs it through a prescribed course.

In a continuing process, how does one define the class of causal events in a causal chain—where does cause stop and effect begin? By taking time slices of pairs of responses, one could label the earlier response, be it the child's or attending adult's, as the "cause" of the next response, which is then labeled the "effect." But it, in turn, becomes the cause of the next action, which is first an effect and then a cause, and so on. One can view the relationship in the larger context, which one can model and describe not in cause-and-effect terms but as an interactive process. One can then determine how closely that model corresponds to the reality of adult/spastic-child interactions. Further, such a model may lead to predictions such as the pattern that the adult's level of concern will take as interaction proceeds and as the adult comes to suspect the child can do more than is being shown. Such predictions, too, can be checked against data. Modeling, predicting, and then checking the predictions against data is a very useful way of validating models of complex relationships.

Thus, whereas even causation considers one class of events at a time, the analysis of a causal process or chain considers a longer temporal sequence of classes of events. Whether one studies a causal process, as in this case, or event causation is a matter of emphasis and of how the problem is formulated. Every phenomenon is embedded in a process; that process may result in an event that can be studied—a spastic child solves a problem, a student is admitted to college. Or one may study the process leading to the event—high school preparation for college. Or one may examine critical aspects or indexes of that process—number of positive comments by the adult when the child initiates problem-solving behavior, high school grade point average. The choice is a matter of emphasis and of problem formulation.

The synthesizer, theorizer, and humanist orientations tend to prefer "process" emphases; the analyzer and pragmatist orientations have "event" emphases. Each has its advantages. Many social policies, practical interventions, and instances of social "engineering" are based on "event" analyses that use cause-and-effect reasoning and examine a single class of outcomes in terms of the single or multiple causes of that event. Others believe such efforts might be strengthened by more emphasis on examination of the causal chain.

Multiple-Cause Patterns

Whether or not one wants to become involved in the complexities of the causal process, single-cause relations are such obvious oversimplifications that often they are immediately rejected. A simple analysis may be adequate to describe very powerful variables or conditions that seem to totally dominate a situation, such as rapid learning or extreme anger. But many variables act only in concert with other variables, and their effects are noticeably modulated. Thus, A and C may combine in some pattern to produce B and may do so equally or unequally. And of course more than two variables may combine equally or unequally to produce B.

$$\begin{matrix} A \searrow \\ & B \\ C \nearrow \end{matrix} \quad \text{or} \quad \begin{matrix} A \searrow \\ C \rightarrow B \\ D \nearrow \end{matrix} \quad \text{and so on}$$

Visual acuity, for example, may be the result of the amount of available light and the strength of the person's uncorrected vision:

light → visual acuity ← strength of vision

But these variables may have different weightings in different ranges. Thus, when the light is very low, light may be the dominant factor in visual acuity, regardless of how good the person's uncorrected vision is:

light → visual acuity

Beyond a certain amount of light, however, no increase can overcome the uncorrected vision limitations; indeed, light may actually be too bright and be a negative factor, suppressing visual acuity rather than contributing to it.

Another pattern is the presence of an intervening variable A, which acts on C, which, in turn, produces B. For example, hostile individuals often are anxious, but one may argue that the hostility is repressed and that the anxiety springs from their concern that the repression may not be totally effective and hostility may break through. So repression is an intervening variable.

hostility → repression → anxiety

In still another pattern, two causative variables may be affected by a third variable:

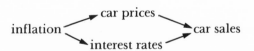

Inflation causes the Federal Reserve Board to raise interest rates and also increases car prices. Both these effects depress car sales. As one can see, as we look at more and more complex patterns, we begin building models of the causative chain.

Alternative Causes and Contingent and Contributing Conditions

As noted earlier, one definition of *cause* is "the necessary and sufficient set of conditions for the effect to appear." But suppose that we have a situation in which the effect appears without what were thought to be necessary conditions. Or suppose the effect appears when a necessary condition is present, but that condition is not enough to bring it about—it is not sufficient. And finally suppose it appears under conditions that are not sufficient in and of themselves to bring it about and, since they are not always present, are apparently not necessary either? Table 3 indicates these four possibilities.

Table 3. Possible Combinations of Necessity and Sufficiency.

| | | Cause is sufficient for the effect | |
		Yes	No
Cause is necessary for the effect	Yes	Only a single set of conditions	A contingent condition
	No	An alternative set of conditions	A contributing condition

Necessary and Sufficient—a Single Set of Conditions. Any time the effect appears, the cause is present; any time the cause is present, the effect is also present. This statement assumes that there is a single set of conditions that brings about this effect, a very difficult proposition to demonstrate. How does one know that any time the cause appears, the effect does? Does one know that any time the effect appears, the cause is present? This is another instance of inference of the kind we encountered in the discussion of external validity (GP) and generality. Unless one had access to all the phenomena in the universe, one couldn't be sure. All that one can do is *infer,* from the instances one has observed, what the more general situation may be. If the effect appears every time this particular set of conditions is present and never appears when it is absent, such evidence is enough to make us more confident about the necessity and sufficiency of a set of conditions.

In a typical control-group experiment, the ability to produce the effect in the experimental group is persuasive evidence for the sufficiency condition: It *did* produce the effect. But the absence of effect in the control group does not prove the necessity condition. There could be other instances in which this cause was absent but the effect appeared; we don't know. A single instance is *not* enough to presume a necessary cause for similar cases; only by generalizing over a number of such instances could we begin to presume that the effect occurred only under that one particular set of causative conditions.

Again, however, as with our experience with inference, a single instance in which the effect does not appear as it should is enough to limit the generality of the relationship or to suggest the relationship may not exist. Thus, if there is a single instance in which the effect occurs without the set of previously established presumably necessary and sufficient conditions, we know that there are alternative conditions under which it might appear.

For example, consider the question "Why do students seek to become teachers of handicapped children?" Possibly because a sibling was born with a handicap and they weren't; by helping others similarly incapacitated, they show their love for their sibling and assuage their guilt. That may be a sufficient condition for becoming a special education teacher, but the fact that there are students in the program who have no handicapped sibling shows it is not a necessary condition.

Not being sure that we have identified the *one and only* cause is not particularly serious, however, since we are usually satisfied if we can find even one way of predicting and controlling a situation. For most practical situations, knowing a sufficient (an alternative) cause gives us the needed power to change conditions.

Sufficient but Not Necessary—an Alternative Set of Conditions. Every time this set of conditions appears, the effect appears; but the effect also appears when the set of conditions is not present. I have already commented on and illustrated alternative causes in discussing the problem of attaining adequate evidence to infer sufficient and necessary conditions. Consider another example, however: A child's low self-esteem may come from not achieving as her peers are or from achieving very well but being continually criticized for not doing still better; they are alternative causes. Or are they? There is the additional problem of whether low levels of self-esteem from two different causes are the same self-esteem. A finer analysis of the effect might show them to be different—still another complexity we need to watch for.

As noted previously, whenever we identify a sufficient set of conditions, unless we can exclude all alternative causes we are not sure that these conditions are necessary. We shouldn't too rashly assert, therefore, that this set of conditions is the only way to bring about this effect. Even if we are correct that the necessary conditions are contained in the set we have identified, frequently we include too much. Does the prospective special education teacher have to feel guilty about the fact that it is the sibling, not himself, who is handicapped? Maybe it is enough just to have been raised in a household where the problems of the handicapped person are apparent.

The distinction between a both necessary and sufficient cause and one that is only sufficient is useful in gaining knowledge about our world. Often we want to know whether an effect has alternative causes before setting policy. If the cause we have identified is only a sufficient but not necessary cause of the phenomenon, then there will be other causes and hence other ways of controlling the effect. For example, if having a certain set of genes is a sufficient but not necessary cause of intelligence, then seeking ways to develop intelligence is a worthwhile effort. But if heredity is the necessary and sufficient condition, as some claim, then the search for new training programs is a waste of research funds—which they also allege. The extreme difficulty of showing that a cause is both necessary and sufficient tends to encourage the search for alternative causes, especially when the presumed causative factor may be denied certain individuals or is difficult or costly to attain.

   Necessary but Not Sufficient—a Contingent Condition. A contingent condition is one that is always present when the effect appears; it may also appear when the effect is not present, since it is not enough in and of itself to cause the effect. Note that here we have switched from "the cause" to "a condition," as in a standing condition that is a part of the situation, in contrast to a causative condition that, on its introduction, completes the set of sufficient conditions to produce the effect. Ability to correctly discriminate the letters of the alphabet is necessary to reading but not sufficient for reading to result without additional skill development. The skills of subtracting and multiplying are necessary to long division but will not produce it. Wherever there is a hierarchy of knowledge skills such that complex behaviors require prior learning of simpler ones (entry-level skills or abilities), contingent conditions exist. Once again, however, there is the potential problem of including too much in the contingent conditions. For example, note that it is the discrimination of letters of the alphabet one from another that is required, not necessarily being able to name them or give their sounds. The latter skills are often taught in reading as contingent conditions but may not actually be.

   Meehl (1977) suggests that, in the contingent case, the cause may have a threshold or step-function characteristic, since the effect appears only as a certain threshold is reached or as the cause rises to the level of the step needed for the effect to occur.

   Contingent relationships are demonstrated by showing that below some level of a condition, the effect never appears but that as one approaches the threshold level, it may. Above that level, there is often little or no relation between the level of the cause and that of the effect, but sometimes there is. A minimum level of oxygen is necessary for a fire. Levels of oxygen above the minimum increase the temperature of the fire. However, consider intelligence and teaching.

Teachers need some minimum mental ability level to be good teachers. Especially given measurement error, as one approaches that minimum level, there are increasing numbers of competent teachers. Above that level so many other factors determine teaching ability that there is little or no relation between mental ability and the teacher's competence. Some very mentally able persons are poor teachers (possibly they do not tolerate persons less able than they), and some close to the minimum may be excellent teachers—motivated, patient, responsive, warm, friendly.

An effect may have multiple contingent conditions. This is obvious in the case of fire: A combustible substance, oxygen, and high temperatures are all contingent conditions. In the case of teaching ability, love of children, learning ability, communication facility, and academic achievement might all be contingent conditions.

Neither Necessary nor Sufficient—a Contributing Condition. With a contributing condition, the effect may appear in the absence of the cause, and the cause in the absence of the effect. But the effect is more likely to appear in the presence than in the absence of the cause. Admiring and wanting to be like one's teachers as one progressed through school is neither a necessary nor a sufficient condition for becoming a teacher, but it is a contributing condition. Unequal distribution of goods—wealth and poverty—is neither a necessary nor a sufficient condition for crime, but it is clearly a contributing condition.

It may help us understand contributing conditions to realize that they are sometimes at stages in the causal chain far removed from the effect. Thus their impact is to establish favorable conditions for the effect but not determining ones. Another way of describing a contributing cause is to say that it increases the probability that the effect will occur.

How to Discern These Conditions from Data

How does one differentiate one of these sets of conditions from another in data? Do they show up differently? Let us look at each instance.

Necessary and Sufficient Conditions. The design for developing data might typically be an experimental situation in which a difference between means of an experimental and control group shows the effect and the treatment includes one's hypothesized necessary and sufficient conditions. If the conditions include continuous variables and the effect is related to the strength of the variables, the relationship would be shown most easily by a correlation coefficient—a Pearson product-moment correlation if it is a linear relation, a correlation ratio or other nonlinear correlation if it is not. Because it is very difficult to infer causation from correlations appearing in retrospective data gathered after the effect has occurred, the data-gathering conditions need to be as close to those of the experimental method as possible.

If the effect is a step function—that is, an all-or-none reaction—then either a point biserial or a tetrachoric or similar correlation with the cutting point at the threshold would show it. If both cause and effect are step functions, a phi coefficient or fourfold point correlation is in order.

The effect would also show as a difference between means of the control group (absence of the set of conditions) and the experimental group (presence of the set), using a t test. Where one uses multiple strengths of the set of variables, analysis of variance could be used.

Alternative Causes. For alternative causes the relevant statistics and data-gathering conditions are the same as for necessary and sufficient conditions. However, since the effect may be caused by conditions other than the one being investigated, to the extent that one or more alternative causes are present in the situation being studied, the effect will appear when the cause may or may not be present, so a correlation will be lower than it would be under necessary and sufficient conditions. How much lower will depend on how many other causes there are and how prevalent these are in the situation studied. Assume that having a handicapped sibling is sufficient to cause a person to wish to be a special education teacher. A correlation can be derived from Table 4. The correlation would be lowered by other sufficient conditions for becoming a teacher of the handicapped that occurred among students with no handicapped siblings, cell C. Further, if there are entries in cell B, which there surely will be, then having a handicapped sibling must not be a sufficient condition, since that condition is present for those in cell B, who are not in the teacher program.

Table 4. Analysis of Having Handicapped Siblings as a Cause of Becoming a Teacher of Handicapped Children.

| | | Student's program | |
		Teacher of the handicapped	Other
Handicapped siblings in student's family	One or more	A	B
	None	C	D

Contingent Conditions. A continuously variable contingent condition is not well reflected by linear correlation coefficients; the effect, if it does appear, will typically show as a low correlation. The reason is that, in these instances, one typically has a triangular distribution for the lower levels of cause, because at the lowest levels of cause the effect does not appear, and only as it approaches the threshold does the effect appear. Above that threshold, there may be no relation to the size of the cause whatsoever, and correlation in that region would be zero. Thus one corner of the scatterplot of a contingent condition would always be empty of cases and the diagonally opposite corner full of scattered cases. A Pearson product-moment correlation would underestimate such a relationship, since the means of the columns would give the appearance of a curvilinear relationship. A correlation to sense nonlinear relationships would do better. Probably the best test is that for a Guttman simplex; the simplex is another way of stating contingent conditions (Guttman, 1953).

Contributing Conditions. A correlation coefficient will show a continuously variable contributing condition, but since the contributing condition only makes the effect more likely, the correlation will be quite low. It may be so low that whether one assumes a linear or nonlinear fit may make little difference. Because we are frequently dealing with conditions at earlier than the immediate stages in the causal chain, path analysis and modeling may be useful techniques. These techniques require some understanding of where the conditions are effective in relation to other conditions and whether there are active instances in which they are especially effective. For example, social sensitivity would be especially important in instances of conflict; a model to predict success as a teacher might provide for special weighting for a showing of social sensitivity under conflict conditions.

Dichotomous Conditions, Continuous Variables, and Causation

Reduction of data, which is essential in science, simplifies the description of the world to those aspects indispensable for describing and controlling it. It is important to uncomplicate one's description as much as possible consistent with accuracy of interpretation and maintenance of the ability to predict and control. But sometimes an attempt at reduction goes too far, as, for example, when we dichotomize a continuous variable to high/low conditions or, more commonly, in administering a single strength of treatment when the treatment could be applied in a variety of strengths. The treatment is either present at the strength used with the experimental group or absent, as it is in the control group. But that treatment strength may or may not be above the threshold at which the effect appears. In addition, the effect produced may or may not be above the level that can be sensed in the study. Building on the work of Bertrand Russell and Norman Campbell, Cook and Campbell (1979, p. 12) show how entirely different conclusions about the nature of the causal relationship result simply from changing the threshold at which the cause or effect is recognized as present or absent.

Delineating Types of Causes

As in dichotomizing continuous data, under some circumstances it is difficult to distinguish the different conditions. For example, if one views poverty across a wide variety of circumstances, it appears to be a contributing factor to crime. But for some individuals poverty may be a sufficient cause for crime—an alternative cause. Under other circumstances it acts like a contingent cause: Crime occurs mainly below a certain level where other factors, such as sickness in the family, are more determining. For the goal of solidly building a behavioral science, we want to delineate carefully the different kinds of relationships; such delineation will result in more fully specified explanations. As noted in the discussion of modeling and path analysis, the explanation is key to knowing what kind of relationship to look for. Careful and painstaking data analysis tells us how to modify the explanation so that future predictions may be more faithfully fulfilled.

Complex Process Causation Conditions

In a process, or system, relationship, in which feedback affects subsequent events, complexities can arise from the way feedback affects the system. Feedback can have several effects. For example, it can cause an amplification, or increase, in effect. This is the instance in which we are most familiar with the term *feedback*, as when a sound amplifier is turned up too loud. The amplified sound from a speaker enters the microphone, is further amplified, exits the speaker, enters the microphone again, and so on. It builds into the high-pitched squeal we call "feedback." In behavioral terms, amplification can be seen in reinforcement: Positive reinforcement of a response increases the frequency of that response in future activity. Feedback can also suppress or decrease, as in punishment, which results in a decrease in the activity.

Feedback can maintain a level or range, as in homeostasis (exemplified by the thermostat). It can also be used to optimize some aspect. In economics, prices can be set to maintain a given demand, as the diamond cartel has done, or to maximize profit by adjusting to demand. Feedback from two or more criteria can be used to find the point at which one simultaneously optimizes multiple goals. For example, structuring the learning environment and tasks increases achievement but suppresses creativity. The teacher seeks to provide enough structure to increase achievement as much as possible consistent with also stimulating as much creativity as possible.

Moderator relationships also exist—the relationship changes in the presence of a third variable. In the prediction of achievement by verbal ability tests, for example, sex is a moderator variable in that prediction is much better for females than males. In males, presumably, various motivational factors diminish the contribution of verbal ability to achievement. Another example is the effect of group size on the control of conscience over behavior. The normal control present in solitary or small-group situations is lost in crowd or mob situations.

Both these instances can also be explained by an analogy with catalysts in chemistry. The presence of a variable or condition results in a change in the relationship without that variable's acting as cause or active agent. For example, the control of behavior normally exerted by a person's conscience ceases to function as restrictively when the person feels herself a part of a crowd; the group imposes a kind of catalytic action on the conscience, suppressing its effectiveness and legitimizing behavior that would be unacceptable in a small group or alone.

One can explain these examples in still another way, using a separate construct for each situation and describing the boundary conditions within which a generalization about the construct holds. Thus, the construct "conscience" is used only to explain the behavior of a solitary person or a small group, and "group conscience" that of a crowd. One sets boundary conditions for the construct by its definition, which is congruent with the generality of the explanation, theory, or rationale explaining how "conscience" or "group conscience" works. In contrast, by explaining the different behavior of conscience by group size, the catalytic moderator explanation, one keeps the same terms and explains what would otherwise be different constructs (conscience or group conscience) by the presence of a third variable. This kind of explanation seems to have more possibilities and is a stronger, more powerful, and more unified explanation or theory. Within it, boundary conditions become part of the explanation. More sophisticated theory results as one modifies the explanation to fit new data and learns more about the situation.

Additional Causation Patterns

Meehl (1977), using medical causation for his examples, catalogues a variety of cause-and-effect conditions for those who wish to explore additional complexities. As an example, he notes that we may have combinations of conditions—presence/absence and a threshold. The gene for a disease such as phenylketonuria that prevents the child from utilizing food with a particular characteristic must be present, *and* sufficient food with that characteristic must be ingested, for the problem to arise.

Meehl (1977) also discusses the INUS condition, first described by Mackie (1965). It disassociates explanation from prediction, as we saw the humanist does to explain individual situations. *INUS* stands for the perplexing combination of the individually *I*nsufficient but *N*ecessary factors in a set of conditions that are jointly *U*nnecessary but *S*ufficient to bring about an effect. This is Mackie's way of describing a cause of a particular event in which each of a set of factors is *insufficient* in and of itself to bring about the effect, but each is *necessary* in this particular constellation of conditions, which as a whole is *sufficient* to bring about the effect although, as a combination, they are *unnecessary* because other constellations of conditions might also bring about the same effect. Consider the conditions that may cause a particular fire: a short in the fuse box, no sprinkler, flammable material near the box, dry wood above it, and a stairway to carry the fire to the rest of the house. No one of these is sufficient— the electrical short, the flammable material, the dry wood, the stairway. Nor are these particular items necessary—for instance, lightning could have substituted for the electrical short or spontaneous combustion in the flammable material. But the entire complex of circumstances is necessary in this constellation—for example, the nearness of the flammable material to the short, the stairway to carry the flame to the rest of the house. The entire set of circumstances is sufficient to "cause" the effect. Such explanations are a common feature of historical works and case studies, hence also of the work of the humanist orientation. And as with all sufficient but not necessary sets of conditions, there may be alternative sets. For example, research may uncover a particular pattern of circumstances that yields high production in factories or high achievement in schools, but there may be several such patterns that also produce those results. Identification of a set of INUS conditions usually leads one to look at other INUS sets producing the same phenomenon to find commonalities that may turn out to be contributing or contingent conditions for producing the phenomenon.

Perhaps this is enough to indicate the suggestive and stimulating nature of Meehl's work. Even in medicine, Meehl is unable to find ready examples for all the complex patterns he suggests. Yet, once they are identified, researchers are alerted to such possibilities so that they might be recognized if the appropriate data pattern is discovered.

Classification Schemes as Causal Explanations

Interest in the use of classification schemes to explain phenomena is increasing. Their use involves classifying new phenomena into a set of previously observed ones that have some already recognized pattern, regularity, or similarity. Kaplan (1965), in a chapter devoted to what he calls noncausal explanation, refers to two such types of explanation: (1) taxonomic schemes, of which the research orientation typology described in this book is an example, and (2) patterns of temporal laws, of which children's growth patterns are an example. Other examples of taxonomic schemes are Jung's personality types (Jung, 1971) and the *Taxonomy of Educational Objectives* (Bloom, 1956; Krathwohl, Bloom, and Masia, 1964). Kaplan says that taxonomic schemes are "weakly" explanatory. He notes that scientists can agree on the usefulness of a taxonomic scheme even when they cannot formulate the causal laws that undergird it. It seems, however, and Kaplan agrees this may be so, that the merits of such a scheme probably "depend on how clearly and neatly it can be related to causal principles" (Kaplan, p. 148).

Classifying a phenomenon with similar ones tells us something about it and what we can expect, even when we do not know the causal basis. It is important to note that predictions can be made and confirmed from such explanations and that the criteria of internal validity (LP) and external validity (GP) apply to such studies. In the absence of a causal understanding of the process, explanation credibility might be weak. Like the predictions made by the pragmatist, which carry with them strong possibility of control, such "explanations" are of considerable interest to us, even though, in the interests of science, we will eventually want to understand the "why" and provide a causal explanation.

Kaplan (1965) notes that purposive statements—explanations that attribute a causal character to behavior that is intentional—serve the same kind of function. Bees' gathering of nectar is purposeful behavior, but we think of it as instinctive rather than motivated. Motivation implies conscious choice, as when a student does homework instead of watching television. In these instances purposive explanations, which are admittedly fictional constructs, may be useful.

Eventually we will want to replace a purposive explanation with a more basic causal explanation. But Kaplan argues that explaining behavior in terms of "motivations" is useful provided we can in some way back up the statement that motives exist. Certainly such explanations have proved useful in the behavioral sciences even though the relations may not eventually prove to be causal when better ones are found. Some researchers would argue that purposive explanations are a kind of causal explanation, rather than noncausal as Kaplan argues. Again, as has been clear throughout this chapter, much depends on the particular definition of cause.

This chapter has suggested the variety of cause-and-effect relations that can exist and provided sources of others. It may also have use in suggesting ways a relationship can be more completely specified, ways that, when used to describe the precise nature of the relationship, make it easier to show congruence of explanation and prediction—congruence between the relationship as described and the data as analyzed. More precise (strong!) predictions and better science can result. More complete understanding of the complexities of the terms *cause* and *effect* may help us all to avoid or at least be aware of the ambiguity of the terms, their frequent poor fit, and attendant problems.

Additional References

A number of useful and reasonably readable treatments of causation exist that go beyond this discussion. Examples are Ellsworth in psychology (1977), Köbben in anthropology (1973), Heise in sociology (1975), and in a more general framework with medical examples, Meehl (1977). Cook and Campbell (1979) have a very clear, readable summarization of the progression of philosophical positions. See also Sosa (1975) and Beauchamp (1974).

10

Applying the Framework to Actual Studies

I have applied the criteria of internal validity (LP) and external validity (GP) to the Coleman study comparing public and private school achievement in the chapters discussing those constructs, but there has been no application of the whole framework, or model, to a study. This chapter provides two examples.

To facilitate the use of the criteria, I have developed a checklist that embodies the implications developed in the previous chapters and, in some instances, goes somewhat beyond them. The checklist makes the criteria available in a single place, the appendix, and in reasonably concise form. It is developed as a series of questions following the order in which they are discussed in the previous chapters. Most of the questions are so framed as to apply to critiquing a published study, which is its use here. But the checklist is equally useful for developing a research proposal, planning a study, or drafting the report of a study; its use for these purposes is recommended. Where items are more applicable to proposal and report writing or research plan development, that is so indicated. The checklist is sequenced as the boxes are numbered in Figure A-1 (in the appendix), and the sections of the discussion use these numbers to simplify reference both to the figure and to the checklist.

Ideally I might apply the checklist to an example of each of the orientations, but unfortunately space is insufficient. Instead I shall apply the checklist to a quantitative, analyzer-orientation study and a qualitative, synthesizer-orientation study in this chapter.

Application of the Checklist to a Quantitative Study

The analyzer, quantitative study chosen is that of Zimbardo, Andersen, and Kabat (1981), on the development of paranoid feelings by persons who are not aware that they are temporarily deaf. It is reprinted here as it appeared in *Science.**

This study is fairly typical of an analyzer's work in that it sets up a hypothesis based on observations (often by others) and proceeds to confirm them. It is atypical only in that it lacks the usual headings that serve to mark sections of the text dealing with the introduction, procedure, data, analysis, and interpretation. Each professional journal sets its own style, and this one omits headings, presumably to save space. The sections appear in their usual order, however.

Induced Hearing Deficit Generates Experimental Paranoia

Abstract. *The development of paranoid reactions was investigated in normal people experiencing a temporary loss of hearing. In a social setting, subjects made partially deaf by hypnotic suggestion, but kept unaware of the source of their deafness, became more paranoid as indicated on a variety of assessment measures. The results support a hypothesized cognitive-social mechanism for the clinically observed relationship between paranoia and deafness in the elderly.*

Clinical observation has uncovered a relationship between deafness and psychopathology (*1–3*). In particular, when deafness occurs later in life and the hearing loss is relatively gradual, paranoid reactions are often observed (*4–14*). Delusions of persecution and other paranoid symptoms, first noted by Kraepelin (*6*) in 1915, seem especially prevalent among the hard-of-hearing elderly (*7–9*). Audiometric assessment of hospitalized, elderly patients (with age and other selection factors controlled statistically) has revealed a significantly greater degree of deafness among those diagnosed as paranoid than among those with affective disorders (*10–12*).

Maher (*15*) suggested that one process by which deafness may lead to paranoid reactions involves an initial lack of awareness of the hearing defect by the person, as well as by interacting others. Paranoid thinking then emerges as a cognitive attempt to explain the perceptual anomaly (16) of not being able to hear what people in one's presence are apparently saying. Judging them to be whispering, one may ask, "about what?" or "why me?" Denial by others that they are whispering may be interpreted by the hard-of-hearing person as a lie since it is so clearly discrepant with observed evidence. Frustration and anger over such injustices may gradually result in a more profound expression of hostility.

Observers, without access to the perceptual data base of the person experiencing the hearing disorder, judge these responses to be bizarre instances of thought pathology. As a consequence, others may exclude the hard-of-hearing person, whose suspiciousness and delusions about their alleged plots become upsetting (17). Over time, social relationships deteriorate, and the individual experiences both isolation and loss of the corrective social feedback essential for modifying false beliefs (18, 19). Within a self-validating, autistic system, delusions of persecution go unchecked (20). As such, they eventually become resistant to contrary information from any external source (21). In this analysis, paranoia is sometimes an end product of an initially rational search to explain a perceptual discontinuity, in this case, being deaf without knowing it.

We now report an experimental investigation of the development of paranoid reactions in normal subjects with a temporary, functional loss of hearing. Across a variety of assessment measures, including standard personality tests, self-reports, and judgments of their behavior by others in the situation, these subjects became significantly more paranoid than did subjects in two control conditions. The effect was transient and limited to the test environment [by the specificity of the instructions, by extensive postexperimental interviews (debriefing procedures), and by the healthy "premorbid" status of each participant]. Nevertheless, qualitative observations and objective data offer support for the role of deafness-without-awareness as a causal factor in triggering paranoid reactions. Although the subjects were young and had normal hearing, these results have obvious bearing on a possible cognitive-social mechanism by which deafness may eventuate in paranoia among the middle-aged and elderly.

Participants were 18 college males selected from large introductory classes. In the selection process, each student (i) demonstrated that he was highly hypnotizable according to the Harvard Group Scale of Hypnotic Susceptibility (22) and the Stanford Scale of Hypnotic Susceptibility, form C (23); (ii) evidenced posthypnotic amnesia; (iii) passed a test of hypnotically induced partial deafness; (iv) scored within the normal range on measures of psychopathology; and (v) attended at least one of two hypnosis training sessions before the experiment.

Six participants were randomly assigned to the experimental treatment in which partial deafness, without awareness of its source, was hypnotically induced. The remaining participants were randomly assigned to one of two control groups. In one of these groups, partial deafness with awareness of its source was induced to demonstrate the importance of the knowledge that one's difficulty in understanding others is caused by deafness. In the other control group, a posthypnotic suggestion unrelated to deafness was experienced (a compulsion to scratch an itchy ear) along with amnesia for it, to establish whether merely carrying out a posthypnotic suggestion with amnesia might be sufficient to yield the predicted results. Taken together, these two groups provide controls for experimental demand characteristics, subject selection traits (hypnotic susceptibility), and the rational basis for the experienced sensory anomaly (24).

During group training sessions, each subject was instructed in self-hypnosis and completed consent and medical history forms, a number of Minnesota Multiphasic Personality Inventory (MMPI) scales (25), and our clinically derived paranoia scale (26). In the experimental session, subjects were hypnotized, after which they listened through earphones to deep relaxation music and then heard taped instructions for one of the three treatments. The use of coded tapes randomly selected in advance by one of the researchers (L.K.) made it possible for the hypnotist (P.Z.), experimenter (S.A.), observers, and confederates to be ignorant of the treatment assignment of the subjects. All subjects were given the suggestion to begin experiencing the changed state when they saw the posthypnotic cue ("FOCUS") projected on a viewing screen in the laboratory. In order to make the task socially realistic and to conceal the purpose of the experiment, each subject was led to believe he was participating, along with two others (who were confederates), in a study of the effects of hypnotic training procedures on creative problem solving. Because of the hearing defect that subjects were to experience, all instructions and tasks were projected automatically by timed slides, the first of which was the posthypnotic cue. While working on a preliminary anagram task, the two confederates engaged in a well-rehearsed, standard conversation designed to establish their commonality, to offer test probes for the subject's deafness, and to provide verbal content that might be misperceived as antagonistic. They recalled a party they had both attended, laughed at an incident mentioned, made a funny face, and eventually decided to work together, finally asking the subject if he also wanted to work with them.

The instructions had previously suggested that group effort on such tasks is usually superior to solitary responding. The subject's behavior was videotaped, observed directly by two judges from behind a one-way mirror, and scored independently by the confederates immediately after the session. After this conversation, the three participants were asked to develop stories about pairs of people in ambiguous relationships [Thematic Apperception Test (TAT)]. On the first task, they had the option of working together or of working alone. Thus, an interdependence among confederates and the subject was created [important in the natural etiology of paranoia (17, 19, 21)], which centered around developing a common creative solution. On the second TAT task, participants had to work alone.

After these tasks were completed, each confederate was instructed by the slides to go to a different laboratory room while the subject stayed in the room to complete evaluation forms, including the MMPI and others. Extensive debriefing followed (27), and to remove any tension or confusion, each subject was rehypnotized by the experimenter and told to recall all the events experienced during the session. Subjects were reevaluated in a 1-month follow-up.

Major results are summarized in Table 1, which presents group means and one-tailed t-test values derived from a single a priori planned comparison that contrasted the experimental group with the two control groups taken together (28). This analysis followed standard analysis of variance tests. As predicted, the experience of being partially deaf, without being aware of its source, created significant changes in cognitive, emotional, and behavioral functioning. Compared with the control groups, subjects in the deafness-without-awareness treatment became more paranoid, as shown on an MMPI paranoia scale of Horn (25, p. 283) and on our clinically derived paranoia scale (26). Experimental subjects also had significantly elevated scores on the MMPI grandiosity scale of Watson and Klett (25, p. 287)—one aspect of paranoid thinking. Experimental subjects perceived themselves as more irritated, agitated, hostile, and unfriendly than control subjects did and were perceived as such by confederates ignorant of the treatment. When invited to work with confederates on the TAT task, only one of six experimental subjects elected to do so; in contrast, 9 of 12 control subjects preferred to affiliate ($z = 4.32$, $P < .001$).

The TAT stories generated by the subjects were assessed in two ways. Subjects' own ratings of the creativity of their stories

Table 1. Mean scores on dependent measures distinguishing experimental from control subjects.

	Treatment				
	Deafness without awareness (N = 6)	Control		t (15)	P
Dependent measures		Deafness with awareness (N = 6)	Post-hypnotic suggestion (N = 6)		
Paranoia measures *					
MMPI–Paranoia	1.50	.33	–.17	1.838	< .05
MMPI–Grandiosity	1.33	–.83	–1.00	1.922	< .05
Paranoia clinical interview form	.30	–.09	–.28	3.667	< .005
TAT					
Affective evaluation	83.35	16.65	33.50	2.858	< .01
Self-assessed creativity	42.83	68.33	73.33	3.436	< .005
Self-rated feelings					
Creative	34.17	55.83	65.83	2.493	< .05
Confused	73.33	39.17	35.00	2.521	< .05
Relaxed	43.33	81.67	78.33	2.855	< .01
Agitated	73.33	14.17	15.33	6.586	< .001
Irritated	70.00	25.00	7.00	6.000	< .001
Friendly	26.67	53.33	56.67	2.195	< .05
Hostile	38.33	13.33	13.33	2.047	< .05
Judges' ratings					
Confused	40.83	27.08	17.67	1.470	< .10
Relaxed	34.17	54.59	65.42	2.839	< .01
Agitated	51.25	24.59	13.75	3.107	< .005
Irritated	45.84	18.92	11.25	3.299	< .005
Friendly	23.34	48.34	65.00	3.385	< .005
Hostile	18.75	5.00	1.67	2.220	< .05

*These measures were taken before and after the experimental session; reported means represent difference scores (after minus before).

indicated that experimental subjects judged their stories to be significantly less creative than did subjects in either of the control groups. Second, the stories were scored (reliably by two judges) for the extent to which subjects evaluated TAT characters. An evaluative-judgmental outlook toward other people is a hallmark of paranoia. The experimental subjects used significantly more evaluative language, both positive and negative (for example, right-wrong, good-bad) (t = 2.86, $P <$ .01) than controls did. In addition, they differed significantly (z = 5.00, $P <$ .001) from the controls in their greater use of positive evaluative language. Experimental subjects reported feeling no more suspicious than did control subjects. These last two findings weaken the possible criticism that the results were based simply on anger induced by the experimental manipulation.

Both groups experiencing a hearing deficit reported, as expected, that their hearing was not keen, but reported no other sensory difficulties. Those who were partially deaf without being aware of the source of the deafness did experience greater confusion, which is likely to have motivated an active search for an appropriate explanation. Over time, however, if their delusional systems were allowed to become more coherent and systematized, the paranoid reaction would be less likely to involve confusion. Ultimately, there is so much confidence in the proposed paranoid explanatory system that alternative scenarios are rejected.

Despite the artificiality of our laboratory procedure, functionally analogous predicaments occur in everyday life. People's hearing does deteriorate without their realizing it. Indeed, the onset of deafness among the elderly is sometimes actively denied because recognizing a hearing deficit may be tantamount to acknowledging a greater defect—old age. Perhaps self-deception about one's hearing deficit may even be sufficient, in some circumstances, to yield a similar response, namely, a search for a more personally acceptable alternative that finds fault in others rather than in oneself. When there is no social or cultural support for the chosen explanation and the actor is relatively powerless, others may judge him or her to be irrational and suffering from a mental disorder. Although our subjects were young and had normal hearing, these findings have obvious bearing on a possible cognitive-social mechanism by which deafness may lead to paranoia among the middle-aged and elderly.

Philip G. Zimbardo
Susan M. Andersen*

*Department of Psychology,
Stanford University,
Stanford, California 94305*

Loren G. Kabat

*Health Sciences Center,
State University of New York,
Stony Brook 11794*

References and Notes

1. B. Pritzker, *Schweiz. Med. Wochenschr.* 7, 165 (1938).
2. F. Houston and A. B. Royse, *J. Ment. Sci.* 100, 990 (1954).
3. M. Vernon, *J. Speech Hear. Res.* 12, 541 (1969).
4. K. Z. Altshuler, *Am. J. Psychiatry* 127, 11 and 1521 (1971).

5. Personal communication from J. D. Rainer (14 July 1980), who has studied the psychiatric effects of deafness for the past 25 years at the New York State Psychiatric Institute.
6. E. Kraepelin, *Psychiatrie* 8, 1441 (1915).
7. D. W. K. Kay, *Br. J. Hosp. Med.* 8, 369 (1972).
8. F. Post, *Persistent Persecutory States of the Elderly* (Pergamon, London, 1966).
9. H. A. McClelland, M. Roth, H. Neubauer, R. F. Garside, *Excerpta Med. Int. Congr. Ser.* 4, 2955 (1968).
10. A. F. Cooper, R. F. Garside, D. W. K. Kay, *Br. J. Psychiatry* 129, 532 (1976).
11. A. F. Cooper, A. R. Curry, D. W. K. Kay, R. F. Garside, M. Roth, *Lancet* 1974-II, 7885 (1974).
12. A. F. Cooper and R. Porter, *J. Psychosom. Res.* 20, 107 (1976).
13. A. F. Cooper, *Br. J. Psychiatry* 129, 216 (1976).
14. D. W. K. Kay, A. F. Cooper, R. F. Garside, M. Roth, *ibid.* 129, 207 (1976).
15. B. Maher, in *Thought and Feeling,* H. London and R. E. Nisbett, Eds. (Aldine, Chicago, 1974), pp. 85-103.
16. G. Reed, *The Psychology of Anomalous Experience* (Houghton Mifflin, Boston, 1974).
17. E. M. Lemert, *Sociometry* 25, 2 (1962).
18. L. Festinger, *Hum. Relat.* 7, 117 (1954).
19. N. A. Cameron, in *Comprehensive Textbook of Psychiatry,* A. M. Freedman and H. I. Kaplan, Eds. (Williams & Wilkins, Baltimore, 1967), pp. 665-675.
20. A. Beck, in *Thought and Feeling,* H. London and R. E. Nisbett, Eds. (Aldine, Chicago, 1974), pp. 127-140.
21. W. W. Meisner, *The Paranoid Process* (Jason Aronson, New York, 1978).
22. R. E. Shor and E. C. Orne, *Harvard Group Scale of Hypnotic Susceptibility, Form A* (Consulting Psychologists Press, Palo Alto, Calif., 1962).
23. A. M. Weitzenhoffer and E. R. Hilgard, *Stanford Hypnotic Susceptibility Scale, Form C* (Consulting Psychologists Press, Palo Alto, Calif., 1962).
24. A fuller presentation of procedures is available by request.
25. W. G. Dahlstrom, G. S. Welsh, L. F. Dahlstrom, *An MMPI Handbook,* vol. 2, *Research Applications* (Univ. of Minnesota Press, Minneapolis, 1975).
26. We derived this scale specifically for this study; it consisted of 15 self-declarative statements responded to on 7-point rating scales. The scale was drawn from a clinical study of paranoia (*14*).
27. L. Ross, M. R. Lepper, M. Hubbard, *J. Pers. Soc. Psychol.* 35, 817 (1977).
28. W. L. Hays, *Statistics for Psychologists* (Holt, Rinehart & Winston, New York, 1965), p. 465.
29. This report is dedicated to Neal E. Miller as part of a commemoration by his former students of his inspired science teaching. We wish to acknowledge the expert and reliable research assistance of Harry Coin, Dave Willer, Bob Sick, James Glanzer, Jill Fonaas, Laurie Plautz, Lisa Carrol, and Sarah Garlan. We thank Joan Linsenmeier and David Rosenhan for critical editing of the manuscript.
*Present address: Department of Psychology, University of California, Santa Barbara 93106.

3 December 1980; revised 23 February 1981

1.0 Question Choice and Formulation

The authors give a quite thorough explanation of how paranoia might evolve, using both old and recent references to establish
that there is a relationship between deafness and psychopathology in
general and especially between deafness and paranoia. As with many
analyzer studies, the idea was suggested by the observations and
experiences of others. The explanation is highly plausible as
developed.

The methodology of the study is unusual in its use of hypnosis.
The authors, however, either presumed the audience accepts it as a
technique or believed they could do little to convince a hostile
audience of the validity of the technique in the space they would likely
be allotted. No space is devoted to an explanation of this aspect of the
study. This is an excellent example of a trade-off one makes in the
face of resource limitations—in this instance, the space available for
such an article in a journal like *Science*. As noted earlier, appropriate
allocation of this resource is frequently overlooked.

2.0 Weighting of Internal Validity (LP) and External Validity (GP)

The study is weighted almost totally toward internal validity
(LP), although clearly it is intended to apply to more than the group
from which the subjects were drawn. This weighting is appropriate,
since it is clear that the link between paranoia and deafness is still
being established.

2.1 Internal Validity (LP)

2.11 Explanation Credibility

The explanation is well developed and is highly credible. The
relation of the hypothesis to the study is clear.

2.12 Translation Fidelity

Subjects. Since a presumably universal relationship is being
investigated, it ought to apply to any person with a mild, unnoticed
hearing disability. Presumably college males are as good as anyone on
whom to experiment. The one question, which is repeatedly noted, is
that the subjects are young and not deaf. Is the process different with
older people? Zimbardo and his coauthors think not. Some readers
might not agree, although I would.

Another concern is that the subjects are all male. Again, since
the proposition is a universal, it ought to apply equally to men and

women, and subjects of one sex ought to be as good as the other. However, for those who are aware that males are more aggressive and see aggressiveness as a factor in paranoia, some question might arise about the appropriateness of an all-male sample.

Situation. The same can be said for situation—the college scene is as good as any if one accepts the authors' proposition as universal.

Observations. The Harvard and Stanford hypnotic susceptibility scales are referenced and are established tests in their field. In addition, subjects were apparently pretested to ensure that they would display induced deafness with posthypnotic suggestion, and only subjects who would were accepted. Further, the confederates used probes to ensure that the induced deafness was present.

A well-established, empirically validated measure of paranoia, the Minnesota Multiphasic Personality Inventory (MMPI), was used. Also used was the well-known Thematic Apperception Test, but as a subjectively interpreted test, it may be less trusted by some and depends on trained scorers for its validity.

Subject behavior was observed by concealed judges and also videotaped. The confederate interaction was rehearsed and standardized so that judges were observing different reactions to the same social situation, thereby making comparisons easier and more reliable. However, no indication was given of the judges' rate of agreement of their ratings.

The MMPI has both construct and predictive validity in relation to paranoia. The validity of the clinical interview form is never really established except to indicate that it is based on earlier research work. The use of multiple methods of assessing paranoia lends credence to the study if they all give the same results.

Treatment. Perhaps the most potentially controversial aspect of the study is the treatment by hypnosis, which left two of the groups with the posthypnotic suggestion of partial deafness, one group aware of the deafness, the other unaware. Persons who have seen hypnosis demonstrations will not find it either strange or impossible that this was undoubtedly effective as a treatment. Those who accept it as such will no doubt consider it an ingenious solution to the problem of how to subject this question to experimental control.

The standard conversation of the two confederates, the cover story that it was a study of the effects of hypnotic training on creative problem solving, the tasks in which the subject was engaged, the presentation of instructions by automatically timed slides, and the administration of the evaluation forms were all part of the treatment. The rehearsed and standardized behavior of the confederates and the use of automatically timed slides ensured that the treatment was the same for all. Except that it is a laboratory rather than field procedure, the treatment seems reasonable.

Basis of Comparison. The use of two control groups, one of which is aware of the deafness, the other not, is a very clever control for the knowledge factor. The use of multiple measures of paranoia increases one's confidence that changes would be observed if they occurred and that it was paranoid behavior that was being measured.

Procedure. There may be some question about the time allowed for the paranoia to develop, since the experiment apparently lasted only a short time. It is not clear exactly how long, but the treatment and development of paranoia appear to have all occurred in a single experimental session. The question for translation fidelity is whether the change in the paranoia scales that occurred is indicative of the kind of paranoia that deaf people experience and whether, indeed, a real paranoia can build up in such a short time. Is it a precursor of the serious condition that deaf individuals display? It seems likely that it is, but here is a point where individuals might differ in their assessment of translation fidelity.

In the discussion of rival explanations I shall note other important features of the procedure such as random assignment to groups and administration of treatment so that experimenters were blind to which of the three treatments the individual was receiving.

2.13 Demonstrated Relationship

2.131 Evidence Authenticity

In the absence of any reason to believe the data were artificial, this category is not relevant to this study. The reputation of an established researcher, the presentation of data that look reasonable, publication in a peer-reviewed journal all tend to allay such concerns. Since the data were directly gathered by the investigators or under their control, authenticity in the sense of subjects' faking the data is also not a problem.

2.132 Precedence of Cause

As in all experiments in which administration of treatment is under the investigator's control, precedence of the treatment prior to the appearance of the effect is easy to establish.

2.133 Presence of Effect

Assuming that one has accepted the instruments as faithful translations of the concepts involved in the study, the question is whether these registered an effect.

The fact that there are eighteen tests of significance does inflate the probability that one of the tests that were significant at the 5 percent level was the result of chance, since on the average, with purely random data, its chances are one in twenty. Seventeen of eighteen significant tests are at the 5 percent level or less, and ten of the eighteen are significant at the 1 percent level or less. Moreover, all the effects are in the predicted direction, and in random data they would go both ways.

Further, the tests contrasted the experimental group with the combined control groups. If deafness itself had any effect on paranoia, even when one knew one's hearing was impaired, this would be a conservative test. The distance between experimental and control groups would be narrowed if paranoia also developed with knowledge of deafness. Although it is a conservative test, the effect showed, thereby indicating robustness and strength.

2.134 Congruence of Explanation and Evidence

The evidence, with one exception, reached levels usually considered statistically significant. The tests were directional, one-tailed tests, the direction of expected effect having been predicted as that indicating increased paranoia. Thus a strong directional hypothesis was made and confirmed.

2.14 Rival Explanations Eliminated

As noted earlier, the presence of a control group, especially one that has been given the treatment in every respect except that subjects knew their hearing was impaired, is a very tight control. Unless there is some association between susceptibility to hypnosis and paranoia, random assignment of individuals to groups also exerted tight control by eliminating the alternative explanation of differences between groups. Prior screening and random assignment to groups made it unlikely that one group's tendency toward paranoia was greater than another's to start with.

The fact that individuals who are susceptible to hypnosis are also extremely suggestible does imply that they might be particularly sensitive to the actions of others. Perhaps such persons might, therefore, show changes in attitude toward others more readily if they felt they were being left out of social intercourse. Thus the group used by the researchers might be prone to show the effect more quickly than persons less susceptible to suggestion. That does not necessarily invalidate the results, however, so long as one assumes that the difference is one of the threshold of sensitivity to others rather than a difference in personality makeup.

Rosenthal's work (1976) indicates that very frequently the researcher's expectations either lead the subjects to behave as they were expected to or lead the researcher to believe that they did so. The study did try to control this in that the directions for posthypnotic suggestion were given by tape, arranged by one of the researchers so the others would not know which treatment a subject was experiencing. But it is also noted that the standard conversation of the confederates included "test probes for the subject's deafness." It would seem that at least the confederates, and possibly the other observers as well, would be aware which subjects had received a posthypnotic suggestion of deafness. They would not know whether the subject was aware of the deafness, however. So there is partial control of the observations. The expectancy effect would not influence the MMPI, Thematic Apperception Test, or self-rating data.

The use of a control group with awareness of deafness ensured that lack of awareness was important in producing the effect; it is part of the set of conditions necessary for the effect to appear. A third control group carrying out a neutral posthypnotic suggestion ruled out simply the carrying out of posthypnotic suggestion as a reasonable explanation.

The self-reported feelings of confusion, agitation, and irritation that appeared in the experimental group were unique to that group and so are confounded with its unique treatment. Only one of six accepted the invitation to work with the confederates, in contrast to nine of the twelve control subjects. Whether this finding is evidence of confusion or paranoid behavior is a matter to consider. The association is rejected in the report, which suggests that the confusion would have subsided if subjects had had adequate time for their delusional systems to become "more coherent and systematized." The researchers reject this alternative explanation, especially considering the more direct evidence of paranoia in the MMPI and TAT.

All in all, it is a carefully controlled study, one of the better of the kind one expects from analyzers.

2.15 Credible Result

Most of the results to this point are indicative of strong internal validity (LP). Are the results credible? There seems no reason to believe them to be unusual results for these subjects, situations, procedure, and so forth. The subjects, situation, tests, basis of comparison, and procedure were used inventively and creatively but not in ways that would impair their credibility.

I am aware of no other study even close to this creative use of hypnosis that would permit comparison of these results with others.

Except as one is concerned about the expectancy effect or the confounding of confusion and paranoia in self-ratings, and assuming one accepts the paranoia experienced by older deaf persons as a more serious extension of that experienced by these young subjects (translation fidelity), one would have to conclude that Zimbardo, Andersen, and Kabat have built a study with strong internal validity (LP). It does appear that there is a relationship between feelings of paranoia and deafness in this group, which was chosen for its susceptibility to hypnosis.

2.2 External Validity (GP)

2.21 Explanation Generality

As noted with respect to internal validity (LP), the generality claimed is apparently quite broad; the proposition is perceived as a universal. There is no indication that the results regarding the linkage of paranoia to deafness are even bound by American culture, although it appears from the articles cited that previous observation of the phenomenon is limited to data from Europe and the United States. It is not apparent what, if any, role the culture plays.

2.22 Translation Generality

The subjects and situation chosen certainly lie within the universal group to which the findings should apply. However, they could hardly be considered a representative sample in the sense of broadly including the variety of persons to whom it should apply. That all subjects were college students (recruited from the proverbial introductory undergraduate class, no less), young, male, and susceptible to hypnosis raises questions, depending on which of these characteristics one thinks might represent a limit on the generality of the proposition.

The tests do appear to include the major hypnosis susceptibility scales. The MMPI is representative of the instruments of its type, those with empirically validated keys. It is not clear how well the clinical interview form is representative of those with keys built on the most common symptoms, but given the reputation of the principal investigator, one would expect that it would be a workmanlike job.

Questions about the translation fidelity of the paranoia induced were raised with respect to internal validity (LP) and obviously apply here as well. Is paranoia induced in a very short time, such as this experimental procedure apparently took, the same as that which develops over a prolonged period of deafness? It would appear to be qualitatively the same, but some readers may have reservations.

The most serious question may be that raised earlier about the possible link between susceptibility to hypnosis and susceptibility to apparent rejection by others—paranoia. Again there is no reason to believe that the kinds of feelings differ, only the likelihood that these individuals might have them. But again, if the reader is concerned that a qualitative difference might exist in the kinds of individuals involved, then this might be a problem in translation, and the sample might be perceived as a rather special group, so that the finding is not widely generalizable.

2.23 "Demonstrated Generality"

The judgment having been made in internal validity (LP) that there was an effect as predicted with a group in which it was supposed to appear allows one to infer that at least for this group there is "demonstrated generality."

2.24 Restrictive Explanations Eliminated

There do not appear to be alternative explanations that would impair the generality of the findings. Certainly, none of the common ones apply.

2.25 Replicable Result

The generality of the results seems to be possibly limited by the two concerns raised so far: (1) the relation of the paranoia induced in the short time the study required to that induced over a considerable period in persons who are deaf and not aware of it, (2) the similarity of individuals who are susceptible to hypnosis to the population of deaf persons who have been shown to have the feelings of paranoia. The first of these concerns was also raised with respect to internal validity (LP). In assessing internal validity (LP), it was assumed that there was a difference in the strength but not in the nature of the paranoid feelings. There seems to be no reason not to assume that here also.

The second concern is a little more difficult to allay. It is not established that the two populations are similar. There is a possible suspicion that the experimental group may be more sensitive to the suggestions of others. Where the target population is not directly sampled, as in this case, the researcher should dispel concerns that the sampled population may be different. Depending on the seriousness of one's reservations on this point, this is a generalizable finding.

The use of all male undergraduate college students is a limiting factor. This is especially true for those who see male aggressiveness as a potential factor in paranoia; generalization to females might be limited. As with all experiments that differ from the real-life counter-part, one would feel much more certain if it had dealt with individuals who were found to be going deaf and were not aware of it. Such a study could be done on a longitudinal basis, but it is doubtful that a human-subject protection committee would deem this an important enough relationship to allow an experiment in which individuals were not told they were going deaf and assumed they had normal hearing. Thus, this simulation may be as close to gathering generalizable evidence as we are able to come.

Note the ethical limitation. The limits and constraints of a study may appear in a wide variety of places throughout any study. In this study they happen to appear here.

3.0 Credibility with Audience

One caveat already noted is that the use of hypnosis might have varying reception through the broad audience that reads *Science*. The study does include a well-known and accepted test, the MMPI, as well as the authors' own clinically derived paranoia scale. Further, it uses self-evidently valid self-report evidence on paranoid characteristics as additional evidence. Thus paranoid behavior is established in several ways.

Except for the hypnosis aspect, the rest of the study is conven-tional and uses standard techniques in standard ways. It appears to be aimed at an analyzer audience and meets its criteria quite well, especially in building a tight design and using the experimental method.

The authors clearly tried to anticipate questions and objections to the study. For example, they anticipate and answer the question of how the directions were given to the hearing-impaired subjects—they were flashed on a screen.

The scoring of TAT stories is likely to be subject to poor objectivity. The authors note that stories were scored by two judges who were reliable in their scorings (although they might have given a correlation coefficient to provide evidence of what they termed "reliable").

The confederates engaged in "a well-rehearsed, standard con-versation designed to establish their commonality . . . and to provide verbal content that might be misperceived as antagonistic." Thus the researchers ensured that all subjects were exposed to a reasonably standardized stimulus that developed the behavior to be judged.

4.0 Information Yield

It is often difficult to judge information yield in a published study: If the report tells only about the main effect, one doesn't know whether that is because nothing else happened or because side effects were not noted. Nor does one know about aberrations in data gathering. Only if they are mentioned does one know resources were allocated for this purpose, for routine but empty-handed searches are rarely mentioned. Similarly, unless it is mentioned, one doesn't know whether resources were used for building future studies based on this one.

One can, however, judge whether enough information was gathered on the main effect to make the case. It did seem to have been in this study.

Although information yield may not appear important in judging a study, it is very important in developing a study.

5.0 Resource Allocation

Resource allocation is apparent only if done badly. The planning that goes into a study is not apparent in the product except to those who have done such studies. In this respect, it is like information yield, which is also a resource allocation function. And also like information yield, it is a critical function in the development of a study but difficult to say anything about when judging the write-up.

Allocation of such resources as funding and research time is apparent only indirectly, by what they produce. One resource allocation decision that is directly visible is the space allocated for the report and the way it is used. Because such space is very limited, its use reflects the concerns the authors expect will be important in the minds of the audience and those that they can do something about. For example, the youth of the sample is noted at different points; the authors realized this would be questioned. So is the subjects' confusion as an alternative explanation. Niceties of the control provided by the design are pointed out. Strangely, by contrast, the sample's maleness is just casually noted. Of particular interest is the lack of comment on the use of hypnosis, a technique that was sure to be considered pseudoscientific by some in the audience. Apparently the authors concluded that either the audience would accept it on the basis of past knowledge or it wouldn't no matter what they could say about it in the brief space they had for the whole article. So they traded off that use of space for issues they could do something about. For instance, they used considerable space to document the relation of deafness and psychological problems, particularly paranoia. Apparently they believed this part of their argument needed support and they could use their space effectively to do it. Use of the very limited publication space obviously involves trade-offs just as many other aspects of the study do.

This study is a well-done study with few criticisms, and none of those involves apparent resource allocation problems.

Limits and Constraints

Resource Limits

As with resource allocation, little can be said about resource limits unless the sample is too small or the study has skimped in some other way. Indeed, in this study the sample of only six subjects in each group was small, but it was sufficient to show the expected effect. Especially with so small a sample, the authors could, however, have said whether each of the six experimental subjects seemed to show the effect or whether there were any exceptions.

Ethical Standards

Subjects were required to complete consent and medical history forms at the outset of the study. There clearly was a concern with the subjects' mental health. We are told that subjects were debriefed extensively and were rehypnotized and told to recall all events experienced during the session. Subjects were also reevaluated in a one-month follow-up, presumably to be sure there were no residual problems.

Institutional Constraints

The only institutional constraints appear to have been those imposed by the Stanford University human-subject protection committee, and these are probably reflected in the precautions noted under "Ethical Standards."

Overall Comment

The argument flows very well from the outset to the end. The authors summarize the results and suggest implications. The reader comes away with a good overall perspective on the study, neither having been overwhelmed by details nor feeling that essential aspects have been omitted.

Application of the Checklist to a Qualitative Study

The examples used in the book so far have been largely quantitative studies; yet, the model applies to qualitative studies as well. Qualitative studies, like the example chosen here, often describe a situation and the interplay of the various aspects, with one or more generalizations emerging. The example chosen is the bulk of a chapter from *Outsiders: Studies in the Sociology of Deviance,* by Howard Becker (1963).* This is the first section of one of two chapters dealing with dance musicians, a group perceived to have a "culture and way of life that is sufficiently bizarre and unconventional for them to be labeled outsiders by more conventional members of the community" (p. 79). The chapter is reasonably typical of qualitative research and was done by a recognized researcher accomplished in the method. In the chapter previous to the quoted one, Becker notes that the material was gathered by participant observation while he played piano professionally in Chicago. Like many other working musicians after World War II, he was taking advantage of the GI Bill to attend college. He later played in Champaign–Urbana and in Kansas City. He took notes only in Chicago but says that his later experiences in no way contradicted his earlier observations. There was no formal interviewing, just notes on the individuals he interacted with during a variety of "gigs."

Careers in a Deviant Occupational Group: The Dance Musician

I have already discussed, particularly in considering the development of marihuana use, the *deviant career* (the development, that is, of a pattern of deviant behavior). I would like now to consider the kinds of careers that develop among dance musicians, a group of "outsiders" that considers itself and is considered by others to be "different." But instead of concentrating on the genesis of deviant modes of behavior, I will ask what consequences for a person's occupational career stem from the fact that the occupational group within which he makes that career is a deviant one.

In using the concept of career to study the fate of the individual within occupational organizations, Hughes has defined it as "objectively . . . a series of statuses and clearly defined offices . . . typical sequences of position, achievement, responsibility, and even of adventure. . . . Subjectively, a career is the moving perspective in which the person sees his life as a whole and interprets the meaning of his various attributes, actions, and the things which happen to him."[1] Hall's discussion of the stages of the medical career focuses more specifically on the career as a series of adjustments to the "network of institutions, formal organizations, and informal relationships" in which the profession is practiced.[2]

The career lines characteristic of an occupation take their shape from the problems peculiar to that occupation. These, in turn, are a function of the occupation's position vis-à-vis other groups in the society. The major problems of musicians, as we have seen, revolve around maintaining freedom from control over artistic behavior. Control is exerted by the outsiders for whom musicians work, who ordinarily judge and react to the musician's performance on the basis of standards quite different from his. The antagonistic relationship between musicians and outsiders shapes the culture of the musician and likewise produces the major contingencies and crisis points in his career.

Studies of more conventional occupations such as medicine have shown that occupational success (as members of the occupation define it) depends on finding a position for oneself in that influential group or groups that controls rewards within the occupation, and that the actions and gestures of colleagues play a great part in deciding the outcome of any individual's career.[3] Musicians are no exception to this proposition, and I shall begin by considering their definitions of occupational success and the way the development of musical careers depends on successful integration into the organization of the music business.

1. Everett C. Hughes, "Institutional Office and the Person," *American Journal of Sociology,* XLIII (November, 1937), 409–410.

2. Oswald Hall, "The Stages of a Medical Career," *American Journal of Sociology,* LIII (March, 1948), 327.

3. See Everett C. Hughes, *French Canada in Transition* (Chicago: University of Chicago Press, 1943), pp. 52–53; and Melville Dalton, "Informal Factors in Career Achievement," *American Journal of Sociology,* LVI (March, 1951), 407–415, for discussions of the influence of the colleague group on careers in industrial organizations; and Hall, *op. cit.,* for a similar analysis of colleague influence in the medical profession. Hall's concept of the "inner fraternity" refers to that group which is so able to exert greatest influence.

There is more to the story of the musician's career, however. The problem of freedom from outside control creates certain additional career contingencies and adds certain complications to the structure of the occupation; I consider these next.

Finally, the musician's family (both the one he is born into and the one he creates by marrying) has a major effect on his career.[4] Parents and wives are typically not musicians and, as outsiders, often fail to understand the nature of the musician's attachment to his work. The misunderstandings and disagreements that arise often change the direction of a man's career and, in some cases, bring it to an end.

Cliques and Success

The musician conceives of success as movement through a hierarchy of available jobs. Unlike the industrial or white-collar worker, he does not identify his career with one employer; he expects to change jobs frequently. An informally recognized ranking of these jobs—taking account of the income involved, the hours of work, and the degree of community recognition of achievement felt—constitutes the scale by which a musician measures his success according to the kind of job he usually holds.

At the bottom of this scale is the man who plays irregularly for small dances, wedding receptions, and similar affairs, and is lucky to make union wages. At the next level are those men who have steady jobs in "joints"—lower class taverns and night clubs, small "strip joints," etc.—where pay is low and community recognition lower. The next level is comprised of those men who have steady jobs with local bands in neighborhood ballrooms and small, "respectable" night clubs and cocktail lounges in better areas of the city. These jobs pay more than joint jobs and the man working them can expect to be recognized as successful in his community. Approximately equivalent to these are men who work in so-called "class B name" orchestras, the second rank of nationally known dance orchestras. The next level consists of men who work in "class A name" bands, and in local orchestras that play the best night clubs and hotels, large conventions, etc. Salaries are good, hours are easy, and the men can expect

4. See the discussion in Howard S. Becker, "The Implications of Research on Occupational Careers for a Model of Household Decision-Making," in Nelson N. Foote, editor, *Household Decision Making* (New York: New York University Press, 1961), pp. 239–254; and Howard S. Becker and Anselm L. Strauss, "Careers, Personality, and Adult Socialization," *American Journal of Sociology,* LXII (November, 1956), 253–263.

to be recognized as successful within and outside of the profession. The top positions in this scale are occupied by men who hold staff positions in radio and television stations and legitimate theaters. Salaries are high, hours short, and these jobs are recognized as the epitome of achievement in the local music world, and as jobs of high-ranking respectability by outsiders.

A network of informal, interlocking cliques allocates the jobs available at a given time. In securing work at any one level, or in moving up to jobs at a new level, one's position in the network is of great importance. Cliques are bound together by ties of mutual obligation, the members sponsoring each other for jobs, either hiring one another when they have the power or recommending one another to those who do the hiring for an orchestra. The recommendation is of great importance, since it is by this means that available individuals become known to those who hire; the person who is unknown will not be hired, and membership in cliques insures that one has many friends who will recommend one to the right people.

Clique membership thus provides the individual with steady employment. One man explained:

> See, it works like this. My right hand here, that's five musicians. My left hand, that's five more. Now one of these guys over here gets a job. He picks the men for it from just these guys in this group. Whenever one of them gets a job, naturally he hires this guy. So you see how it works. They never hire anybody that isn't in the clique. If one of them works, they all work.

The musician builds and cements these relationships by getting jobs for other men and so obligating them to return the favor:

> There were a couple of guys on this band that I've got good jobs for, and they've had them ever since. Like one of those trombone players. I got him on a good band. One of the trumpet players, too. . . . You know the way that works. A leader asks you for a man. If he likes the guy you give him, why every time he needs a man he'll ask you. That way you can get all your friends on.

Security comes from the number and quality of relationships so established. To have a career one must work; to enjoy the security of steady work one must have many "connections":

> You have to make connections like that all over
> town, until it gets so that when anybody wants a man
> they call you. Then you're never out of work.

A certain similarity to the informal organization of medical practice should be noted. Musicians cooperate by recommending each other for jobs in much the same way that members of the medical "inner fraternity" cooperate by furnishing each other with patients.[5] The two institutional complexes differ, however, in that medical practice (in all except the largest cities) tends to revolve around a few large hospitals which one, or a few, such fraternities can control. In music, the number of possible foci is much greater, with a correspondingly greater proliferation of organization and, consequently, there are more opportunities for the individual to establish the right connections for himself and a lessening of the power of any particular clique.

In addition to providing a measure of job security for their members, cliques also provide routes by which one can move up through the levels of jobs. In several cliques observed, membership was drawn from more than one level of the hierarchy; thus men of lower position were able to associate with men from a higher level. When a job becomes available higher in the scale, a man of the lower level may be sponsored by a higher-ranking man who recommends him, or hires him, and takes the responsibility for the quality of his performance. A radio staff musician described the process in these terms:

> Now the other way to be a success is to have a
> lot of friends. You have to play good, but you have to
> have friends on different bands and when someone
> leaves a band, why they're plugging to get you on. It
> takes a long time to work yourself up that way. Like I've
> been 10 years getting the job I have now.

If the man so sponsored performs successfully he can build up more informal relationships at the new level and thus get more jobs at that level. Successful performance on the job is necessary if he is to establish himself fully at the new level, and sponsors exhibit a great deal of anxiety over the performance of their protégés. The multiple sponsorship described in this incident from my field notes illustrates this anxiety and its sources in the obligations of colleagues:

5. Hall, *op. cit.*, p. 332.

A friend of mine asked me if I was working that night. When I told him no, he led me over to another guy who, in turn, led me to an old fellow with a strong Italian accent. This man said, "You play piano, huh?" I said, "Yes." He said, "You play good, huh?" I said, "Yes." He said, "You play good? Read pretty good?" I said, "Not bad. What kind of a deal is this?" He said, "It's at a club here in the Loop. It's nine to four-thirty, pays two-fifty an hour. You're sure you can handle it?" I said, "Sure!" He touched my shoulder and said, "OK. I just have to ask you all these questions. I mean, I don't know you, I don't know how you play, I just have to ask, you see?" I said, "Sure." He said, "You know, I have to make sure, it's a spot downtown. Well, here. You call this number and tell them Mantuno told you to call—Mantuno. See, I have to make sure you're gonna do good or else I'm gonna catch hell. Go on, call 'em now. Remember, Mantuno told you to call."

He gave me the number. I called and got the job. When I came out of the booth my friend who had originated the deal came up and said, "Everything all right? Did you get the job, huh?" I said, "Yeah, thanks an awful lot." He said, "That's all right. Listen, do a good job. I mean, if it's commercial, play commercial. What the hell! I mean, if you don't then it's my ass, you know. It isn't even only my ass, it's Tony's and that other guy's, it's about four different asses, you know."

In short, to get these top job positions requires both ability and the formation of informal relationships of mutual obligation with men who can sponsor one for the jobs. Without the necessary minimum of ability one cannot perform successfully at the new level, but this ability will command the appropriate kind of work only if a man has made the proper connections. For sponsors, as the above quotation indicates, the system operates to bring available men to the attention of those who have jobs to fill and to provide them with recruits who can be trusted to perform adequately.

The successful career may be viewed as a series of such steps, each one a sequence of sponsorship, successful performance, and the building up of relationships at each new level.

I have noted a similarity between the musician's career and careers in medicine and industry, shown in the fact that successful functioning and professional mobility are functions of the individual's relation to a network of informal organizations composed of his colleagues. I turn now to the variation in this typical social form created by the strong emphasis of musicians on maintaining their freedom to play without interference from nonmusicians, who are felt to lack understanding and appreciation of the musician's mysterious, artistic gifts. Since it is difficult (if not impossible) to attain this desired freedom, most men find it necessary to sacrifice the standards of their profession to some degree in order to meet the demands of audiences and of those who control employment opportunities. This creates another dimension of professional prestige, based on the degree to which one refuses to modify one's performance in deference to outside demands—from the one extreme of "playing what you feel" to the other of "playing what the people want to hear." The jazzman plays what he feels while the commercial musician caters to public taste; the commercial viewpoint is best summarized in a statement attributed to a very successful commercial musician: "I'll do anything for a dollar."

As I pointed out earlier, musicians feel that there is a conflict inherent in this situation, that one cannot please the audience and at the same time maintain one's artistic integrity. The following quotation, from an interview with a radio staff musician, illustrates the kind of pressures in the top jobs that produce such conflict:

> The big thing down at the studio is not to make any mistakes. You see, they don't care whether you play a thing well or not, as long as you play all the notes and don't make any mistakes. Of course, you care if it doesn't sound good, but they're not interested in that. . . . They don't care what you sound like when you go through that mike, all they care about is the commercial. I mean, you might have some personal pride about it, but they don't care. . . . That's what you have to do. Give him what you know he likes already.

The job with most prestige is thus one in which the musician must sacrifice his artistic independence and the concomitant prestige in professional terms. A very successful commercial musician paid deference to artistic independence while stressing its negative effect on career development:

> I know, you probably like to play jazz. Sure I understand. I used to be interested in jazz, but I found out that didn't pay, people didn't like jazz. They like

rumbas. After all, this is a business, ain't that right? You're in it to make a living or you're not, that's all. And if you want to make a living you can't throw jazz at the people all the time, they won't take it. So you have to play what they want, they're the ones that are paying the bills. I mean, don't get me wrong. Any guy that can make a living playing jazz, fine. But I'd like to see the guy that can do it. If you want to get anywhere you gotta be commercial.

Jazzmen, on the other hand, complain of the low position of the jobs available to them in terms of income and things other than artistic prestige.

Thus the cliques to which one must gain access if one is to achieve job success and security are made up of men who are definitely commercial in their orientation. The greatest rewards of the profession are controlled by men who have sacrificed some of the most basic professional standards, and one must make a similar sacrifice in order to have any chance of moving into the desirable positions:

See, if you play commercial like that, you can get in with these cliques that have all the good jobs and you can really do well. I've played some of the best jobs in town—the Q— Club and places like that—and that's the way you have to do. Play that way and get in with these guys, then you never have to worry. You can count on making that gold every week and that's what counts.

Cliques made of jazzmen offer their members nothing but the prestige of maintaining artistic integrity; commercial cliques offer security, mobility, income, and general social prestige.

This conflict is a major problem in the career of the individual musician, and the development of his career is contingent on his reaction to it. Although I gathered no data on the point, it seems reasonable to assume that most men enter music with a great respect for jazz and artistic freedom. At a certain point in the development of the career (which varies from individual to individual), the conflict becomes apparent and the musician realizes that it is impossible to achieve the kind of success he desires and maintain independence of musical performance. When the incompatibility of these goals becomes obvious, some sort of choice must be made, if only by default, thus determining the further course of his career.

One response to the dilemma is to avoid it, by leaving the profession. Unable to find a satisfactory resolution of the problem, the individual cuts his career off. The rationale of such a move is disclosed in the following statement by one who had made it:

> It's better to take a job you know you're going to be dragged [depressed] with, where you expect to be dragged, than one in music, where it could be great but isn't. Like you go into business, you don't know anything about it. So you figure it's going to be a drag and you expect it. But music can be so great that it's a big drag when it isn't. So it's better to have some other kind of job that won't drag you that way.

We have seen the range of responses to this dilemma on the part of those who remain in the profession. The jazzman ignores audience demands for artistic standards while the commercial musician does the opposite, both feeling the pressure of these two forces. My concern here will be to discuss the relation of these responses to career fates.

The man who chooses to ignore commercial pressures finds himself effectively barred from moving up to jobs of greater prestige and income, and from membership in those cliques which would provide him with security and the opportunity for such mobility. Few men are willing or able to take such an extreme position; most compromise to some degree. The pattern of movement involved in this compromise is a common career phenomenon, well known among musicians and assumed to be practically inevitable:

> I saw K—— E——. I said, "Get me a few jobbing dates, will you?" He said, imitating one of the "old guys,"[6] "Now son, when you get wise and commercial, I'll be able to help you out, but not now." In his normal voice he continued, "Why don't you get with it? Gosh, I'm leading the trend over to commercialism, I guess. I certainly have gone in for it in a big way, haven't I?"

At this crucial point in his career the individual finds it necessary to make a radical change in his self-conception; he must learn to think of himself in a new way, to regard himself as a different kind of person:

6. "Old guys" was the term generally used by younger men to refer to the cliques controlling the most desirable jobs.

This commercial business has really gotten me, I guess. You know, even when I go on a job where you're supposed to blow jazz, where you can just let yourself go and play anything, I think about being commercial, about playing what the people out there might want to hear. I used to go on a job with the idea to play the best I could, that's all, just play the best I knew how. And now I go on a job and I just automatically think, "What will these people want to hear? Do they want to hear Kenton style, or like Dizzy Gillespie [jazz orchestras], or like Guy Lombardo [a commercial orchestra], or what?" I can't help thinking that to myself. They've really gotten it into me, I guess they've broken my spirit.

A more drastic change of self-conception related to this career dilemma is found in this statement:

I'll tell you, I've decided the only thing to do is really go commercial—play what the people want to hear. I think there's a good place for the guy that'll give them just what they want. The melody, that's all. No improvising, no technical stuff—just the plain melody. I'll tell you, why shouldn't I play that way? After all, let's quit kidding ourselves. Most of us aren't really musicians, we're just instrumentalists. I mean, I think of myself as something like a common laborer, you know. No sense trying to fool myself. Most of those guys are just instrumentalists, they're not real musicians at all, they should stop trying to kid themselves they are.

Making such a decision and undergoing such a change in self-conception open the way for movement into the upper levels of the job hierarchy and create the conditions in which complete success is possible, if one can follow up the opportunity by making and maintaining the proper connections.

One way of adjusting to the realities of the job without sacrificing self-respect is to adopt the orientation of the craftsman. The musician who does this no longer concerns himself with the *kind* of music he plays. Instead, he is interested only in whether it is played *correctly,* in whether he has the skills necessary to do the job the way it ought to be done. He finds his pride and self-respect in being able to "cut" any kind of music, in always giving an adequate performance.

The skills necessary to maintain this orientation vary with the setting in which the musician performs. The man who works in bars with small groups will pride himself on knowing hundreds (or even thousands) of songs and being able to play them in any key. The man who works with a big band will pride himself on his intonation and technical virtuosity. The man who works in a night club or radio studio boasts of his ability to read any kind of music accurately and precisely at sight. This kind of orientation, since it is likely to produce just what the employer wants and at a superior level of quality, is likely to lead to occupational success.

The craftsman orientation is easier to sustain in the major musical centers of the country: Chicago, New York, Los Angeles. In these cities, the volume of available work is great enough to support specialization, and a man can devote himself single-mindedly to improving one set of skills. One finds musicians of astounding virtuosity in these centers. In smaller cities, in contrast, there is not enough work of any one kind for a man to specialize, and musicians are called on to do a little of everything. Although the necessary skills overlap—intonation, for instance, is always important—every man has areas in which he is just barely competent. A trumpet player may play excellent jazz and do well on small jazz jobs but read poorly and do much less well when he works with a big band. It is difficult to maintain pride as a craftsman when one is continually faced with jobs for which he has only minimal skills.

To sum up, the emphasis of musicians on freedom from the interference inevitable in their work creates a new dimension of professional prestige which conflicts with the previously discussed job prestige in such a way that one cannot rank high in both. The greatest rewards are in the hands of those who have sacrificed their artistic independence, and who demand a similar sacrifice from those they recruit for these higher positions. This creates a dilemma for the individual musician, and his response determines the future course of his career. Refusing to submit means that all hope of achieving jobs of high prestige and income must be abandoned, while giving in to commercial pressures opens the way to success for them. (Studies of other occupations might devote attention to those career contingencies which are, likewise, a function of the occupation's basic work problems vis-à-vis clients or customers.)

1.0 Question Choice and Formulation

Becker's problem appears to have grown out of his previous research. This fact is both reassuring, since it indicates there is some basis for the expectations, and troubling, if one thinks these expectations might have influenced data collection. Only if one is concerned that the ignored observations are contrary to expectations is this a problem. Without being present during the observations, one rarely knows in a qualitative study. Only if the study is replicated and the evidence is consistent is the doubt totally removed. In qualitative research, credibility with the audience, convincing it of the researcher's integrity, is essential to allaying such concerns. This is further commented on in the section "Demonstrated Result."

2.0 Weighting of Internal Validity (LP) and External Validity (GP)

The study appears to be about equally weighted toward both of these, hoping to show that the explanations match reality and that the reality applies to mainstream musicians. This is appropriate but a large order for a single study.

2.1 Internal Validity (LP)

2.11 Explanation Credibility

Assuming that the researcher is working in a synthesizer mode, looking for relationships and generalizations, rather than a humanist's telling an informing story, one of the first things one must do is to ascertain what generalizations, if any, are being put forward and what their explanations are. In some qualitative reports, where generalizations appear absent, the material is purely descriptive, and although criteria for accuracy of description might apply, much of the checklist—basis of comparison, demonstrated result, rival explanations eliminated, and so on—would not. In this instance, one must sort out what it is Becker sees as the generalizable material one should carry away from one's reading.

Becker seems to be claiming three generalizations: (1) Musicians build their careers by climbing a series of steps, "each one a sequence of sponsorship, successful performance, and the building up of relationships" that will lead to new sponsorships to attain new levels. (2) As one climbs through the levels, desire for artistic freedom (which is a sign of professional prestige) conflicts with job prestige in such a way that one cannot have both; climbing the ladder gains job prestige, but one loses artistic control to one's clients and audiences, who require one to play what they want to hear rather than what one feels. (3) To maintain self-respect, the musician "no longer concerns himself with the *kind* of music . . . [but] whether it is played *correct-*

ly, . . . whether he has the skills . . . to do the job the way it ought to be done."

Is this explanation of the musician's career credible? To those of us outside the musicians' realm, it has both plausible and implausible elements. The descriptions of the social elements and of the conflict between commercial music and jazz sound real enough. But the lack of emphasis on skill runs contrary to the layperson's view. Skill seems to enter only in that the person is capable of taking the next step and, when one has turned commercial, as the source of self-respect. Superior skill, which seems to be what every layperson is looking for in musicians, seems to have little or no place in the rise through the levels. Since one's rise is dependent on building relationships, which takes time, it seems superior skill may not even be a factor in a quicker rise through the levels. Is this correct? One wonders whether Becker is accurate for the great bulk of dance musicians but not for the really talented. The latter is really a generality question, taken up under external validity (GP).

2.12 Translation Fidelity

Here we are concerned with the translation of the explanation to the real world. In qualitative research, there is usually little problem with translation fidelity, since the terms of the explanation are derived from the data, and one's only concern is whether the proper terms have been chosen to describe what appears in the data. Unfortunately, in most qualitative research, the only data displayed are those given in carefully selected quotations from field notes, often quotations from individuals. This may provide too little evidence for judgment, but one looks at it for inconsistencies in the usage of terms between text and field notes or within the text itself. There appears to be none in Becker's text.

One also asks whether the subjects were members of the target group to which the generalization is to apply (not necessarily whether they were representative, as in external validity (GP)). They clearly were here.

2.13 Demonstrated Relationship

Once again one is looking at the relationships among the data one is provided with, the quotations from field notes, and their interpretation to see whether the explanation is supported. Here the choice of quotations from the field notes is crucial for the researcher, since an irrelevant field note to support a point begins to raise questions about what is being advanced.

The quotations with regard to building a network of relationships that help the musician obtain work all seem to support the point well.

The quotation about Mantuno and the need to reassure him that the musician had the necessary skill makes the point well that there is anxiety that those recommended may not live up to the recommendation. It reinforces the notion that it is the contact rather than actual playing skill that permits one to move up, since Mantuno apparently made no request for a demonstration. Such a request would be routine for many positions, but here it might be perceived as evidence of distrust of the recommendation. So that particular field note reinforces the earlier point about the importance of the social network *vis-à-vis* ability. Finally, the quotations regarding the implications of going commercial or developing a craftsmanship orientation to maintain self-respect do not really bear on that point. They all deal with the problem of going commercial and the pressures to do so. The idea of a craftsmanship orientation may be correct, but it is derived from field notes that are not quoted in the text.

As one can sense, with so few data, a great deal must be left to the integrity of the investigator. So few data are cited in a qualitative report, relative to the abstracted descriptions of them and explanations of them, that one often has to depend on small clues to get a sense of whether the investigator is trustworthy. An example of such evidence is when he tells you he does not have the data for a generalization. Becker does this: "Although I gathered no data on the point, it seems reasonable to assume that most men enter music with a great respect for jazz and artistic freedom." This material flows reasonably from the rest of the material, and he could have passed it off as data-based. It is reassuring that he tells you the contrary.

2.14 Rival Explanations Eliminated

Are there rival explanations that could explain the data as well as the ones advanced? None of the standard rival explanations seems a reasonable candidate here.

Are there rival explanations for the generalizations? It is hard to tell without more data, but little is said about the socialization of musicians and whether that socialization might not, in some instances, result in congruence between what the public likes and what the musician wants to play. Are some socialization routes more likely to result in congruence than others and thus to avoid the conflict Becker sees as inevitable? (Some of this concern is answered in the previous chapter, where Becker indicates that the musician sees himself as an isolate against the squares of the world, who do not have the mysterious artistic gift that sets him apart.) And there is still the question whether skill might play a larger part in the rise of a musician than Becker's script seems to allow for. Once one gets on the ladder in a steady job, doesn't skill count for more than is indicated? Or is that just the American dream of an unstreetwise nonmusician?

2.15 Credible Result

Finally, one must examine the whole of Becker's case, checking it against whatever other evidence one has and deciding whether the explanation claimed is valid. The parallel to the medical profession is pointed out early and the medical generalization is based on prior research, which is cited, but there seems to be no direct evidence bearing on musicians. Except as one has a musical background or access to one through family or friends, most of us do not have a basis in personal experience to determine whether what Becker advances "rings true." We are therefore thrown back entirely on our analyses of the prior four judgments. These are largely positive but do raise some questions. Overall, Becker seems to get relatively high but not perfect marks in internal validity (LP). Had he correctly anticipated some of the questions raised and included more relevant quotations from his field notes regarding craftsmanship, he could have markedly strengthened the internal validity (LP) of the study.

2.2 External Validity (GP)

2.21 Explanation Generality

Does Becker intend his explanation to apply mainly to the run-of-the-mill musician, and does he exclude those with exceptional musical ability? It is not clear from his report; yet, the layperson's image of the musician is more likely to come from the highly talented whose lives are revealed in magazine articles, award ceremonies, and countless television interviews. I would have to infer that he is concerned mainly with the mainstream of musicians, since he says nothing about talent in the material dealing with his explanation. He apparently had experience with a variety of orchestras and dance bands. That places boundaries around his generalizations which are not stated but which must be inferred, and the inference is by no means a certain one. Becker would undoubtedly intend the idea of deviance to apply to the talented as well, but their opportunity to control their fate may be somewhat greater; it is not clear.

2.22 Translation Generality

Does Becker include the kinds of individuals in his sample to whom he wishes to generalize? Again, it is not clear. There was no systematic sampling of individuals or situations. For situations, the samples are limited to two large cities and one small one, all in the Midwest, and not including such centers as New York and Los Angeles. Becker seems to believe that the size of the city makes a difference in whether an individual can specialize in order to show craftsmanship, but aside from that, he seems to believe the rest of the description holds. If one agrees with Becker, and most of us will not have the background that provides a basis for disagreement, representativeness for mainstream musicians seems present.

2.23 "Demonstrated Generality"

Does the explanation fit the instances that provide the data, and are these representative of the range of instances to which one hopes to generalize? There is no way of telling the latter from the small number of quotations given. The ones that appear are relevant and do support the explanations. But how representative they are of the field notes, only Becker knows. One has to trust the qualitative researcher in such instances and hope he will warn us when the field notes cited are relevant but atypical. A researcher with integrity will.

2.24 Restrictive Explanations Eliminated

As with internal validity (LP), most of the common rival explanations that would restrict generality do not apply. It is not clear to what extent in gathering the data Becker may have tipped his hand about what answers he expected. It is not clear whether he went into the study with expectations that finding a position for oneself with an influential group was important and that "the actions and gestures of colleagues play a great part in deciding the outcome of any individual's career." The dates of prior research indicate that he had found this formulation before writing the chapters with which we are concerned, but it is not clear how the date of that formulation relates to the data gathering for those chapters. The question is whether the findings could be a function of experimenter expectancy. One can't tell from the evidence given, and Becker's information on methods is somewhat sketchy. He does comment in the previous chapter, however, that "I seldom did any formal interviewing, but concentrated rather on listening to and recording the ordinary kinds of conversation that occurred among musicians. Most of my observation was carried out on the job and even on the stand as we played" (p. 85). These remarks seem to suggest that he was unlikely to have led his respondents to give the sought-for answers. If there were a bias, it would be in his recording of the conversation, and there is little basis for judgment here one way or the other except his general reputation as an accomplished user of the method.

2.25 Replicable Result

Would these same generalizations result if one increased one's sample of respondents? Would they result in other cities? With the full range of musical talent? If one used individuals to do the interviews who were not privy to Becker's prior expectations? These are some of the questions that run through one's mind in making this judgment. There are no past results with which to compare this study, so that aspect, which is often a part of this judgment, is not appropriate in this instance.

The evidence that is given is put together well; it has internal consistency; it seems to convey the feeling that we are dealing with a person with integrity and one who has personally experienced and therefore knows the music scene. Thus, it reduces to the matter of whether one trusts the investigator, since what evidence there is from field notes is generally favorable. If one does, then the study has both internal validity (LP) and external validity (GP).

3.0 Credibility with Audience

We saw that, in admitting he lacked data, Becker built credibility with the audience. He is an experienced investigator, using his favorite and previously highly successful method, so that helps his credibility. The method is one that is commonly used by synthesizers and it was used conventionally, all in his favor. The fact that, as a participant observer, he could actually be a professional musician and be accepted as such should have resulted in excellent observation opportunities not available to an investigator without those skills, who could not have built as successful a cover.

We did find several questions, however. Had he anticipated and allayed them, it would have raised his credibility; leaving them unanswered damaged it somewhat but not greatly.

4.0 and 5.0 Information Yield and Resource Allocation

As in most research reports, there is little basis for judging these very important aspects of the implementation of research. One can, however, often tell when they are done badly, and there is no such evidence here. In evaluating efficiency and effectiveness, for instance, there is no way to judge from the evidence whether the field notes have been milked for the major generalizations that could be squeezed from them.

Limits and Constraints

Resource Limits

Though critical in building a study, resource limits are not very evident in a reported study unless the amount of data gathered is obviously too small. There is no evidence of the amount gathered, but neither is there any evidence that the data were inadequate. Apparently the data were gathered over two years, 1948–1949, which is a substantial period of observations.

Ethical Standards

There is no evidence that there were ethical problems of any kind in the data-gathering process. Anonymity has been preserved.

Institutional Constraints

Again, institutional constraints do not seem relevant to this study, since institutions as such were not involved.

Overall Comment

The study seems to be well done. Although the argument seems generally plausible, the layperson without music background to check it against cannot read it without questions. One may still wonder about the role of ability, but for the mainline musician, the way Becker describes it may well be how it is. The explanation is presented well, and quotations from field notes are appropriate and generally supporting.

11

Comparing the Framework with Other Ways of Conceptualizing Research Criteria

This chapter relates linking and generalizing power to the two main competing formulations. The most prominent of these is that devised by Campbell and Stanley (1963) and later modified in Cook and Campbell (1979). Most researchers would agree that it and its modifications have become the standard against which any other must be judged. The other is that of Cronbach, which has not been available long enough to determine whether it will replace or how it will modify the earlier formulations.

This chapter is not intended to develop further the formulation of internal validity (LP) and external validity (GP) but, rather, aims at increasing the understanding of these terms by comparing them with other formulations. It will also prepare the reader who has not yet encountered those formulations so that she will be ready to recognize the way they differ from the formulation in this book. For those who brought with them a knowledge of prior formulations, it places the formulation of this book in that stream of development; it shows how this book's framework builds on prior formulations and goes beyond them. Such understanding is necessary for the peers who will judge it and, it is hoped, find it useful.

All three formulations are concerned with the problem of inferring whether relationships exist and how generally they apply.

The Campbell and Stanley formulation and its successors, however, are described in the more limiting terms of experimentation and causality, although Campbell has contributed very significantly to our understanding of how knowledge develops as well as the area of causation (for example, 1969, 1974, 1977, 1979). The problem for all three formulations is to identify the characteristics of a study that permit one to infer relationships.

Those familiar with Campbell and his work, particularly the conceptualization of internal and external validity, and its modifications may wonder why alternative conceptualizations need be considered. Since the revision by Cook and Campbell split the initial formulation into four validities, it is clear that Campbell was not entirely happy with the original. Kruglanski and Kroy (1976) provide a useful critique that describes some of the problems of that framework. Cronbach's formulation and the internal validity (LP)/external validity (GP) formulation described herein are attempts to overcome problems that have become apparent. One way to handle some of the problems is the development of additional validities; Cook and Campbell added two. Brinberg and McGrath (1982) have suggested twelve additional internal validities and three additional external validities. This increasing complexity initially seems undesirable, but on reflection, it is clearly necessary if that is the way the process of research is most clearly modeled. If we are to know how to build strong studies, then our model must be as complete as possible. Greater completeness is one intent of the internal validity (LP)/external validity (GP) formulation described herein, although that formulation also results in a somewhat complex set of criteria.

The additional validities of Brinberg and McGrath suggest another problem of the internal/external validity formulation, that of terminology. Most persons first meet the concept of validity in the context of tests and measurement, and it continues to be associated with that context. Although construct validity is used by Cook and Campbell much as it is in testing, the other validities are new ones, and they use the term *validity* in a somewhat different sense. At one time, I considered using only the terms *linking power* and *generalizing power*. Then *validity* could be confined to testing. But it is clear that *internal* and *external validity* are too well established in the literature for that to be practical; the social cost of trying to change the terminology is too high. I have therefore used the modified terms *internal validity (LP)* and *external validity (GP)* to indicate that these are related but broader terms.

Finally, Cronbach in devising reproducibility and I in this formulation have been concerned about the way people think about relationships and the way they build studies to show them. If possible, the distinctions among concepts ought to be made at useful and natural points. Aristotle is said to have argued that we should "carve nature at its joints." It has yet to be determined whether the internal validity (LP)/external validity (GP) formulation has found the "joints" any better than alternatives, but that is one of its goals.

Internal Validity (LP)/External Validity (GP) and Internal/External Validity

There is a subtle but important difference in approach between the internal validity (LP)/external validity (GP) formulation and the internal/external validity formulation of Campbell and Stanley (1963) and its later reformulation by Cook and Campbell (1979). The internal validity (LP) formulation starts from the premise that the function of science is accumulation of knowledge and that knowledge is carried mainly in abstract descriptions of phenomena. It therefore asks the question "What is needed to move ahead the process of knowledge building?" The answer is "To know what it is that allows one to build a consensus among others that one has a valid knowledge claim." It is the decision of others that will ultimately determine the acceptability of that claim. Accordingly, this discussion starts with how the claim to knowledge is presented as a deductive scheme, starting with an explanation or theory, if there is one, and moving through the various kinds of evidence that link the researcher's demonstration to a reduction in uncertainty that a relationship exists. It seeks to answer the question "What decisions enter into the acceptance of a knowledge claim so that we can build as strong knowledge claims as our results permit?"

Cook and Campbell (1979) state that they have merely subdivided Campbell and Stanley's concepts of internal and external validity, adding statistical conclusion validity and construct validity, and tried "to make the difference among types [of validity] explicit" (p. 39). They base their approach on the "four major . . . questions that the practicing researcher faces. These are: (1) In the given investigation, is there a relationship between the two variables? (Internal validity) (2) Given that there is a relationship, is it plausibly causal from one operational variable to the other or would the same relationship have been obtained in the absence of any treatment of any kind? (Statistical conclusion validity) (3) Given that the relationship is plausibly causal and is reasonably known to be from one variable to another, what are the particular cause-and-effect constructs involved in the relationship? (Construct validity) and (4) Given that there is probably a causal relationship from construct A to construct B, how generalizable is this relationship across persons, settings, and times? (External validity)" (p. 39). As they note, "Our approach is entirely practical. . . . There are no totally compelling logical reasons for the distinctions" (p. 39).

Of course, as it turns out, these are among the basic questions that must be answered by any formulation but are less than the whole story. As embodied in internal validity (LP)/external validity (GP), they are part of the larger matrix of questions that forms the sequential logic of the knowledge claim as it flows through the chain of reasoning. That they relate to only part of the chain is made clear when we set the two frameworks opposite each other, showing parallels between pairs of terms, as in Table 5.

The correspondence between the two formulations is examined more closely in the following sections.

Internal Validity (LP) and Internal Validity

As I noted in Chapter Three when introducing the terms, internal validity is related to, but not the same as, internal validity (LP). Cook and Campbell define internal validity as "the validity with which statements can be made about whether there is a causal relationship from one variable to the other *in the form in which the variables were manipulated or measured*" (p. 38, emphasis added). This statement is, I believe, a logical problem in the formulation. As stated, an underlying causal relationship of interest is implied, but as Cronbach (1982) points out, internal validity really refers to the relationship at the instant in time at which the study was done. It infers there *was* a relationship in a historical sense at that time. External validity is the inference that there is now and in the future such a relationship. Although Cook and Campbell's language in the quotation may be confusing on this point, Cronbach's interpretation seems valid in the context of the rest of the formulation (see the earlier long quotation beginning "four major . . .") and the fact that external validity is defined as the generalization to other persons, places, and *times*. As Cronbach points out, internal validity defined as a historical event is of little use to anyone. Indeed, this may be why, as noted earlier, a number of research methods texts changed the definition to one consistent with this book's formulation.

Internal validity (LP), by contrast, is the judged validity with which statements can be made about a study that the relationship proposed as linking the variables is the only appropriate interpreta-

**Table 5. Correspondence Between
Internal Validity (LP)/External Validity (GP) Formulation and
the Internal/External Validity Formulation of Cook and Campbell.**

Internal Validity (LP)/External Validity (GP) Formulation	Internal/External Validity Formulation
Internal Validity (LP)	Internal Validity
1. Explanation credibility	—
2. Translation fidelity	Construct validity
3. Demonstrated relationship	Statistical conclusion validity
4. Rival explanations eliminated	Internal validity
5. Credible result	—
External Validity (GP)	External Validity
1. Explanation generality	—
2. Translation generality	Construct validity
3. "Demonstrated generality"	External validity
4. Restrictive explanations eliminated	External validity
5. Replicable result	External and construct validity

tion of the evidence. Note that this deals with the relationship between the variables *as they are conceptualized.* As if to emphasize the difference, Cook and Campbell continue with the statement quoted above: "Internal validity has nothing to do with abstract labeling . . . it deals with the *relationship* between the research operations *irrespective of what they represent"* (p. 38, emphasis in original).

Another possible distinction, depending on how one defines cause, is that internal validity refers only to causal relationships; certainly the development of internal validity is done entirely in a causal framework in both Campbell and Stanley (1963) and Cook and Campbell (1979). Internal validity (LP) applies to any form of relationship. It could, for instance, be a reciprocal one with feedback modifying each successive action. As noted in Chapter Nine, there are many ways of formulating a relationship.

Operationally, internal validity requires determining the relationship direction (which variable is the cause?), ascertaining that cause preceded effect, and eliminating "threats to validity," rival alternative explanations. For a causal relationship, internal validity (LP) includes the criterion of precedence of cause as well, but only if it is relevant to the conceptualization. Otherwise, it is concerned with congruence between the relationship that was predicted and what actually was found.

Eliminating "threats to validity" is operationally identical to "rival explanations eliminated" in the internal validity (LP) formulation.

The preceding considers what Cook and Campbell call "internal validity." The other half of Campbell and Stanley's original "internal validity" is Cook and Campbell's "statistical conclusion validity." It is quite close to "demonstrated relationship." But the latter is also a broader category, since in it the relationship may be demonstrated by any means: statistical evidence, case studies, persuasive examples, and so on. As previously noted, however, Cook and Campbell are concerned mainly with experimentation, which usually deals with statistics, so in that context, this part of internal validity is quite appropriately named for their purposes. *Demonstrated relationship* seems an appropriate name for a framework intended to apply to a broad range of research methods.

As Table 5 shows, two parts of the internal validity (LP)/ external validity (GP) formulation, "explanation credibility" and "credible result," are not part of Cook and Campbell's internal/ external validity formulation. Let us look at these parts of internal validity (LP) in relation to the conceptualization of internal validity.

Explanation credibility, which is only in the internal validity (LP) formulation, is an extremely important part of a strong chain of reasoning. It is one of the few parts of the framework that appear in every one of the research orientations except the pragmatist. It is our main means of discerning whether we have a Type I or Type II error. As noted earlier, it sets one's initial attitude toward acceptance or rejection of the study and thus is likely to influence one's reaction to it in its entirety. It is very important in building a consensus of judgments.

Cook and Campbell agree on the importance of an abstract formulation to both the theory-oriented and the applied researcher. Working at the abstract level is inescapable in theory building, but it is important to applied researchers as well, "for it is hardly useful to assume that the relationship between the two variables is causal if one cannot summarize these variables other than by describing them in exhaustive operational detail . . . one wants to be able to make generalizations about . . . terms that have a referent in . . . theory or everyday abstract language" (p. 38).

The internal validity (LP) formulation, as well, starts the knowledge claim with whatever "theory or everyday abstract language" is used to describe the phenomenon under study and asks about the credibility of whatever explanation or theory is put forth. The formulations agree on the importance of relating to everyday terms. However, judgment of the credibility of the explanation may be implicit, but it is certainly not an explicit and emphasized part of either the Campbell and Stanley or the Cook and Campbell formulation. Equally important, in the textbook treatments of internal validity, explanation credibility does not appear as a part of the internal validity formulation, even by those who misinterpret internal validity as the relationship between cause and effect as conceptualized rather than between their operational definitions. So the emphasis on explanation credibility as a base for the determination of internal validity (LP) is unique to it.

Because most studies begin with an explanation, hypothesis, or question in the presentation of results (though by no means in the sequence of work—see Chapter Two), the accurate translation of this explanation into the operations of the study is an important step. Kruglanski and Kroy (1976) noted the need for construct validity in determining the existence of a relationship at the abstract level, referring to its placement in external validity as a "misclassification of validity types." Thus "translation fidelity," the translation of everyday or technical terms into operations in a study, enters into internal validity (LP). But this translation is called "construct validity" in Cook and Campbell's formulation and is seen as relevant only in the external validity context.

In addition, construct validity refers only to measures of effect and fidelity of treatment in the Cook and Campbell formulation. It seems apparent that a need equally exists to examine the translation of the explanation, question, hypothesis, or model to subjects, to situation, to point in time, and to the way things are operationalized in the statement of procedure. Thus "translation fidelity" is a more inclusive concept than "construct validity."

"Rival explanations eliminated" has an exact counterpart in the elimination of "threats to validity." It is the main focus of attention and a major contribution of the Campbell/Stanley and Cook/Campbell formulations. It is also an important part of internal validity (LP) but not the main focus of attention.

Finally, internal validity (LP) includes the judgment of the credibility of the result, which has no counterpart. Comparison of the results of a study with previous experience is an important part of uncertainty reduction, as Campbell clearly explains in his own writing, but it seems not to have been formally included in the Campbell/Stanley or Cook/Campbell formulation.

External Validity and External Validity (GP)

The terms *construct validity* and *external validity* in Cook and Campbell seem to divide Campbell and Stanley's external validity on the basis of which of the six design facets in the chain of reasoning are referred to. For example, construct validity refers to the generalizability of other forms of treatment and other measures of effect (observation); Cook and Campbell's external validity refers to the generalizability to other persons (subjects), places (situations), or times (procedures).

This perspective on the study is quite different from external validity (GP), so that it is difficult to relate the parts of the two. Some correspondences in Table 5 are merely approximate.

As with internal validity (LP), comparing the Cook/Campbell external validity formulation with that of external validity (GP) shows at least one part not to be covered, just like "explanation credibility" in internal validity (LP): There is no counterpart of "explanation generality." The matter of a theory, rationale, or explanation that suggests the generality one ought to expect seems to be an essential part of the logic of many studies but is not covered by external validity. The reasonableness of the generality claimed for an explanation often critically predisposes the audience either favorably or negatively to the claimed generality for a study, so it seems it should be a part of any formulation.

"Translation generality" bears somewhat the same relation to "construct validity" in external validity (GP) as its parallel category did in internal validity (LP), but, again, it is a broader concept. It asks whether the claimed generality is represented in the selection of the various design choices: subjects representative of the target population to which one expects to generalize, situations representative of the target situation, and so on. Further, it asks, "Are the boundary conditions specified or implied in the explanation represented in all these choices as well?" As noted before, construct validity is limited to measures and treatment.

"Demonstrated generality" asks whether the relationship was demonstrated across the variety of instances included in the study and what the answer implies for the target variety of instances to which one hopes to generalize. It is an inferential leap from these instances to assume the relationship also holds in the total set of instances they represent. The logic is essentially the same as that implied in the thought experiments that make up external validity. It includes a judgment of the generality to other persons, situations, and times.

External validity also calls for the elimination of any reasonable "threats to validity," restrictive explanations that would limit generality. This, of course, is parallel to "restrictive explanations eliminated" in external validity (GP), but the fact that these explanations restrict generality is not noted.

The counterpart in external validity (GP) of the fifth decision, "replicable result," appears to combine the judgment of generality to other persons, places, and times with the judgment of generality implicit in construct validity. Though not stated in terms of replicability, many of the judgments are similar. Construct validity seems to involve dual judgments, of accuracy and of typicality, or representativeness. Are the constructs accurately represented in the study? This is the counterpart of translation fidelity. Second, are the operations typical of what is meant by the terms used to describe the treatment and effect so that findings would generalize to other operational definitions of them? This is the counterpart of translation generality. Both are involved in judging "replicable result." But replicable result also considers past research evidence, which is not part of the external validity formulation. Nor does the external validity formulation involve considering whether, in thought experiments, one could replicate the study. Are there ambiguities in design or procedure, instances which aren't clearly enough specified and which therefore interfere with the tightness of the chain of reasoning?

Distinguishing Between Judging That a Relationship Exists and That It Has Generality

Another way of looking at the difference between the two formulations is in terms of where they break the chain of reasoning: the break between internal and external validity, on the one hand, and between internal validity (LP) and external validity (GP), on the other. Both make the break around the point in the chain where the data have been analyzed, the results are on hand, and it is a matter of interpreting them. The internal/external validity formulation breaks internal from external validity just *before* one concludes the hypothesis has been supported in the sense that the cause-and-effect relationship hypothesized exists; one knows that it did in a historical instance if the study has internal validity (for example, "In these data manifest-anxiety scores are, on the average, higher for women than men"). Generality to the present and future is a matter of external validity. The internal validity (LP)/external validity (GP) formulation breaks the chain just *after*. It permits one to conclude that the hypothesis is supported for this study and that the variables are related at least insofar as translation fidelity indicated the operational definitions were appropriate (for example, "In this study women are more anxious than men"). Judging the generality of this statement is then a matter of determining the external validity (GP) of the study.

This breaking point seems to be a better place "to carve nature at its joints," since it is the confirmation of the hypothesis for this instance that one is initially concerned about. As noted early in Chapter Three, one finds that internal validity, even when the originating authors are cited, is sometimes defined in terms of the *variables themselves* being related rather than just their *operational definitions* as Campbell and Stanley and Cook and Campbell specify. A dozen examples of textbooks were cited there that use that definition. One doesn't know, of course, whether these authors intended to change the definition, but their use of it this way lends credence to the "naturalness" of the breaking point.

Once again, however, what is "natural" is in part a matter of one's orientation to research. From the standpoint of the pragmatist, the only trustworthy facts are those given by what operationally happened. The interpretation of those facts, the explanation, is always a matter of conjecture and is subject to revision. Pragmatists would locate the breaking point as is done in the internal/external validity formulation. But as previously indicated, pragmatists are unique in their disdain for explanations, and even they do not ignore them but use them for their own purposes.

All the other orientations—analyzer, synthesizer, theorizer, multiperspectivist, and humanist—view science as advancing primarily by means of understandings and explanations. Thus it is support of the explanation that is initially sought, and one can then determine its generality. Looked at from this standpoint, the break should be located as it is in the internal validity (LP)/external validity (GP) formulation. So perhaps, in part, which formulation is preferred is a matter of research orientation—as many things seem to be.

Reproducibility and Internal Validity (LP)/External Validity (GP)

Cronbach (1982), in an excellent and stimulating chapter, "The Limited Reach of Internal Validity," suggests as a substitute for the internal/external validity formulation the concept of reproducibility. He defines three levels of it, which are refinements of Lykken's (1968) three levels of replicability: literal, operational, and constructive replication. Lykken's formulations were devised in the context of animal studies, which are presumably more replicable than human ones. Cronbach's appear in the context of a discussion of the evaluation of educational and social programs, but one finds many issues of research directly discussed in the book and many others for which the implications are clear. Thus, as is true of many such seminal works, his writing has very much greater applicability than the title suggests. Another interesting three-level formulation is found in Fiske (1978, p. 182), who suggests the terms *replicability, reproducibility,* and *generality* for increasing levels of generality.

Clearly the concept of reproducibility or replicability is a powerful one. The idea can also be conceptualized as "robustness" (Wimsatt, 1981). A robust treatment will replicate regardless of circumstances, persons, and so forth. I have been using a chain analogy; the philosopher Charles Peirce used a similar structure, a cable analogy, to suggest the workings of replicability. Each replication is like one of the small, weak strands from which a cable is constructed. Taken together, they can form a cable of Herculean strength. Such is the power of replication or, in Cronbach's terms, reproducibility. It is an interesting concept that spans internal/external validity and internal validity (LP)/external validity (GP) and combines them in a single term.

Both Cronbach and Lykken find it useful to break reproducibility into three levels. Cronbach's levels are intended as "thought experiments" to help one judge the reproducibility of the results of a given study. His first level, like Lykken's "literal replication," asks, "How closely will the results of a second study agree . . . if the procedures of the first . . . are exactly repeated on fresh samples. . . ?" (1982, p. 122).

How is this first level of reproducibility related to the internal validity (LP)/external validity (GP) formulation? It appears to be part of the question asked in the fifth judgment of internal validity (LP), "credible result." In this, the last of the five, one decides whether the result is a typical result or a fluke, an outlier. Adding additional cases to the original study sample in a thought experiment would be a way of judging whether the result is typical or atypical. But any of the original conditions might have been unusual as well, not just the sample of subjects. If the study was done around the Christmas holidays or when the subjects were "hung over" after a big social occasion, the results might be unique. Actually running additional subjects in a real separate trial could help pick up such factors; even when everything else is assumed constant, it might bring out an intrusive effect not previously recognized. But remember, this is a thought experiment, and aberrant conditions of this kind would have to be described (but their effect not recognized) by the original researcher—not very likely. So, in general, such aberrant conditions will not be caught by the thought experiments of first-level reproducibility, although they might be by its third level. Judging the typicality of the result is the thought experiment involved in internal validity (LP). Further, the latter thought experiment uses consistency with previous relevant studies to help make that judgment. In reproducibility terms, previous studies that relate to portions of the thought experiment may be considered partial replications.

Cronbach's second level, like Lykken's "operational replication," follows the "original procedures according to the best available description of them" (1982, p. 123). How closely this can be done will depend, of course, on how completely and precisely the procedures are described as well as how thoroughly all the unspoken but routine conventions of good practice in the field were followed (for example, one-tailed statistical tests with directional hypotheses, 5 or 1 percent level of significance). Too brief descriptions, especially if unconventional procedural aspects are not detailed, make for poor replicability.

A real value of the second level is that it forces one to rethink the procedure to seek ambiguities that might be crucial in influencing the result. One's judgment of how well the researcher resolved these ambiguities contributes to reproducibility.

The second level of reproducibility could relate to either internal validity (LP) or external validity (GP), depending on the characteristic involved. For instance, were nonreturns from a questionnaire study sampled and analyzed to ensure that their responses would not have differed from those returned? Lack of clarity on this point would affect internal validity (LP). A case in which it is not clear whether the first treatment interfered with the second might affect external validity (GP). The rethinking of procedure involved in the second level is the same kind of questioning involved in the thought experiments of replicable result in external validity (GP). So the second level relates to both internal validity (LP) and external validity (GP)—and so also to both internal and external validity.

The third level for Cronbach involves asking how closely new results would agree with the original study if one specified the target population of subjects, the treatment, and the effect to be observed, leaving the researcher to "choose procedure for himself in a reasonable manner" (p. 123). Lykken's "constructive replication" is slightly different in that the researcher designs the study given only "a clear statement of the empirical fact" to be replicated (p. 156).

The third level would appear to be closest to "replicable result," the fifth and final judgment of external validity (GP). It is also a thought experiment about the replicability of the study with new subjects, situations, times, and versions of the treatment, new measures of treatment fidelity and of effect, as well as possibly a new basis of comparison and procedure. So Cronbach's formulation and the other two end up at about the same place: with a judgment of whether the relationship exists and of its generality. But they use different intermediate cutting points for the concepts involved and, for that matter, different conceptualizations about how to get there.

There is an additional level that could be built into "replicable result," the fifth judgment of external validity (GP); it is hinted at but not operationalized by Lykken. At one point he suggests that one avoid imitation of the original study in the redesign. This concern arises from the possibility suggested by Cronbach and Meehl (1955) that similarities in method might either cause an apparent relationship or at least enhance the strength of the relationship found.

This possibility raised by Cronbach and Meehl suggests that it might be appropriate to add a fourth level of reproducibility to Cronbach's formulation. At this level, the researcher must find reasonable alternatives to all aspects of the original study—subjects, situations, design, and procedure—being especially careful not to use any ways of measuring or treating that were used in the original unless not using them would sufficiently change the replication to invalidate it. This variation would ensure that a successful replication would not result from similarities in method. Such a stipulation probably should be a part of the thought experiment in the replicable result judgment of external validity (GP) as well.

Other Aspects than Internal Validity and External Validity

One of the important characteristics of a useful formulation is that it examines the problem from the standpoint of what goes into the judgments of studies and therefore helps one build a study that results in the desired judgments. Cook and Campbell and Campbell and Stanley took a big step toward this characteristic in analyzing various experimental designs to determine the extent to which they protected against rival explanations, or, as they called them, threats to validity. Their work has been particularly useful in strengthening studies. The internal validity (LP) and external validity (GP) formulation, in addition to the differences in the conceptualization of internal and external validity, goes beyond them to call attention to five aspects to optimize as well as the three limits and constraints. Of these eight additional aspects, only the weighting of internal to external validity is discussed in the original formulations. Whereas most of the eight are relevant to judging and critiquing studies, they all are much more important in the formulating and planning of studies and should help strengthen that process.

Conclusion

We have examined in detail three formulations of the problem of building a study that reduces the uncertainty that a relationship exists and adequately demonstrates the generality of that relationship. What are the characteristics of a study that builds a chain of reasoning to achieve these goals?

Campbell's formulations alone and with associates have markedly advanced this field. The internal validity (LP)/external validity (GP) formulation has benefited markedly from Campbell's work. Experimental design has been strengthened by his philosophical writing and analyses and operationally, among other contributions, by his specification of the common threats to validity. That the concepts of internal and external validity have proved useful is indicated by their widespread adoption.

The logic followed in that formulation, however, inevitably results in a division of internal from external validity at, for many researchers, a place they either did not or prefer not to recognize. As Cronbach deftly notes, Campbell and Stanley define "internal validity as pertinent only to an interpretation of a particular historical event. The interpretation is not a prediction about other instances, not a lawlike statement. Only in a trivial sense is it 'explanatory'" (1982, p. 127). Support of the hypothesis tested is a matter of construct validity, which is considered associated with external validity.

Cronbach's simplification of the whole field to the powerful concept of reproducibility is elegant. And as might be expected of a master student as well as practitioner of the field, his book is studded with gems about how to do evaluations. What advice Cronbach gives on "reproducible" studies seems to stem more from his conceptualization of evaluation than from the conceptualization of reproducibility. It is possible that reproducibility is more useful in evaluating than in building studies.

In formulating internal validity (LP)/external validity (GP), my aims have been (1) to provide as complete a set of criteria of a good research study as possible, (2) in doing so, to "carve nature at its joints" by distinguishing internal validity (LP) from external validity (GP) at a more "natural" and useful place, (3) to indicate the critical importance of the explanation to the chain of reasoning designed to develop a consensus, (4) to broaden the concept of construct validity to the translation of all aspects of the hypothesis into operations in the study, (5) to illustrate the interdependence of the various parts of the study in terms of trade-offs and the flow of the chain of reasoning, (6) to place internal validity (LP) and external validity (GP) in the context of the other decisions and constraints that affect a study, and (7) to indicate how various parts of the behavioral science orientation spectrum view the criteria. The formulation seems to include the very important questions posed by the Campbell/Stanley and Cook/ Campbell formulations. It is hoped that this new framework will lead to stronger research studies and perhaps still more advanced conceptualizations of research criteria.

Epilogue

What Has Been Attempted

My aim in this book has been to—

1. Differentiate the creative process of research from the process of staking a knowledge claim; research methods books all too often make it appear that these two processes are the same.
2. Analyze what is involved in staking a claim and, using the chain-of-reasoning model, describe how the claim is built.
3. Make apparent the difference between knowing, a personal judgment, and knowledge, a consensus of such judgments.
4. Show that getting a knowledge claim accepted means building a study that will command a consensus of knowing judgments.
5. Show how studies can be conceptualized in their presentation as a chain of reasoning to achieve such a consensus and point out useful parallels in the chain analogy.
6. Provide as complete a picture as possible of the decisions involved in designing, building, and judging a chain of reasoning.
7. Define internal validity (LP) and external validity (GP) in such a way as to relate to the chain of reasoning, to include the very important questions posed by the Campbell/Stanley and Cook/Campbell formulations, and to distinguish internal validity (LP) from external validity (GP) at a more "natural" place, to "carve nature at its joints."
8. Go beyond the earlier formulations to indicate the critical importance of the explanation.

9. Broaden the concept of construct validity to a translation of all aspects of the hypothesis into operations in a study, in the consideration of both internal validity (LP) and external validity (GP).

10. Illustrate the interdependence of the various parts of the study and place internal validity (LP) and external validity (GP) in the context of optimization, which makes apparent the necessity of trade-offs.

11. Provide a set of criteria that encompasses both causal and non-causal hypotheses and both qualitative and quantitative studies—indeed, any study that submits empirical evidence to support a knowledge claim regarding a generalizable relationship.

12. Make clear the importance of the audience in creating a consensus, showing how one must build on what its members already accept as knowledge, meet the criteria they deem important, and anticipate concerns they may have about the study.

13. Call attention to the role of problem formulation and resource allocation in building a successful study as well as the role of limits and constraints.

14. Show that there are different orientations to what the behavioral sciences ought to look like, that these orientations can be formed into a typology, that the orientations have implications for what knowledge is and for research methods, that the types differ in which criteria they deem important, and that, therefore, knowing the types in one's audience is important in designing or reporting a study.

15. Indicate how various parts of the behavioral science orientation spectrum view the criteria, what is a strength and a weakness of each approach, what emphasis is important, and what is of less importance or ignored.

16. Point up the problems in inferring causation and make more salient some of the more complex as well as the simple patterns of causation.

17. Indicate the complexity of decision making in designing and reporting a study so it is clear why the development and design of a study is still something of an art and why reasonable persons often differ: on the best design, on what in a study is of most value, and on what should be traded off for the greatest gain.

The picture is a complex one; we prefer simple ones. Is the greater complexity worth the greater verisimilitude? When a single research method and orientation are involved, the picture is simpler, but even then, it helps to place one's own orientation within the perspective of the others; doing so may suggest possibilities not previously considered.

It is hoped, of course, that this formulation will be useful. From describing the process of research, identifying the facets involved, conceptualizing the relevant criteria in their larger context, and making explicit aspects we sensed were there but had not formulated, stronger behavioral research should result. The checklist should facilitate bridging from the abstract framework to the reality of practice and make the conceptualization useful.

Perhaps, also, the typology of research orientations will make clearer the contributions of the variety of viewpoints so there may be less defensiveness on the part of some orientations, fewer criticisms by other orientations, and a greater ability to get on with the task of building a behavioral science with stronger studies and contributions by all.

Appendix

Checklist—Criteria
of a Research Study

How does one apply the criteria in judging a published research study? In planning a new study? In drafting a research report? To facilitate such use, this appendix makes the implications discussed in the previous chapters available in reasonably concise form and in one central place. In addition, it states implications which would have interrupted the flow of the discussion of the model but which nonetheless derive from it and need to be made apparent. Developed as a series of questions, it follows the model as previously outlined. Most of the questions are framed to critique a published study. Occasional items in the checklist (for example, 1.0-A-d and 1.0-D) are not particularly relevant for critiquing but may be important for research proposals or plans. Such items are so indicated. Many items are adapted from a similar checklist for research proposals that appears in *How to Prepare a Research Proposal* (Krathwohl, 1977, revision due in 1985).

The checklist is arranged as the boxes are numbered in Figure A-1. The three limits and constraints can be considered to surround the other decisions and are important before, during, and after a plan is built. In this instance I will consider them afterward, so they appear at the end of the checklist. In planning a study, however, these are items one would want to consider early in the study, so remember to do so when so using the checklist. The placement of some items such

Figure A-1. The Complete Model.

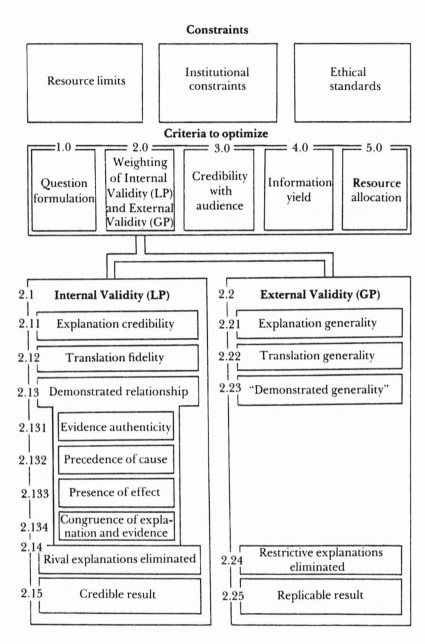

as this, though appropriate for critiquing a study in which those decisions are already made, may not be optimal for developing a study.

The checklist begins with the five conditions to be optimized and takes them in order across the row in Figure A-1, going into detail with respect to internal validity (LP) and external validity (GP) to consider the subconditions that enter into those decisions.

Characteristics to Optimize

1.0   *Question Choice and Formulation*

- A.   Does the study connect to previous work in the field and, if possible, build on it?
    - a.   Have materials been carefully selected that most directly bear on the problem? Do they include the *recent* literature in *both* content and method?
    - b.   Have they been summarized so that the reviewer need not know the critical articles to sense their significance?
    - c.   Have studies been critically reviewed and flaws noted?
    - d.   Have ongoing studies been included? (This item is more relevant for research proposals—it helps to show that other ongoing work does not duplicate one's request.)
    - e.   Have primary as well as secondary sources been examined?
    - f.   Where appropriate, has methodologically relevant as well as content-relevant material been reviewed?
    - g.   If there is a theoretical base for the study, has it been explored and related to the problem? If the study tests or extends theory in some way, is that indicated?
    - h.   If there is no relevant literature, is there an indication of why not?
    - i.   Has a ring been drawn around the problem so it is clear what is included and what left out?
    - j.   If there are hypotheses, do they flow from the problem statement? Are they the strongest hypotheses that can be drawn from the explanation advanced?
    - k.   Is it clear how well this study will mesh with the cited studies?

B.   Is the general methodology being followed appropriate for the problem stated? In a research proposal, consider whether the investigation of the problem is feasible methodologically and with the instrumentation available. Is more claimed in the problem statement than the procedures support? Conversely, are there sections of the procedure and analysis that are not reflected in the problem statement but should have been?

C.   In considering the evaluation of a treatment, has thought been given to whether the study will have the desired impact on those to whom it is directed? Will they be likely to change their minds if they see evidence contrary to the position they hold? Are there ways of proceeding that will involve them? If it is unlikely that evidence will change the mind of anyone with sufficient influence to change the situation, should this study be carried out anyway?

D.   Is this a routine approach to a problem for which new approaches should be explored? (Particularly important to consider in designing research proposals.)

E.   Is the phenomenon kept in holistic perspective so the problem is properly related to its conceptual context?

2.0   *Weighting of Internal Validity (LP) and External Validity (GP)*

A.   Is the study properly weighted toward an appropriate balance between internal validity (LP) and external validity (GP)? Has the relationship been adequately demonstrated so that generality is of primary interest, or are there still serious questions about the existence, extent, or nature of the relationship?

B.   Is the problem a good compromise between the control needed to show a relationship and the breadth needed to show its generality (the bandwidth/fidelity problem)?

C.   Is this a public policy matter in which the generality of the possible relationship is as much a concern from the beginning as the existence and nature of the relationship?

2.1   Internal Validity (LP)

2.11   Explanation Credibility

A.   Is the proposed explanation of each relationship adequately developed so that it can be judged?

B.   Is the explanation plausible? Credible and persuasive?
C.   Where pertinent, is the relationship of the explanation to underlying theory developed?
D.   Are the hypotheses or questions credibly supported by the explanation?

2.12   Translation Fidelity

A.   Is the explanation appropriately translated into questions, hypotheses, expectations, predictions, or a model? Do they follow or flow reasonably from the explanation or theory advanced? Are they an appropriate test of the theory? (If this question is relevant, see Platt, 1964.)
B.   Was each part of each question or hypothesis appropriately translated into procedure?
   a.   Was the selection of subjects appropriate? Whether representative or not, are subjects members of the group to which the results would be expected to apply?
   b.   Whether representative or not, were the situations chosen for gathering the data among those to which the results would be expected to apply?
   c.   Was the procedure for administering the treatment consistent with the explanation? Was there assurance that the treatment was appropriately administered? Were multiple levels of the treatment used so that the nature of the relationship of treatment to effect could be discerned (rather than just its presence or absence)? If there was no treatment, was the operational definition of the independent variable consistent with the explanation?

        For case studies, was the description of the situation consistent with the explanation? Was the situation adequately described with respect to the causative factors as well as the effect?
   d.   Were the operational definitions of the variables to be observed consistent with the explanation and, unless otherwise specified, with the usual connotations and denotations of those variables? Where new measures were used, was evidence of validity, reliability, and objectivity provided as appropriate?

e.   Was the procedure by which variables, persons, or situations were observed consistent with the explanation?

f.   Is the contrast between treatment and no-treatment conditions in the design of the study consistent with the explanation?

2.13   Demonstrated Relationship

2.131   Evidence Authenticity

A.   Is the evidence what it is purported to be? (This is taken for granted when one personally gathers it but may be important with historical evidence or when others do the data gathering; for example, a lazy interviewer may make up an imaginary interview.)

2.132   Precedence of Cause

A.   Where a cause-and-effect relationship is being studied, is there good reason to believe, or evidence to show, that cause preceded effect?

2.133   Presence of Effect

A.   If statistics were used to assess the effect:

a.   Were the sampling methods used consistent with the statistical model?

b.   Was the unit of sampling consistent with that implied by the problem statement?

c.   Were controls of pertinent extraneous variables needed? Was stratification used for such control? If stratification or clustering was used, was the basis given?

d.   In complex designs, was the sample size per cell adequate?

e.   Was an estimate of the power of the statistical test indicated so that if an effect of interest occurred, it was sensed as statistically significant?

f.   Where statistical assumptions were violated, were appropriate corrective measures used?

g.   Where nonprobability methods were used, was that use justified?

h.   Was the statistical analysis correctly carried out and interpreted?

B.   Was as precise a prediction made of the expected effect as the explanation allowed? Was not only the direction of the expected effect predicted but as much of its timing, strength, duration, and pattern of change over time (for example, forgetting or learning curve) as the explanation permitted?

2.134 Congruence of Explanation and Evidence

A.   If there was a prediction, was it confirmed? In all details? If there was a prior explanation, does that explanation fit the evidence?

B.   If adjustments are necessary to make the explanation or prediction fit the evidence, are those adjustments made but sufficiently separated from the initial interpretation of the data so that it is clear that they need to be validated by further evidence?

2.14   Rival Explanations Eliminated

A.   The design of the study is the main protection against rival explanations of the phenomenon. Have common design errors been avoided, eliminating the commonest rival explanations?

a.   History: Other causes of the effect occurred during the study.

b.   Maturation: Changes occurred in the subjects during the study, biologically or psychologically (for example, subjects grew tired, learned to handle their anxiety, or developed greater physical coordination).

c.   Testing: Later test results were affected by earlier test experiences.

d.   Instrumentation: Changes in the way measures were used or observations collected during a study make apparent changes in the effect.

e.   Statistical regression: The average scores of groups selected on the basis of a high or low cutoff score regress toward the average of the group from which they were originally selected.

f.   Selection: Biases result from differential factors affecting the recruitment of individuals for the various comparison groups (such as use of volunteers for the treatment but not the control group).

      g.   Mortality: Biases result from the differential loss of individuals from comparison groups (for example, nonrespondents in a questionnaire study).

    B.   Certain common features of research studies will control for many of the preceding rival explanations, although not all are feasible in experimental studies and even more are not possible in nonexperimental studies. If they were feasible, were such procedures as appropriate control groups, double-blind conditions, unobtrusive observation and treatment, and random assignment to groups used? Was the control group given all aspects associated with the treatment except the experimental aspect?

    C.   Were there rival explanations not covered by the common categories of such explanations?

2.15   Credible Result

    A.   Are the results consistent with published studies or with the closest studies that exist? If not, are the differences explainable?

    B.   Are there other reasons for supposing this result is a fluke? A highly unusual result? An outlier?

    C.   What is the overall internal validity (LP) of the study? Is the audience's uncertainty about the existence of the relationship reduced? Significantly reduced or just weakly?

2.2   External Validity (GP)

2.21   Explanation Generality

    A.   Is the generality to be expected of the hypothesis, question, proposition, theory, or explanation stated, or must it be inferred? If stated, is it reasonable and are the boundaries, if any are set, appropriate?

    B.   If it is implied that the proposition is a universal, is that reasonable? Are there boundaries that ought to have been noted?

2.22   Translation Generality

    A.   Subjects: Was the population from which the sample was drawn that which was described or inferred in the explanation? Were the subjects completely representative of the target group to which generality was expected to be inferred?

B. Situation: Was the situation drawn from those to which one would expect to be able to generalize? How completely representative was it of those situations?

C. Observations and measures: Are these representative of the constructs and concepts used in the explanation? Are they representative of the measures typically used to measure those concepts? Were the concepts as described what one typically expects them to be? If not, is justification given for the deviation? Are measures and observations consistent with this deviation? Were the characteristics of measures described?

D. Treatment: Was the way the treatment was defined and administered representative of the treatment characteristics and administration conditions to which one would expect to generalize? Were special and obtrusive observations that might affect the result necessary for evaluating the treatment? Will they normally be part of the treatment when one generalizes?

E. Basis of comparison and procedure: Was there anything special about the basis of comparison or procedure (for example, the time when the study was done, such as during the Christmas holidays) that might affect the study results? Would it limit generality?

2.23 "Demonstrated Generality"

A. If the relationship was demonstrated, did it appear over the broad set of instances one would have expected from the generality being projected?

2.24 Restrictive Explanations Eliminated

Have these rival explanations, which have the effect of limiting the intended generality, been avoided?

A. Common design errors:
   a. Selection/maturation interaction: Biases may result if members of the groups involved were selected on different bases (for example, volunteers in one group, nonvolunteers in the other) and this difference is compounded and made more potent (or weakened) by maturation factors (for example, volunteers were older and therefore in a different part of their growth cycle).

b. Selection/treatment interaction: The effect of groups selected on different bases, as above, is compounded and made more potent by one group's being more attracted to the treatment than another.

c. Testing/treatment interaction: The testing affects the way subjects respond to the treatment. Examples are pretest sensitization (a pretest alerts subjects to the important parts of the lesson on which they will later be tested) and posttest effect (the posttest is a learning experience that makes the treatment more effective).

d. Multiple-treatment interference: Where multiple treatments are applied to the same subjects, a prior treatment may affect the results of a later one.

e. Reactive effects: A number of reactive effects result from the subjects' awareness that they are in a special situation:

i.   The "Hawthorne effect"—merely receiving special attention differentiates subjects from comparison groups not receiving that attention.

ii. Rivalry—control groups strive to outdo treatment groups in a contest atmosphere.

iii. Compensation—administrators try to compensate nontreatment groups for their not being favored. Parents may demand such treatment.

iv. Novelty effect, associated with the use of the new, whatever it is.

v.   Annoyance, disorganization, and other effects resulting from the disruption of routine.

f. Experimenter expectancies—subjects may react to the experimenter's expectations, usually by trying to please the experimenter but on occasion antagonistically.

B. Are there other rival explanations not covered by a–f above, especially ones unique to the study, that would limit the intended generality?

2.25 Replicable Result

A. To what extent is the replicability of the result dependent on the particular conditions of the study? This involves a series of thought experiments:

a. Subjects: Would the result replicate with other samples of subjects just like these? With other samples of subjects from the same population? Is the population sampled representative of the target group to which one wishes to generalize?

b. Situation: Would the result replicate in a similar situation, or is this particular situation unique in some important way that affected the results? Is it representative of those to which one hopes to be able to generalize?

c. Observation: Would the effect also appear with different instrumentation or different observation procedures for the same variables?

d. Treatment: Would other versions of the treatment that would conceptually be considered the same kind of treatment be effective as well?

e. Basis of comparison: Could the effect also be shown with other designs?

f. Procedure: Could the effect be shown with alternative procedures designed to accomplish the same purposes? Would it appear at different times than the original study?

(Questions a and b and the "times" question in f concern generality of the hypothesis or proposition over persons, situations, and times. Questions c, d, and e and the rest of f concern the extent to which the methodology of the study is a constraining factor, or whether the result would generalize beyond this study's methods.)

B. Are these results consistent with past ones? If not, why not? Does the reason reflect in any way on the generality of what was studied?

C. To what extent would the results seem to generalize to situations that are very much like that studied but are not directly sampled?

3.0   Credibility with Audience

A. What criteria are the most important to the audience being addressed? Was the audience's research orientation taken into account? Did the study adequately meet the criteria of importance to that orientation? Were multiple orientations anticipated and adequately met, if that is appropriate?

B.   Did the study build on findings that have been accepted as knowledge by that audience?

C.   Did the study use instruments or observation procedures that are acceptable and understood by the audience? If not, was an adequate case made for the instruments or observation procedures used?

D.   Did the study use conventional procedure? If not, was there an explanation and appropriate justification for the deviance?

E.   Did the study use analytical procedures and statistics familiar to and understood by the audience? If the procedures are unfamiliar, did it explain them intelligibly enough that they would be comprehended and the audience would understand the interpretation advanced?

F.   Were appropriate compromises made where design trade-offs were necessary? Were these pointed out and justified in the presentation to make clear they were conscious choices rather than aspects that were overlooked?

G.   Did the study correctly anticipate details of methodology that help the perceptive reader to judge the study? There is a fine balance between smothering the reader in detail—to which editors usually object—and giving just enough to satisfy the reader of the investigator's integrity and competence. Did the write-up find this middle ground? Sometimes appendixes are effective in keeping such detail out of the way of the main presentation but making it available.

H.   Is the hasty reader signaled to the critically important parts of the write-up? It is always best to assume that readers are under time pressure or in a situation where it is difficult to concentrate; prepare the write-up to aid them. Good writing, like good acting, uses nonverbal gestures—punctuation, underlining, spacing, paragraphing, diagrams, and other devices that command the reader's eye.

4.0   *Information Yield*

A.   Was sufficient information gathered about the main effect(s) to build a strong chain of reasoning?

B. Was the data-gathering system monitored so that aberrations would have been noticed?

C. Did the design permit observation and recording of potential side effects of the treatment?

D. In a research proposal the opportunity should be taken to try out things that might lead to future studies. Will the information gathered be that which would best assist in the formulation of successive studies? Is that effort at an appropriate level relative to the main focus and, if this study is part of a research program, to the long-term goals?

5.0   Resource Allocation

A. Were resources allocated appropriately?

    a. Was each link in the chain of reasoning made as strong as the others—no overemphasis on one step at the inappropriate expense of another, like sampling at a cost to instrumentation?

    b. Where links in the chain are mutually supportive, as at the design stage, were weak links compensated for by building extra strength into other links?

    c. Was the most efficient and effective use made of resources?

B. If the study had to be redesigned to stay within resource limits, were the cuts made in appropriate places? Was the problem kept within the same context that the researchers had intended to investigate?

C. Was the expected space available for publication used in the most effective way to answer such concerns as might be anticipated, concentrating on those for which the communication medium being used could be effective?

D. In a research proposal or plan, are provisions made for the unexpected—dropout of subjects, report costs, transportation of subjects or pay for relief persons or substitutes, extra analyses, Murphy's law?

E. In a research proposal or plan, is a work plan developed so that expectations and plans are appropriate and the best use made of resources? So that appropriate parts of the project mesh together with proper timing and sequence? Does the plan include a reasonable time estimate for the various parts? Are starting dates realistic and in accord with the vagaries of the calendar, vacations, and so on?

Limits and Constraints

The general question considered throughout this section is whether the study was developed within the constraints and limits that must be observed. For a research proposal or plan, the question is whether an adequate and appropriate study can be developed within these limits and constraints.

Resource Limits

A.   Were additional resources sought if these were necessary to preserve the integrity of the investigation?

B through E apply primarily to proposals and planning:

B.   Can a useful investigation be conducted with the resources available? Will it be an adequate one? Is it possible to complete the study within the resource limits?

C.   Are constraints on personal and professional time planned for and observed as well as monetary limits?

D.   Where funds are requested from an outside agency, is allowance made for overhead charges?

E.   Where plans exceed available resources, is the possibility considered of breaking the study into successive phases each of which might be more easily supported as a separate project?

Ethical Standards

A.   Were ethical standards observed?

   a.   Were the standards of the profession observed (for example, American Psychological Association, 1981)?

   b.   For research proposals and planning, if human or animal subjects are involved, and if the agency for which the researcher works receives any federal funds, will the appropriate subject protection committees clear the study (some states require this too)?

    c.   Were the provisions of the various privacy acts observed? Was adequate care taken to assure the privacy of the individuals regardless of whether the acts apply or not?

    d.   Was not only the physical but also the mental well-being of the subjects assured? If there are problems in this regard, was the justification not only made to the protection committee but also included in presentation of the study? Were informed consent forms obtained, if appropriate? Was the fact reported?

Institutional Constraints

A.   Was it possible to get institutions to cooperate with the study? Did this occur easily or were there turndowns? If the latter, are those that cooperated different from those that refused? Is the difference one that might in some way affect the study results? Note: The latter may have serious consequences for external validity (GP).

B and C apply primarily to research proposals and planning:

B.   Is it possible to develop the study within such limits on changes in routine and procedure as the institutions set? Would "business as usual" interfere in significant ways with the study?

C.   What are the limits on such procedures as restricting treatment to one group and denying it to another that might benefit from it? Where this is done, are adequate provisions made for later treatment of the denied group?

Other Criteria, Hints, and Suggestions

A.   Does the argument flow from the outset to the end with no break? Does each step build on the previous one? No aspects started and then dropped? No aspects developed as a surprise at a later step, the groundwork not having been laid earlier?

B.   Are key terms defined early, so the reader learns them and gets used to them?

C.   Does the write-up give a proper overall perspective, keeping parts in appropriate relative emphasis?

D.   For work in progress, has the study write-up, proposal, or design been reviewed by someone who can view it objectively? Does the proposal communicate to such nonspecialists as are likely to review it or to be in the administrative chain of responsibility either in one's own institution or in the reviewing agency?

Key Concepts

Audience credibility. The credibility with one's audience needed to build a consensus; "validity depends . . . on the way a conclusion is . . . communicated . . . plausibility . . . lies in the ear of the beholder" (Cronbach, 1982, p. 108) *(p. 141).*

Basis of comparison. The nature of the comparative sample that is used to determine the change in research variables. Usually refers to study design, such as comparing a control group with an experimental group or using subjects as their own controls by collecting pre and post measures *(p. 48).*

Congruence of explanation and evidence. Agreement between what the explanation leads one to expect and what the evidence shows *(p. 92).*

Construct validity. "The approximate validity with which we can make generalizations about higher-order constructs from research operations" (Cook and Campbell, 1979, p. 38) *(p. 272).*

Credible result. A result that is plausible when viewed against both previous experience in the area and the four other parts of internal validity (LP) *(p. 101).*

Demonstrated generality. A result that appeared in all instances in which it would be expected given the generality inferred or claimed *(p. 120).*

Note: The page number in italic refers to a text discussion of the concept.

Demonstrated relationship. The relationship under inquiry occurred in this instance: the evidence is authentic, an effect is present, cause preceded effect, and the evidence is congruent with the prediction or explanation *(p. 89)*.

Evidence authenticity. The evidence is what it purports to be *(p. 90)*.

Explanation credibility. The explanation is plausible, believable to the point of being persuasive *(p. 79)*.

Explanation generality. The generality stated or implied in the explanation proposed for a relationship *(p. 116)*.

External validity. "The approximate validity with which conclusions are drawn about the generalizability of a causal relationship to and across populations of persons, settings, and times" (Cook and Campbell, 1979, p. 39) *(p. 272)*.

External validity (GP). How unequivocally the evidence supports the generality—across subjects, situations, measures, treatments or independent variables, study designs, and procedures—claimed for the relationship *(pp. 58, 113)*.

Information yield. Evidence generated as a result of efforts to reduce uncertainty about one's main knowledge claim, to ensure accurate interpretation of one's evidence, to pick up side effects, and to facilitate formulating future studies *(p. 145)*.

Institutional constraints. The limits imposed by institutions on studies to keep things operating normally and to avoid results that reflect negatively on the institution *(p. 151)*.

Internal validity. "The validity with which statements can be made about whether there is a causal relationship from one variable to another in the form in which the variables were manipulated or measured" in a particular study (Cook and Campbell, 1979, p. 38) *(p. 268)*.

Internal validity (LP). How conclusively the evidence supports the relationship proposed to link variables and excludes other interpretations *(pp. 57, 79)*.

Measures or observations. Evidence collected to show that a change, an effect, or some event occurred; to ensure that the treatment was administered as intended; or to ensure that various groups were equivalent *(p. 48)*.

Precedence of cause. There is evidence that the cause occurred before the effect *(p. 90)*.

Presence of effect. There is evidence that an effect worthy of noting did recur *(p. 91)*.

Procedure. Who gets what measures and what treatment, as well as when and how *(p. 48)*.

Replicable results. Results would be reproducible in relevant wider contexts, such as different subjects, situations, times, treatment form or format, measures, study design, and procedures *(p. 123)*.

Reproducibility. The extent to which the results of a study can be replicated at level 1, just as it was done but with a new sample of subjects; at level 2, as best one can with the description of the study supplied; and at level 3, given only the findings from the reference study, with a new study that one develops to replicate them *(p. 274)*.

Resource allocation. The allocation of resources so that the goals of the study are achieved and a strong chain of reasoning is built *(p. 144)*.

Restrictive explanations eliminated. No alternative explanations of the results from a particular study limit claims of generality *(p. 121)*.

Rival explanations eliminated. Plausible alternative explanations of the relationship are eliminated, usually by proper design of the study *(p. 97)*.

Situations. The situations in which the subjects are studied *(p. 47)*.

Statistical conclusion validity. Evaluation of the study. Was it: "(1) . . . sensitive enough to permit reasonable statements about covariation of cause and effect? (2) . . . is there reasonable evidence from which to infer that the presumed cause and effect covary?

and (3) . . . how strongly do the two variables covary?'' (Cook and Campbell, 1979, p. 39) *(p. 270)*.

Subjects. The individuals, groups, institutions, or organizations sampled, thus constituting the units studied. Presumably they are representative of a larger population. Qualitative researchers sensitive to the word *subjects* should read it as *informants* or *hosts (p. 47)*.

Translation fidelity. The accuracy with which the constructs and concepts of the explanation are translated into choices of subjects, situations, measures, treatments, and various operations of a study *(p. 86)*.

Translation generality. The accuracy with which the generality claimed by or inferred about an explanation is translated into the subjects, situations, measures, treatments, and operations of a study that are representative of that generality *(p. 117)*.

Treatment. That which instigates change in the state of a variable; the cause in a cause-and-effect relationship *(p. 48)*.

Weighting of internal validity (LP) and external validity (GP). The design of a study to yield greater support for the conclusion that a relationship exists or for the inference that it has generality *(p. 129)*.

References

Abt, W., and Magidson, J. "Problems in Program Implementation and Evaluation." In H. A. Freeman and R. A. Berk (Eds.), *Contemporary Evaluation Research*. Vol. 4. Beverly Hills, Calif.: Sage, 1980.

Allison, G. T. *Essence of Decision: Explaining the Cuban Missile Crisis*. Boston: Little, Brown, 1971.

American Psychological Association. *Standards for Educational and Psychological Tests*. Washington, D.C.: American Psychological Association, 1974.

American Psychological Association. *Ethical Standards of Psychologists*. Washington, D.C.: American Psychological Association, 1981. (An updated version is included in each issue of the *Biographical Directory*, published by the association every four years.)

Anderson, L., Evertson, C., and Brophy, J. "An Exploratory Study of Effective Teaching in First Grade Reading Groups." *Elementary School Journal*, 1979, *79*, 193–223.

Backer, T. E. *A Directory of Information on Tests*. ERIC TM Report 62-1977. Princeton, N.J.: ERIC Clearinghouse on Tests, Measurement and Evaluation, Educational Testing Service, 1977.

Barzun, J., and Graff, H. F. *The Modern Researcher*. (3rd ed.) New York: Harcourt Brace Jovanovich, 1977.

Beauchamp, L. (Ed.). *Philosophical Problems of Causation.* Encino, Calif.: Dickinson, 1974.

Becker, F. D., and others. "College Classroom Ecology." *Sociometry,* 1973, *36,* 514–525.

Becker, H. S. *Outsiders: Studies in the Sociology of Deviance.* New York: Free Press, 1963.

Becker, H. S., and others (Eds.). *Institutions and the Person: Papers Presented to Everett C. Hughes.* Chicago: Aldine, 1968.

Best, J. W. *Research in Education.* (4th ed.) Englewood Cliffs, N.J.: Prentice-Hall, 1981.

Blau, T. *Dynamics of a Bureaucracy: A Study of the Interpersonal Relations in Two Government Agencies.* Chicago: University of Chicago Press, 1955.

Blau, T. *Dynamics of a Bureaucracy: A Study of the Interpersonal Relations in Two Government Agencies.* (2nd ed.) Chicago: University of Chicago Press, 1963.

Bloom, B. S. (Ed.). *Taxonomy of Educational Objectives: The Cognitive Domain.* New York: Longman, 1956.

Bloom, B. S. "Thought Processes in Lectures and Discussions." *Journal of General Education,* 1953, *7,* 160–169.

Bracht, G. H., and Glass, G. V. "The External Validity of Experiments." *American Educational Research Journal,* 1968, *5,* 437–474.

Bradburn, N. N., Sudman, S., and Associates. *Improving Interview Method and Questionnaire Design: Response Effects to Threatening Questions in Survey Research.* San Francisco: Jossey-Bass, 1979.

Brill, A. A. (Ed. and trans.). *The Basic Writings of Sigmund Freud.* Modern Library edition. New York: Random House, 1938.

Brinberg, D., and McGrath, J. E. "A Network of Validity Concepts Within the Research Process." In D. Brinberg and L. H. Kidder (Eds.), *New Directions for Methodology of Social and Behavioral Science: Forms of Validity in Research,* no. 12. San Francisco: Jossey-Bass, 1982.

Broad, W. J. "Freud and the Structure of Science." *Science,* 1981a, *212,* 137–141.

Broad, W. J. "Congress Told Travel Issue 'Exaggerated.'" *Science,* 1981b, *212,* 421.

Bronfenbrenner, U. "Toward an Experimental Ecology of Human Development." *American Psychologist,* 1977, *32,* 513–531.

Bronowski, J. *The Ascent of Man.* Boston: Little, Brown, 1973.

Browne, J. "The Used Car Game." In M. P. Golden (Ed.), *The Research Experience.* Itasca, Ill.: Peacock, 1976.

Campbell, D. T. "Prospective: Artifact and Control." In R. Rosenthal and R. L. Rosnow (Eds.), *Artifact in Behavioral Research.* New York: Academic Press, 1969.

Campbell, D. T. "Evolutionary Epistemology." In P. A. Schilpp (Ed.), *The Library of Living Philosophers.* Vol. 14: *The Philosophy of Karl Popper.* LaSalle, Ill.: Open Court, 1974.

Campbell, D. T. "Descriptive Epistemology: Psychological, Sociological and Evolutionary." Preliminary draft of the William James Lectures, Harvard University, Spring 1977.

Campbell, D. T. "A Tribal Model of the Social System Vehicle Carrying Scientific Knowledge." *Knowledge,* 1979, *1*, 181-201.

Campbell, D. T., and Stanley, J. C. "Experimental and Quasi-Experimental Designs for Research on Teaching." In N. L. Gage (Ed.), *Handbook of Research on Teaching.* Chicago: Rand McNally, 1963.

Chadwick, B. A., Bahr, H. M., and Albrecht, S. L. *Social Science Research Methods.* Englewood Cliffs, N.J.: Prentice-Hall, 1984.

Chamberlin, T. C. "The Method of Multiple Working Hypotheses." *Journal of Geology,* 1897, *5*, 837. Reprinted in *Science,* 1965, *148*, 754-759.

Cohen, J. *Statistical Power Analysis for the Behavioral Sciences.* New York: Academic Press, 1970.

Cohen, M. R., and Nagel, E. *An Introduction to Logic and the Scientific Method.* New York: Harcourt Brace Jovanovich, 1934.

Coleman, J. S., Hoffer, T., and Kilgore, S. "Public and Private Schools." Draft of a report to the National Center for Education Statistics by the National Opinion Research Center, University of Chicago, under Contract 300-78-0108, March 1981.

Coleman, J. S., and others. *Equality of Educational Opportunity.* Washington, D.C.: U.S. Government Printing Office, 1966.

Cook, T. D., and Campbell, D. T. *Quasi-Experimentation.* Chicago: Rand McNally, 1979.

Cozby, P. C. *Methods in Behavioral Research.* (2nd ed.) Palo Alto, Calif.: Mayfield, 1981.

Cronbach, L. J. *Essentials of Psychological Testing.* (3rd ed.) New York: Harper & Row, 1970.

Cronbach, L. J. "Beyond the Two Disciplines of Scientific Psychology." *American Psychologist,* 1975, *30*, 116-127.

Cronbach, L. J. *Designing Evaluations of Educational and Social Programs.* San Francisco: Jossey-Bass, 1982.

Cronbach, L. J., and Meehl, P. E. "Construct Validity in Psychological Tests." *Psychological Bulletin,* 1955, *52*, 281-302.

Davis, M. S. "That's Interesting! Toward a Phenomenology of Sociology and a Sociology of Phenomenology." *Philosophy of the Social Sciences,* 1971, *1*, 309-344.

Denzin, N. K. *The Research Act: A Theoretical Introduction to Sociological Methods.* (2nd ed.) New York: McGraw-Hill, 1978.

Einstein, A., and Infeld, L. *The Evolution of Physics.* New York: Simon & Schuster, 1938.

Ellsworth, P. "From Abstract Ideas to Concrete Instances: Some Guidelines for Choosing Natural Research Settings." *American Psychologist,* 1977, *32,* 604–615.

Erikson, E. H. *Childhood and Society.* New York: Norton, 1950.

Ferris, T. "The Spectral Messenger." *Science 81,* October 1981, pp. 66–71.

Feyerabend, P. *Against Method.* London: Verso, 1975.

Fiske, D. W. *Strategies for Personality Research: The Observation Versus Interpretation of Behavior.* San Francisco: Jossey-Bass, 1978.

Gans, H. J. "The Participant Observer as Human Being." In H. S. Becker and others (Eds.), *Institutions and the Person: Papers Presented to Everett C. Hughes.* Chicago: Aldine, 1968.

Gates, D., and Smith, J. "Keeping the Flat-Earth Faith." *Newsweek,* July 2, 1984, p. 12.

Gergen, K. J. "The Emerging Crisis in Life Span Developmental Theory." In P. B. Baltes and O. G. Brim (Eds.), *Life-Span Development and Behavior.* Vol. 3. New York: Academic Press, 1980.

Getzels, J. W. "The Problem of the Problem." In R. M. Hogarth (Ed.), *New Directions for Methodology of Social and Behavioral Science: Question Framing and Response Consistency,* no. 11. San Francisco: Jossey-Bass, 1982.

Getzels, J. W., and Csikszentmihalyi, M. *The Creative Vision: A Longitudinal Study of Problem Finding in Art.* New York: Wiley, 1976.

Gilbert, J. P., McPeek, B., and Mosteller, F. "Statistics and Ethics in Surgery and Anesthetics." *Science,* 1977, *198,* 684–689.

Glaser, B. G., and Strauss, A. L. *The Discovery of Grounded Theory: Strategies for Qualitative Discovery.* Chicago: Aldine, 1967.

Glass, G. V. "Experimental Validity." In H. M. Mitzel (Ed.), *Encyclopedia of Educational Research.* (5th ed.) Vol. 2. New York: Free Press, 1982.

Glass, G. V., McGaw, B., and Smith, M. L. *Meta-analysis in Social Research.* Beverly Hills, Calif.: Sage, 1981.

Goldberger, A. S., and Cain, G. G. "The Causal Analysis of Cognitive Outcomes in the Coleman, Hoffer and Kilgore Report." *Sociology of Education,* 1982, *55,* 103–122.

Golden, M. P. (Ed.). *The Research Experience.* Itasca, Ill.: Peacock, 1976.

Goldstein, J. H., and Arms, R. L. "Effects of Observing Athletic Contests on Hostility." *Sociometry*, 1971, *34*, 83-90.

Griver, S. "Coming Close to Curing Leukemia." *Israel Digest*, 1979, *22*, 7.

Guttman, L. "Image Theory for the Structure of Quantitative Variates." *Psychometrika*, 1953, *18*, 277-296.

Hammond, P. E. *Sociologists at Work*. New York: Basic Books, 1964.

Haney, C. "The Play's the Thing: Notes on Social Simulation." In M. P. Golden (Ed.), *The Research Experience*. Itasca, Ill.: Peacock, 1976.

Haney, C., Banks, C., and Zimbardo, P. G. "Interpersonal Dynamics in a Simulated Prison." *International Journal of Criminology and Penology*, 1973, *1*, 69-97.

Hare, P., and Bates, R. "Seating Position and Small Group Interaction." *Sociometry*, 1963, *26*, 480-487.

Hearnshaw, L. S. *Cyril Burt, Psychologist*. Ithaca, N.Y.: Cornell University Press, 1979.

Heise, D. *Causal Analysis*. New York: Wiley, 1975.

Hogarth, R. M. (Ed.). *New Directions for Methodology of Social and Behavioral Science: Question Framing and Response Consistency*, no. 11. San Francisco: Jossey-Bass, 1982.

Holmes, D. S. "Meditation and Somatic Arousal Reduction: A Review of the Experimental Evidence." *American Psychologist*, 1984, *39*, 1-10.

Humphreys, L. *The Tearoom Trade: Impersonal Sex in Public Places*. (2nd ed.) Chicago: Aldine, 1975.

Joint Committee on Standards for Educational Evaluation. *Standards for Evaluation of Educational Programs, Projects, and Materials*. New York: McGraw-Hill, 1981.

Judson, H. F. *The Eighth Day of Creation: Makers of the Revolution in Biology*. New York: Simon & Schuster, 1979.

Judson, H. F. *The Search for Solutions*. New York: Holt, Rinehart and Winston, 1980.

Jung, C. G. "Psychological Types." In *Collected Works of C. G. Jung*. (2nd ed.) Vol. 6. Princeton, N.J.: Princeton University Press, 1971.

Kagan, N. "Influencing Human Interaction." ERIC microfiche #ED 065793, 1972.

Kagan, N., Krathwohl, D. R., and Miller, R. "Stimulated Recall in Therapy Using Videotape—a Case Study." *Journal of Counseling Psychology*, 1963, *10*, 237-243.

Kagan, N., and others. "Interpersonal Process Recall: Stimulated Recall by Videotape in Exploratory Studies of Counseling and Teacher-Learning." ERIC microfiche #ED 003230, 1965.

Kagan, N., and others. "Studies in Human Interaction: Interpersonal Process Recall Stimulated by Videotape." ERIC microfiche #ED 017946, 1967.

Kagan, N., and others. "Interpersonal Process Recall." *Journal of Nervous and Mental Disease,* 1969, *148,* 365–374.

Kagan, N., and others. "Influencing Human Interaction." ERIC microfiche #ED 065793, 1972.

Kaplan, A. "Noncausal Explanation." In D. Lerner (Ed.), *Cause and Effect.* New York: Free Press, 1965.

Köbben, A.S.F. "Cause and Intention." In R. Naroll and R. Cohen (Eds.), *A Handbook of Method in Cultural Anthropology.* New York: Columbia University Press, 1973.

Kounin, J. S. *Discipline and Group Management in Classrooms.* New York: Holt, Rinehart and Winston, 1970.

Kousser, J. M. "History QUASSHed: Quantitative Social Scientific History in Perspective." *American Behavioral Scientist,* 1980, *23,* 885–904.

Krathwohl, D. R. *How to Prepare a Research Proposal.* Syracuse, N.Y.: Syracuse University Bookstore, 1977.

Krathwohl, D. R., Bloom, B. S., and Masia, B. B. *Taxonomy of Educational Objectives: The Affective Domain.* New York: Longman, 1964.

Krathwohl, D. R., Gordon, J., and Payne, D. "The Effect of Sequence on Programmed Instruction." *American Educational Research Journal,* 1967, *4,* 125–132.

Kruglanski, A. W., and Kroy, M. "Outcome Validity in Experimental Research: A Reconceptualization." *Representative Research in Social Psychology,* 1976, *7,* 166–178.

Kuhn, T. S. *The Structure of Scientific Revolutions.* Chicago: University of Chicago Press, 1962.

Kuhn, T. S. *The Structure of Scientific Revolutions.* (2nd ed.) Chicago: University of Chicago Press, 1970.

Lakatos, I. "Falsification and the Mythology of Scientific Research Programmes." In I. Lakatos and A. Musgrave, *Criticism and the Growth of Knowledge.* Cambridge: Cambridge University Press, 1970.

Lakatos, I. *The Methodology of Scientific Research Programmes.* Cambridge: Cambridge University Press, 1978.

Lengermann, J. J. "Exchange Strengths and Professional Autonomy in Organizations." In M. P. Golden (Ed.), *The Research Experience.* Itasca, Ill.: Peacock, 1976.

Levin, J. "Ethical Problems in Sociological Research." In A. J. Kimmel (Ed.), *New Directions for Methodology of Social and*

Behavioral Science: Ethics of Human Subject Research, no. 10. San Francisco: Jossey-Bass, 1981.

Levine, D. "The Evolutionary Crisis of the Social Sciences." Draft, Center for Advanced Study in the Behavioral Sciences, Stanford, Calif., 1981.

Lewis, D. "Causal Explanation." In D. Lewis (Ed.), *Philosophical Papers.* Vol. 2. Oxford: Oxford University Press, in press.

Liebow, E. *Tally's Corner: A Study of Negro Streetmen.* Boston: Little, Brown, 1967.

Lin, N. *Foundations of Social Research.* New York: McGraw-Hill, 1976.

Lindblom, C. E., and Cohen, D. *Usable Knowledge: Social Science and Social Problems.* New Haven, Conn.: Yale University Press, 1979.

Lykken, D. T. "Statistical Significance in Psychological Research." *Psychological Bulletin,* 1968, *70,* 151-159.

Machlup, F. *Knowledge: Its Creation, Distribution and Economic Significance.* Vol. 1: *Knowledge and Knowledge Production.* Princeton, N.J.: Princeton University Press, 1981.

Mackie, J. L. "Causes and Conditions." *American Philosophical Quarterly,* 1965, *2,* 1-20.

McMillan, J. H., and Schumacher, S. *Research in Education: A Conceptual Introduction.* Boston: Little, Brown, 1984.

Magidson, J., and Sörbom, D. "Adjusting for Confounding Factors in Quasi-Experiments: Another Reanalysis of the Westinghouse Head Start Evaluation." *Educational Evaluation and Policy Analysis,* 1982, *4,* 321-329.

Maier, N.R.F. "Reasoning in Humans II: The Solution of a Problem and Its Appearance in Consciousness." *Journal of Comparative Psychology,* 1931, *12,* 181-194.

Medley, D. *Teacher Competence and Teacher Effectiveness.* Washington, D.C.: American Association of Colleges for Teacher Education, 1977.

Meehl, P. E. "Specific Etiology and Other Forms of Strong Influence: Some Quantitative Meanings." *Journal of Medicine and Philosophy,* 1977, *1,* 33-53.

Merton, R. K. *Social Theory and Social Structure.* New York: Free Press, 1968.

Milgram, S. "Behavioral Study of Obedience." *Journal of Abnormal and Social Psychology,* 1963, *67,* 371-378.

Milgram, S. *Obedience to Authority: An Experimental Viewpoint.* New York: Harper & Row, 1973.

Mitchell, T. W., and Klimoski, R. J. "Is It Rational to Be Empirical?

A Test of Methods for Scoring Biographical Data." *Journal of Applied Psychology*, 1982, *67*, 411–418.

Mitroff, I. I., and Kilmann, R. H. *Methodological Approaches to Social Science: Integrating Divergent Concepts and Theories*. San Francisco: Jossey-Bass, 1978.

Moore, H. "Notes on Sculpture." In B. Ghiselin (Ed.), *The Creative Process*. New York: Mentor Books, 1955.

Morgan, G. "Research as Engagement: A Personal View." In G. Morgan (Ed.), *Beyond Method: Strategies for Social Research*. Beverly Hills, Calif.: Sage, 1983a.

Morgan, G. (Ed.). *Beyond Method: Strategies for Social Research*. Beverly Hills, Calif.: Sage, 1983b.

Mouly, G. *Educational Research*. Boston: Allyn & Bacon, 1978.

Nagel, E. "Types of Causal Explanation in Science." In D. Lerner (Ed.), *Cause and Effect*. New York: Free Press, 1965.

National Opinion Research Center (NORC). *High School and Beyond, Information for Users: Base Year (1980) Data, Version 1*. Chicago: National Opinion Research Center, 1980.

Orenstein, A., and Phillips, W. R. *Understanding Social Research: An Introduction*. Boston: Allyn & Bacon, 1978.

Piaget, J. *The Child's Conception of the World*. (S. Tomlinson and A. Tomlinson, Trans.) London: Routledge & Kegan Paul, 1929.

Piaget, J. *The Child's Conception of Physical Causality*. (M. Gabain, Trans.) London: Routledge & Kegan Paul, 1930.

Platt, J. R. "Strong Inference." *Science*, 1964, *146*, 347–353.

Polanyi, M. *Personal Knowledge*. Chicago: University of Chicago Press, 1958.

Pollie, R. "Brother, Can You Paradigm." *Science 83*, 1983, *4* (6), 76–77.

Popper, K. R. *The Logic of Scientific Discovery*. London: Hutchinson, 1959.

Popper, K. R. "Of Clouds and Clocks: An Approach to the Problem of Rationality and the Freedom of Man." In K. R. Popper, *Objective Knowledge: An Evolutionary Approach*. Oxford: Clarendon Press, 1972.

Prescott, P. S. "The Bard of St. Botolph's." *Newsweek*, June 28, 1982, p. 77.

Prewitt, K. Annual Report of the President. In *Annual Reports 1979–80, Social Science Research Council*. New York: Social Science Research Council, 1980.

Reason, P., and Rowan, J. (Eds.). *Human Inquiry: A Sourcebook of New Paradigm Research*. New York: Wiley, 1981.

Rist, R. *The Invisible Children*. Cambridge, Mass.: Harvard University Press, 1977.

Roe, A. *The Making of a Scientist.* New York: Dodd, Mead, 1953a.

Roe, A. "A Psychological Study of Eminent Psychologists and Anthropologists and a Comparison with Biological and Physical Scientists." *Psychological Monographs,* 1953b (2, Whole No. 253).

Rosenthal, R. *Experimenter Effects in Behavioral Research.* (Enl. ed.) New York: Irvington-Halsted, 1976.

Rossi, P. H., and Berk, R. A. "An Overview of Evaluation Strategies and Procedures." In E. L. Baker (Ed.), *Evaluating Federal Education Programs.* Los Angeles: Center for the Study of Evaluation, University of California, Los Angeles, 1980.

Rowe, M. B. "Relation of Wait-Time and Rewards to the Development of Language, Logic and Fate Control. Part I, Wait-Time." *Journal of Research in Science Teaching,* 1974, *11,* 81–94.

Rubin, L. B. *Worlds of Pain: Life in the Working Class Family.* New York: Basic Books, 1976.

Sax, G. *Foundations of Educational Research.* Englewood Cliffs, N.J.: Prentice-Hall, 1979.

Scriven, M. "Self Reference Research." *Educational Researcher,* 1980, *9* (6), 11–18, 30.

Siegel, M. H., and Zeigler, H. P. (Eds.). *Psychological Research: The Inside Story.* New York: Harper & Row, 1976.

Simon, H. A. "A Behavioral Model of Rational Choice." *Quarterly Journal of Economics,* 1955, *69,* 99–118.

Simon, H. A. "Rational Choice and the Structure of the Environment." *Psychological Review,* 1956, *63,* 129–138.

Simon, J. L. *Basic Research Methods in Social Science.* (2nd ed.) New York: Random House, 1978.

Skinner, B. F. *Verbal Behavior.* New York: Appleton-Century-Crofts, 1957.

Skinner, B. F. "The Science of Learning and the Art of Teaching." In B. F. Skinner, *The Technology of Teaching.* New York: Appleton-Century-Crofts, 1968. (Original version published in *Harvard Educational Review,* 1954, *24,* 86–97.)

Slavin, R. E. *Research Methods in Education: A Practical Guide.* Englewood Cliffs, N.J.: Prentice-Hall, 1984.

Slovic, P., Fischhoff, B., and Lichtenstein, S. "Response Mode, Framing, and Information-Processing Effects in Risk Assessment." In R. M. Hogarth (Ed.), *New Directions for Methodology of Social and Behavioral Science: Question Framing and Response Consistency,* no. 11. San Francisco: Jossey-Bass, 1982.

Smith, M. L., Glass, G. V., and Miller, T. I. *The Benefits of Psychotherapy.* Baltimore: Johns Hopkins University Press, 1980.

Sosa, E. (Ed.). *Causation and Conditionals*. London: Oxford University Press, 1975.

Spengler, O. *The Decline of the West*. New York: Knopf, 1926.

Stent, G. S. "Prematurity and Uniqueness in Scientific Discovery." *Scientific American*, 1972, *227*, 84–93.

Strong, E. K., and Campbell, D. P. *Strong-Campbell Vocational Interest Inventory*. Stanford, Calif.: Stanford University Press, 1981.

Summers, A. A., and Wolfe, B. L. "Which School Resources Help Learning? Efficiency and Equity in Philadelphia Public Schools." *Federal Reserve Bank of Philadelphia Business Review*, February 1975, pp. 4–28.

Torbert, W. R. "A Collaborative Inquiry into Voluntary Metropolitan Desegregation." In P. Reason and J. Rowan (Eds.), *Human Inquiry: A Sourcebook of New Paradigm Research*. New York: Wiley, 1981.

Toynbee, A. J. *A Study of History*. London: Oxford University Press, 1948.

Tuchman, B. *The Guns of August*. New York: Macmillan, 1962.

Tversky, A., and Kahneman, D. "The Framing of Decision and the Psychology of Choice." In R. M. Hogarth (Ed.), *New Directions for Methodology of Social and Behavioral Science: Question Framing and Response Consistency*, no. 11. San Francisco: Jossey-Bass, 1982. (Reprinted from *Science*, 1981, *211*, 453–458.)

Tyack, D. "Ways of Seeing: An Essay on the History of Compulsory Schooling." *Harvard Educational Review*, 1976, *46*, 355–389.

Vasta, R. *Strategies and Techniques of Child Study*. New York: Academic Press, 1981.

vonOech, R. *A Whack on the Side of the Head: How to Unlock Your Mind for Innovation*. New York: Warner Books, 1983.

Watson, J. *The Double Helix*. New York: Atheneum, 1968.

Webb, E. J., and others. *Unobtrusive Measures: Nonreactive Research in the Social Sciences*. (2nd ed.) Chicago: Rand McNally, 1970.

Wertheimer, M. *Productive Thinking*. New York: Harper & Row, 1945.

White, T. H. *The Making of the President 1960*. New York: Atheneum, 1961.

White, T. H. *The Making of the President 1964*. New York: Atheneum, 1965.

White, T. H. *The Making of the President 1972*. New York: Atheneum, 1973.

Whitehead, A. N. *Adventures of Ideas*. New York: Free Press/Macmillan, 1933.

Whyte, W. F. *Street Corner Society: The Social Structure of an Italian Slum.* (2nd ed.) Chicago: University of Chicago Press, 1955.

Williamson, J. B., and others. *The Research Craft: An Introduction to Social Research Methods.* (2nd ed.) Boston: Little, Brown, 1982.

Wimsatt, W. C. "Robustness, Reliability, and Multiple Determination in Science." In M. B. Brewer and B. E. Collins (Eds.), *Scientific Inquiry and the Social Sciences: A Volume in Honor of Donald M. Campbell.* San Francisco: Jossey-Bass, 1981.

Winkler, K. J. " 'Disillusioned' with Numbers and Counting, Historians Are Telling Stories Again." *Chronicle of Higher Education,* June 13, 1984, pp. 5-6.

Woody, R. H., and others. "Stimulated Recall in Psychotherapy Using Hypnosis and Videotape." *American Journal of Clinical Hypnosis,* 1965, 7, 234-241.

Wulf, K. M. "Relationship of Assigned Classroom Seating Area to Achievement Variables." *Educational Research Quarterly,* 1977, 2, 56-62.

Ziman, J. *Reliable Knowledge.* London: Cambridge University Press, 1978.

Zimbardo, P. G., Andersen, S. M., and Kabat, L. G. "Induced Hearing Deficit Generates Experimental Paranoia." *Science,* 1981, *212,* 1529-1531.

Zwier, G., and Vaughan, G. M. "Three Ideological Orientations in School Vandalism Research." *Review of Educational Research,* 1984, *54,* 263-292.

Index